PLOWSWORDS

Plowswords

LITERATURE AND THE AGRICULTURAL TRAP FROM SHAKESPEARE TO COETZEE

Cates Baldridge

UNIVERSITY OF VIRGINIA PRESS
CHARLOTTESVILLE AND LONDON

The University of Virginia Press is situated on the traditional lands of the Monacan Nation, and the Commonwealth of Virginia was and is home to many other Indigenous people. We pay our respect to all of them, past and present. We also honor the enslaved African and African American people who built the University of Virginia, and we recognize their descendants. We commit to fostering voices from these communities through our publications and to deepening our collective understanding of their histories and contributions.

University of Virginia Press
© 2024 by the Rector and Visitors of the University of Virginia
All rights reserved
Printed in the United States of America on acid-free paper

First published 2024

1 3 5 7 9 8 6 4 2

LIBRARY OF CONGRESS CATALOGING-IN-PUBLICATION DATA

Names: Baldridge, Cates, author.
Title: Plowswords : literature and the agricultural trap from Shakespeare to Coetzee / Cates Baldridge.
Description: Charlottesville : University of Virginia Press, 2024. | Includes bibliographical references and index.
Identifiers: LCCN 2024000474 (print) | LCCN 2024000475 (ebook) | ISBN 9780813951621 (hardcover ; acid-free paper) | ISBN 9780813951638 (paperback ; acid-free paper) | ISBN 9780813951645 (ebook)
Subjects: LCSH: English literature—History and criticism. | Agriculture in literature. | LCGFT: Literary criticism.
Classification: LCC PR149.A47 B35 2024 (print) | LCC PR149.A47 (ebook) | DDC 820.9/36—dc23/eng/20240225
LC record available at https://lccn.loc.gov/2024000474
LC ebook record available at https://lccn.loc.gov/2024000475

Cover art: shutterstock.com/L. Feddes
Cover design: Kelley Galbreath

To Susan, the kids, and the grandkids,
for showing me where the true bounty is gathered

CONTENTS

	Acknowledgments	ix
	Introduction: Foraging for Happiness	1
1	The Farm Implements of War	17
2	Sowing the Seeds of Our Discontent	31
3	Shelley's and Brontë's Solitary Walkers	62
4	Coetzee's Carcer[e]al State	97
5	The Necessity of Cannibalism	124
6	What Walls Want	160
	Conclusion: The Timescales Fall from Our Eyes	189
	Notes	197
	Works Cited	201
	Index	215

ACKNOWLEDGMENTS

This book was begun during a long-planned sabbatical that happened to fall amidst the Academic Plague Year of 2020–21, a trick of timing that abruptly mandated the cloistered, scribal existence I had planned to embrace anyway. However, given all the ricocheting fears of that time, I think I would be remiss if I failed to thank the public officials of Vermont, who unfailingly delivered unpoliticized science-based information to its citizens, thus allowing me (and I believe many others) to retain enough mental bandwidth to get on with the challenging jobs we had chosen and could not defer.

That leave was facilitated—as were several during decades past—by Middlebury College's Dean of Faculty Development and Research, Jim Ralph. Middlebury has a very generous leave policy, but even the best program requires a competent and dedicated facilitator, and Jim is that indispensable person. He is also the organizer of Middlebury's Carol Rifelj lecture series, which has afforded myself and many others the opportunity to premiere our latest research efforts in front of a sympathetic home audience. The speculations that eventually grew into this book got their first public airing in this richly stimulating venue.

It is a testament to the swiftness and completeness with which this project overtook me that a pair of my colleagues in the English Department—Marion Wells and Dan Brayton—wrote supporting letters to granting agencies in the belief (for I had told them so) that I would be pursing an entirely different topic. If they ever felt any annoyance at my precipitous change of direction, which rendered their thoughtful recommendations moot, they were too gracious to say so. Then, once my new course was set, Dan Brayton furthered it by acting as my guide into the—for me—terra incognita of ecocriticism, toward which precincts I appeared to be hurtling with inadequate knowledge and preparation. I am also indebted to Dan for introducing me to Bill Vitek, director of the New Perennials project at Middlebury, who, like Dan, read sections of the manuscript and offered helpful feedback and invigorating intellectual community. On any given page of this book it may seem as though I am skeptical that agriculture can ever be "fixed," but if it ever can, it seems clear to me that people like Bill and his collaborators at the New Perennials Project and the Land Institute will be at the forefront of that solution.

I must also thank Ellen Oxfeld, a longtime friend in Middlebury's Anthropology Department. When I came to her asking for a reality check about what I was doing, she was the opposite of territorial and indeed seemed pleased—or at least amused—that a literary critic was trespassing within the bounds of her own discipline. On several occasions she was able to either confirm an amateur's hunch or tell him why he was barking up entirely the wrong tree. My general impression after researching this book is that anthropologists are a self-skeptical (and indeed often a self-castigating) community, but I have finished this project quite full of admiration for them, and the same goes for Ellen in particular.

I would further like to thank all those at the University of Virginia Press who have helped this book through a long process of evaluation, revision, editing, and publication, especially Angie Hogan, Ellen Satrom, and Emily Shelton. From the Press's cordial acknowledgment of the manuscript's receipt through the many steps that followed, I have always felt as though I was in the hands of people who are accomplished, committed, professional, and caring. As, long ago, I spent six years as a graduate student at Charlottesville, Angie and her colleagues have facilitated as pleasant an intellectual "homecoming" as ever I could have wished for.

Back in Vermont, I owe a great debt to my wife and partner, Susan Baldridge, who has been marvelously supportive of this project from its initial moment to its last. Not only did she fail to bat an eye when first informed that her husband—whom she believed to be employed by an English Department—was about to write a book that was largely about farmers and hunter-gatherers, but she also continued to evidence the kind of curiosity toward, and engagement with, my labors that is the vital food of every writer, just as it is of every spouse. If I managed to remain calm in the midst of scholarly mazes, hopeful in the face of rejections, cordial in response to readers' reports, and grateful for the task of having to learn difficult new material on a daily basis, this is mostly due to Susan's wisdom, patience, and innate optimism. I am immeasurably grateful that we are, and will continue to be, hoeing our row in each other's company.

PLOWSWORDS

INTRODUCTION

Foraging for Happiness

If it is difficult for us, in the midst of our increasingly virtual reality, to recall that the harvest is still the most important yearly event in our lives, how much more difficult is it to grasp how recent a development, in the arc of our species' existence on this planet, is the harvest itself and all that it annually entails: the sowing, plowing, weeding, storing (i.e., guarding), milling, baking, and so on. But the fact is that if one were to shrink down the 250,000 years that have elapsed since the emergence of modern *Homo sapiens* into the span of a twenty-four-hour day, the tilling of fields dedicated to cereals would only commence a little before eleven in the evening. On such timescales, the practice of agriculture comes to be seen for what it is—a biocultural experiment on which any impartial jury is still out. And yet, on the scale of individual lives, plowing has seemingly been around so long as to be accepted as a given of our existence, as a product not of cultural choices and processes so much as an imperative of our physical condition as multitudes in a world of scarcity. If, for instance, you were to ask people casually encountered what humanity's oldest, most basic foodstuff is, most might understandably yet erroneously answer, "Bread," having so often heard it referred to as the Adamic staff of life. Though even in Genesis there is presumably no bread until Cain, the Bible's first farmer and first murderer and first city-builder, begins milling the grain he has sown.

But once we appreciate the sheer historical novelty of agriculture, the next mental leap that modern anthropologists require of us may feel equally counterintuitive, for they now insist that the emergence of farming imposed upon the human condition a radical increase in toil, violence, disease, famine (yes, famine), and social stratification. This grim view of our Neolithic transition from nomadic hunting-and-gathering bands into the unfree citizenry of walled grain cities has evolved over the last half-century, the product of a nearly complete reversal in anthropological thinking about what the domestication of cereal grasses, feed animals, and, indeed, of human beings themselves meant for the vast majority of people who were not the kings or the temple priests of the first urban centers. Guided by this new understanding of the birth of tillage as a hedonic catastrophe whose consequences we still endure, this book attempts to understand the complicity and resistance of various works of literature to an ideology that paints a farmed world as the only rational, inevitable, and sufficiently abundant one, and that has chronically demonized those who persist in foraging for their sustenance—those who, in other words, feed themselves by means of knowledge rather than toil (Mithen 165), and who express contentment with the present day rather than fretting about tomorrow.

That certain literary texts register ambivalences and anxieties about the imperative to plow—an imperative *supposedly* too commonsensical either to require championing or to prompt doubting—can be easily demonstrated. When, for example, midway through *Wuthering Heights*, Edgar Linton is given the unwelcome news that Heathcliff has returned to the neighborhood and paid a visit to his wife, Catherine, he responds with an astonished oxymoron: "What, the gypsy—the plough-boy?" (74). There is much to unpack in this contradictory pair of labels—or, rather, libels. In a farming culture, to contemptuously call someone a "plough-boy" is to advertise your own leisured position atop the ziggurat of laborious occupations required to sustain that culture. In this respect, Edgar's response is merely one expression among many of the class hatreds that Heathcliff first suffers from and then exploits as Brontë's narrative unfolds. However, within the word "gypsy" there resides a spell that has repeatedly *united* squire and plowboy against a supposedly common and inherently contemptible foe, just as a racial epithet deployed in the American South once joined even the richest and poorest whites in a common cause of suppression and demonization. The "gypsy"—a.k.a. the nomad, the forager, the barbarian, the nonfarmer, he who is ignorant of the plow—*there* is the real threat against whom all, low and high, who care about a "civilized" existence must rally. Such labeling, which is often about color (especially since the early modern period), but always about the way one gets one's dinner, is a habit that has functioned for millennia as the defensive wall engirdling an agricultural city of the mind, sheltering "us," the intellectually enlightened, the physically satisfied, the politically advanced, from the savage, starveling, anarchic mob outside. And yet in *Wuthering Heights* it is not the farmer but the dark-skinned gypsy who—despite all his acts of "savagery"—stands as the text's protagonist. Thus, it might illuminate much about Brontë's novel to inquire whether, and to what extent, she can be numbered among agro-culture's discontents.

If Brontë did in fact dissent from an established church whose founder was Cain, the heresiarch she would have looked to for inspiration was, of course, Rousseau. But while much of Rousseau's political doctrine soon found both visceral revolutionary expression and widespread intellectual acceptance (as well as fierce resistance), his insistence that mankind's primordial catastrophe arose from the planting of cereals rather than the plucking of fruit had to wait two full centuries before it found itself broadly seconded. Indeed, in this respect my own youth was spent under the ancien régime, for I remember being taught in junior high school about what was then still called "the agricultural revolution." It being the early 1970s, the authorities that presided over my classrooms and hallways reliably communicated only fear or disdain toward whatever calls for "revolution" one still occasionally heard on the margins of the public sphere, so I was slightly surprised to find the word used with approbation during third period. The way it was explained to me, this revolution represented our species' great leap forward from savagery into civilization, the moment (comprising a few hundred years, it seemed) when humanity somehow figured out the secret to bending every graph-line skyward (for I was learning to graph as well): more food, more people, more time for thought, more time for play, and, with each generation, more and more of the machines, physical structures, and enlightened attitudes that made modern life so much better than our "caveman" ancestors could have dared to fantasize about. It all centered on the invention of the plow, and on domesticating some lumbering beasts to pull it. Before this great watershed in human affairs, so the story went, life was a continual slog of trudging, scrounging, starving, and of the hurling of spears at animal and human foes; afterward, it was all amber waves of grain and the equally gilded civilization that the harvesting of staples made possible. *Viva la revolución!*, then, since it resulted in, as Joseph Conrad's Marlow drolly puts it, "as sunny an arrangement of small conveniences as the mind of man can conceive" (*Lord Jim* 239). What I could not know at the time was the very long provenance of this story, the fact that it was an ideological accretion—one as old as agriculture itself—and that its neat division of historical eons into a dark age of foraging and a perpetual renaissance of tillage was at sharp variance with what anthropologists had lately begun to report.

By the time I attained middle age, our species' wily self-extraction from the chains of Necessity had been recast as our hubristic stumble into a self-laid snare. Indeed, the revolution had become a trap, for, beginning in the mid-1960s, and with increasing speed and growing confidence thereafter, contemporary anthropology wrought, vis-à-vis the material, psychological, and social advantages of foraging versus farming, a transvaluation of all values. Much of this occurred because, in their precarious redoubts scattered across the globe, hunter-gatherers were finally being listened to with patience and genuine curiosity rather than being peremptorily slandered. Anthropologists imbedded in foraging cultures and committed to a gradual and osmotic understanding of their hosts found themselves dwelling amid peoples possessed of robust bodies, nurturing communities, philosophies of resilient gratitude, and a vast, intricate, and efficacious knowledge of the environmental surround. As it turned out, there was more hunger, violence, domination, disease, and despair to be found in Kansas City than in the Kalahari. And so the proud rampart of the agro-city, once conceived of as the very marker of an escape from scarcity and precariousness, had become something altogether opposite: a yawning chasm, a "great gulf fixed" across which we—the increasingly remorseful damned of vast farming-dependent empires—gazed with envy at those who still wandered amid the delights of their overstoried Edens.

To speak as broadly as the timescales involved demand, we are thus confronted with two narratives concerning agriculture: an older one proclaiming our fortunate, willed arrival, and a newer one regretting our unlucky, deluded straying. Some of the authors whose fictions I scrutinize will appear wholly captive to the prior story—although their obsessive eagerness to confirm its every jot and tittle will betray a cultural unconscious suffering from myriad insecurities where only certainties should seemingly reign. Others, while ostensibly affirming the older narrative, will nevertheless—at the level of metaphor, symbol, and implication—discretely recognize the existence and cautiously explore the wisdom of the alternative account. Others still will self-consciously champion the newer story, harnessing the concepts and vocabulary of contemporary anthropology to paint agriculture as the original sin responsible both for our violent history and our unsustainable present. What unites these texts is the fact that they all represent, consciously or unconsciously, humankind's abandonment of foraging for farming as a problem to be engaged with rather than as a presupposition to be ignored. For all of them, the fact that we plow the earth to get our bread is not a mere given, but a cause for anxiety. My belief is that, by stopping to ask if these texts might be interested (consciously or unconsciously) in our species' adoption of farming as a discrete and discernible subject of judgment and speculation, some things that now seem strange or baffling about them will coalesce into a new clarity, and that this clarity will in turn testify to their engagement with a subject whose dimensions and consequences are vast, foundational, and newly urgent. If these texts fascinated us even before we asked them whether our bodies and souls are better nourished by game or by grain, they are even more compelling once the query is put to them.

Though I believe that in what follows I am (to employ a metaphor precisely as old as agriculture) breaking new ground, it is important to acknowledge that my arguments are partly contiguous with other, well-established areas of scholarship. In close proximity, for instance, lies the vast body of work that addresses Western literature's implication within various intertwining discourses of imperialism, colonialism, and racism. Within this critical enterprise, scholars have extensively chronicled instances where novels, poems, and dramas have laid against various cultural Others the charge that they are "incapable" of farming and thus "merely" forage for their food. Such scholarship insists that the literary works hurling such "indictments" (for they are always framed as such) are deeply complicit in material enterprises of conquest, domination, and genocide. This is undeniable, and in regard to the political ends served by imaginative literature's propensity to denigrate non-European subsistence practices, everything that I offer is extrapolative and amplifying. I am neither trying to deny that a murder has taken place nor to tinker with the findings of guilt and injury that have already been handed down—even if I occasionally point out that the murder weapon, often reported to be a sword, might be better described as a scythe. Rather, my primary interest lies in the moment just after the accusatory cry of *"Forager!"* has been hurled, when its wielders, realizing that (at least for the moment) they still stand face to face with people who differ from them in something as basic as the procurement of nutrition, feel the well-policed boundary markers of their fields begin to fluctuate or fade. It is at this crucial, subsequent moment, when the forest that looms beyond the grain-stalks begins to look more penetrable, more intriguing, more inviting—and, often, precisely because of this, sorely in need of a higher rampart to block out the sight of it—that this book will attempt to capture. Thus, while it often examines texts that give voice in some measure to farming's battle cry against those refusing the plow, its special focus will be upon those instances where, consciously or unconsciously, they seem to express doubt about the inevitability and justice of the crusade.

This study also owes much—and, I hope, contributes something of value—to the ever-burgeoning fields of ecocriticism and the environmental humanities writ large. To offer a synecdochic example of the relationship between, on the one hand, my specific arguments concerning the struggles within literary texts that pit farmers against foragers, and, on the other, the concerns of numerous strands of ecological scholarship, let me offer a passage from J. M. Coetzee's *Life & Times of Michael K*. Here Michael, that happily skinny man, shimmies beneath the lowest strand of a barbed-wire fence: "Ducking through the fences, he could feel a craftsman's pleasure in wire spanned so taut that it hummed when it was plucked. Nonetheless, he could not imagine himself spending his life driving stakes into the ground, erecting fences, dividing up the land. He thought of himself not as something heavy that left tracks behind it, but if anything as a speck upon the surface of an earth too deeply asleep to notice the scratch of ant-feet, the rasp of butterfly teeth, the tumbling of dust" (97). Even as I wish to read Michael's act of escape as a recapitulation of those accomplished by ancient foragers evading the writ of the grain city's walls, I know that both the passage itself, and my approach to it, potentially engage any number of disparate "green" discourses. For Michael, in musing upon the kind of "tracks" he leaves behind him, is clearly articulating the magnitude of his "footprint," in the modern, ecological sense of that term. What I will be doing in the chapters that follow is to investigate how various works of literature measure our species' first (and perhaps still deepest) footprint upon the Earth. As I do so, it will become clear that the proliferating impressions left by our primordial stumble lie at the center of ecocriticism's attention: our replacement of botanical diversity with monocultures, the construction of a human landscape of endemic ugliness, an ever-growing sense of guilt over our extermination of animal life, and soils impoverished by our obsession with enriching and engorging ourselves.

Before I took up this subject—or, more properly, before *it* overtook *me*—I never thought of myself as an ecocritic. Perhaps for this reason, and from a resulting fear of presumption, I have been sparing in my use of ecocritical terms of art. Nevertheless, I have sometimes come upon concepts devised by those in the green humanities that seem pertinent to, and clarifying of, aspects of my own project. One among these is Timothy Morton's notion of the "hyperobject," which can be succinctly defined as an entity "so massively distributed, both in space and time, that [its] reality exceeds being adequately grasped at any particular time or place" (Clark 38). Agriculture certainly qualifies as such an entity—indeed, Morton describes "global agriculture" as "the grandaddy hyperobject, the first one made by humans," and one which has proven itself "toxic from the beginning to human and other lifeforms" (*Dark Ecology* 42–43). Certainly a few of the texts I scrutinize seem at times not to understand that they are talking about agriculture at all; rather, they believe they are tackling some more discrete and bounded subject, such as the work ethic, or Christian morality, or cannibalism, or the general desirability of stout city walls. It is as if they can pick out the promontories that sprout from the hyperobject's surface while simultaneously failing to notice the gradual curvature of the object itself and thus cannot recognize that the terrain they comment upon is the result of a planetary geology that is too vast to take in and too slow-moving to reveal itself as causal to the local landscape. Translated into Marxist terms, the rightness and unquestionability of agriculture vis-à-vis its onetime rival is so deep a cultural assumption that farming's myriad epiphenomena are as close as even the sharpest satire or the most rigorous dissent are likely to penetrate toward the genuine engine of history—and thus we often hear about the bells and whistles but less frequently about the steady hum of the machinery within. But, as Morton himself says, agriculture has always constituted a "gigantic machinery" that "predates industrial Age machinery," and that thus "before the web of fate began to be woven on a power loom, machinery"—both physical and psychic—"was already whirring away" (42). In what follows, then, there will be a Marxian flavor to what I say about various literary responses to this first and still-mightiest producer of commodities, for the hyperobject that is agriculture is, as Marx would have us believe about class struggle, a primum mobile whose workings remain largely invisible to those whose boots are necessarily planted in the soil.

Another resonant term is Glenn Albrecht's "solastalgia," defined as a form of homesickness that one can feel without ever leaving home because one's environmental surround has changed in ways that one finds distressing (Albrecht). And if, as must be the case, it is not only the sheer *sight* of the changed locale that disturbs one but also the altered texture of one's daily *interactions* with that place, then its pertinence to my subsequent chapters becomes clear, though with an important amplification. What seems to occur within some of the texts I cover is that, for their protagonists who till, the intrusion of the forager into their field of vision (agricultural metaphors being unavoidable) brings on a sudden and *shameful* solastagia in the space where nothing but self-congratulation should exist. There he appears, the hunter-gatherer, that barbarian figured by agriculturalist ideology as hungry, wearied, and unhappy—but is it possible to seamlessly depict him in this way, or do traces of his actual satiety, leisure, and contentment leak through into the prescribed libel? If the forager can't fully or consistently be made into the wretch that he must be in order to justify one's own hunger, weariness, and unhappiness, then the sight of familiar fields tilled by the continual sweat of one's brow brings on a *forbidden* solastalgia, a solastalgia that Dare Not Speak Its Name, leading to an episode of solastalgic panic. As we shall find, the crisis that arises when the tree line suddenly parts to reveal an unnervingly unimmiserated Other can become at least a partial explanation for Prospero's thunderings, Crusoe's hyperactivity, Frankenstein's hatred and self-hatred, and Marlow's uneasy fascination. Agriculture, so often sustained and reproduced by structures of social repression, also requires of its practitioners a discipline of self-repression—the willed forgetting of the possibilities offered by a life lived Otherwise.

I can also offer (but will not insist upon) a new coinage, the utility of which my ensuing interpretations seem to suggest. If all texts that deal with the production of cereal grains are ordinarily said to be "agronomic" in nature, it is certainly the case that many of them—including most of the fictions I will soon turn to—can also be rightly described as agro*gnostic*. That is, they assume, like certain gospels of the early Christian era, that an esoteric knowledge (rather than good works) is the key to salvation: the knowledge here being that of how to plow, plant, tend, and harvest staples, and the salvation being one's full attainment of "civilization" (including, of course, the proper worship of an omnipotent sky god). There is, certainly, a sharp irony imbedded in this term, in that our species' transition to agriculture required trading a vast and nuanced gnosis about our surrounding biome for a narrow rubric focused upon the exacting requirements of a handful of grain-bearing annuals. At that point of inflection, our foodways ceased to resemble a vascular network permeating the forest and became instead a very straight road leading, nutritionally, to a very strait gate. And while, in the history of religion, what are known as the Gnostic Gospels lost out to competing spiritual narratives, it would be difficult to imagine a more successful and durable hegemonic formation than agrognostic accounts of how we get our daily bread—for bread, obviously, it must be. Certainly under its long ascension all other stories about how to properly sustain our bodies have quickly and authoritatively been consigned to the junk heap of history as—according to the century concerned—so much savagery, or sin, or Romanticism. Others must determine the utility of such a neologism, and, indeed, if anything in what follows proves useful to ecocritics I will be gratified to find my results exceeding my original intention. Perhaps it can be asserted today, as it used to be said in connection with Marxism, that "we are all ecocritics now." If this is in fact the case, then who can doubt that our times have simply demanded that we become so?

In the chapters that follow, then, I will aim a series of interrelated questions at *The Tempest, Robinson Crusoe, Frankenstein, Wuthering Heights, Heart of Darkness*, and the novels of Coetzee, all of which depict farmers (or those imbued with a tiller's mindset) in conflict with foragers. These questions include: How exactly do these texts construct the supposed advantages of agriculture? What are their assumptions about when, how, and why agriculture historically triumphed over foraging? What aspects of the hunter-gatherer as a figure especially threaten their values? Do they betray any overt or covert envy of the forager's way of living? And, finally, if a text self-consciously understands that agriculture is propped up by a widely extensive and long-operative ideology, what alternative to farming is it implicitly or explicitly proposing? Although it is rarely the self-appointed office of these fictions to directly affirm or refute specific dictums pronounced by the proto- or professional anthropologists of their time, they all employ their respective eras' notions about how and why human beings traded the forest for the farm as prompts for meditations on how we feed (or starve) ourselves spiritually as well as materially. In other words, they consider bread not only as a foodstuff but also as either a symbol of cultural attainment or a symptom of cultural disease, as either manna from heaven or the harvest of Cain. But, being literary texts, they do so by focusing upon the intimate, the physical, and the immediate: at some point in each of our works, a figure standing amid a tilled field will lock eyes with a figure emerging from the forest, and whether the resulting emotion is rage, envy, or something interestingly in-between, it will emanate from the guts and conduce to gestures of violence, to gambits of liberation, to crippling exertions of denial. By definition, literary characters engage us to the extent that, as the saying goes, they refuse to live by bread alone, but when a character disdains that staple altogether, she presents the text that contains her with something rather difficult to digest.

I will first set out the old, triumphalist story of planting, followed by the newer, much more skeptical account of it, each in its own chapter. Thus, chapter 1 will trace the remarkably stable main channel of agricultural ideology as it flows from the first grain cities of ancient Mesopotamia all the way into the rapidly professionalizing human sciences of the nineteenth and twentieth centuries. Along the way, Western habits of labeling land that is not being plowed as "waste" or "empty" places will be touched upon, along with a consideration of the colonial invasions that such notions authorized and sustained. This brisk chronicle of plowing's boastful apologetics, which begins with inscriptions upon temples and pyramids, concludes with Lewis Mumford's opus of 1961, *The City in History*. As we shall see, this justly respected work of synthetic scholarship, despite its tough-minded clarity concerning the arduous lives of ordinary plowers and rakers beneath the walls of Uruk and its progeny, simply cannot bring itself to depict agriculture as causally responsible for the panorama of immiseration it paints. The strength and longevity of the traditional story about farming's benign conquest of the world will thus be underscored through the remarkable similarity of its bookending texts.

Then, in chapter 2, I describe a pair of major challenges to this notion of the agricultural revolution as a beneficent provider of bounties and an ecumenical lifter of burdens. The first emanates from Rousseau, who, while generally agreeing with his fellow "speculative historians" of the Enlightenment that humankind developed through four distinct cultural stages—hunting, pastoralism, agriculture, and commerce—refuses to see the adoption of the plow as anything but a moral, political, and physical catastrophe. It is Rousseau's impassioned dissent from his fellow protoanthropologists, almost all of whom viewed farming as the happy climacteric through which our species passed out of barbarism and into civilization, that will eventually animate the ambivalent depictions of figurative hunter-gatherers by Mary Shelley and Emily Brontë. The remainder of chapter 2 reviews the reversal in thinking concerning foragers that overtook the modern profession of anthropology beginning with the Man the Hunter conference of 1966. It was here that Marshall Sahlins's notion of hunter-gatherers as inhabiting "the first affluent society" was initially aired, a line of revisionist thinking that repositioned foragers as living lives more secure, more healthful, more peaceful, more imaginative, and more firmly anchored in caring communities than their (often aggressive) cousins who trudged behind a plow and team. We shall trace how this intellectual about-face, when fully matured, succeeded in replacing the notion of farming as our species' greatest triumph with that of it as our primordial Fall from happiness.

These introductory labors completed, I turn squarely toward works of imaginative literature, treating some texts briefly and other at some length, according to the varying extent of their engagements with my subject. Chapter 3 begins this process by examining two agroskeptic novels of the Romantic era—Mary Shelley's *Frankenstein* and Emily Brontë's *Wuthering Heights*. These texts' pair of "monstrous" protagonists are, to one degree or another, both figures for foragers and are thus instinctively perceived by others as threats to the values and security of agroculture. But both authors are also sympathetic to Rousseau's insistence that individuals enjoying the first phase of humanity's four-part stadial progression (i.e., hunting and gathering) are happier and more ethical than their descendants who farm. Shelley's Creature, because he is a new-created man, is also necessarily the recapitulation of primordial man and, indeed, lives most of his brief life as a hunter-gatherer. But while Shelley's novel as a whole seems sympathetically curious about the lives of foragers, Victor Frankenstein can only view stage-one existence as synonymous with both cannibalism and incest, instigating a state of interstadial warfare that permanently immiserates both characters. In Brontë's novel, the environs of the Heights support and protect that embodiment of stage-one humanity, Heathcliff, while the Grange, as a walled farm, exemplifies third-stage sedentism and is prey to all its attendant disease, social stratification, and anxiety about the future. Between two realms so anthropologically disparate, there can be no peace and little understanding. Moreover, the fact that the speculative historians took "America" as a model for the prehistoric world as a whole explains Brontë's ambivalence toward the charismatic but "savage" Heathcliff and hints at what type of nonwhite person he is meant to represent.

Chapter 4 covers J. M. Coetzee's depictions of farming and foraging protagonists under the inspiration of contemporary anthropology's replacement of the agricultural revolution with the more dire and ambivalent notion of the "agricultural trap." Coetzee first offers us, in the person of *Waiting for the Barbarians*'s Magistrate, an amateur anthropologist who cannot fathom that both his queasy likeness to the torturer Colonel Joll as well as his inability to appreciate the cultural alternatives offered by the Barbarian Girl are both the result of his unconscious allegiance to an agriculturalist ideology. By contrast, in *Life & Times of Michael K*, the titular character's diet, peregrinations, and easy labors are recognizably those of the academy's refigured hunter-gatherer, demonstrating not only Coetzee's knowledge of recent anthropological theory but also his full assent to that vision of prehistory that sees the rise of tillage as antithetical to human flourishing. The work camps where Michael is serially detained are so many miniature versions of the grain state, offering him only porridge, forced labor, and militarized ramparts. Escaping them, he handily forages off the land, eating frugally but finding what he names "bliss" (Heathcliff's exact word, as it happens) in his freedom from toil, from anxiety about the future, and from what the farming world would mistakenly valorize as "purpose." The camp's medical officer, a baffled agriculturalist who imaginatively follows Michael onto the veld, slowly realizes that his onetime patient embodies a lost gnosis that might offer an attractive, thoroughgoing alternative to his own aggressive, racist, and ecologically unsustainable culture beholden to the plow.

Chapter 5 turns to the subject of cannibalism, or at least to the frequent laying of that spurious yet always explosive charge, examining its deployment in *The Tempest, Robinson Crusoe, Heart of Darkness*, and Coetzee's *Foe*. Among the authors of these texts, only Daniel Defoe actually seems to believe that the practice represents a clear and present danger to civilization, and Crusoe's frenzied insistence on its ubiquity and intoxicating pleasures whip him into a frenzy of sowing, baking, and silo-building that belies agriculture's claim to be a practice needing no apology. Meanwhile, to differing degrees and by different methods, Shakespeare, Conrad, and Coetzee all demonstrate their understanding that the accusation of man-eating is more expedient than accurate, especially when it is aimed at hunter-gatherers, all of them suggesting that the charge serves a purpose akin to that which Freud and Lacan assigned to the incest taboo: a way to shortcut our desire to reexperience a primordial freedom and close communal bonds. In their texts, then, characters hurl the indictment because they see the indulgence of such longings as threats to their own colonialist enterprises, and because they know it will quash any genuine (and therefore politically dangerous) curiosity concerning how foragers actually live and eat.

In chapter 6, I focus my attention on the built environment required by agriculture, given that walls and cereal grains are obligate symbionts—that is, two species that can only live and flourish in each other's presence.

Revisiting Defoe, Shelley, Conrad, and Coetzee, we will consistently find walls figured as monuments of ambivalence, standing simultaneously as, on the one hand, markers and guarantors of the supposed security and permanence of a farmed world, and, on the other, as chronic reminders of the violence, anxiety, and unfreedom required by the agro-cultural order. In the texts discussed here, a life lived behind defensive ramparts is never solely a physical condition but also a captivity within the plowman's mindset, revealing the ways we have divided up, regularized, and patrolled the boundaries of our inner landscapes to resemble that of the fixed fields that dominate our external surround. It is little wonder, then, that characters within each of the texts covered in this chapter betray a secret, shameful envy of the forager's uninhibited and therefore "uncivilized" mobility.

This done, the book concludes by reviewing the difficult shift in perspective required when we attempt to make sense of literary texts (as well as current events and cultural practices) by situating them within vast anthropological timescales instead of within the historical ones with which we are more familiar. Perhaps the largest shift required in exchanging the notion of the agricultural revolution for that of the agricultural trap is the Oedipus-like lurch from a species-identity grounded in hubris to one informed by a mortifying anagnorisis from which recovery seems unlikely. This new mindset involves an admission that, for our authors and for all of us consigned to agro-cultures, the appearance of the hunter-gatherer is now attended by a sense of the uncanny, for she makes us feel suddenly alien and untethered inside the walls of our tiller's domus, a structure upon whose permanence we once relied and in whose wisdom we once rejoiced, but which we now know to be, well, made of straw.

In this chronicling of literary responses to the implications of our decision to forever hoe the rows, I believe I have cast a wide net, though there is one ubiquitous precipitate of *Homo sapiens*' agricultural turn that I will not be dealing with directly. It has likely occurred to some that the art of writing is as much a product of fixed-field tillage as are domesticated cereals, city walls, and class conflict. Indeed, it is well understood that writing first began as a way of specifying exact quantities of grain so that they might be adequately paid for, transported, stored, taxed, and doled out as salary (Scott 21–24, 128–34). But, in what follows, I will not be taking up writing itself as a discrete subject in the way that I readily take up fictional foragers, cannibalism, or wall-building as discrete subjects. My reasons for this reluctance are straightforward. Such a topic is at one and the same time far too vast to be undertaken within the confines of a chapter and far too thoroughly understood already thanks to the main arc of literary criticism itself over the last half century; it is difficult imagine how long such a chapter would need to be or the criteria by which it could determine the inclusion or exclusion of any particular text. If this is work which still requires to be done, then for the present moment it is a labor that must be undertaken by others. The sections of this book address the subjects they do because I believe that so long as I am engaging with them specifically, I am illuminating aspects of familiar texts that have not yet, in light of our evolving understanding of our Neolithic cultural transformation, received all the attention they deserve. When and where I felt I could no longer shine such a light, my own writing discovered its natural end point.

A different kind of reluctance explains why issues of gender are at best sparsely engaged in the sections ahead. To put the matter succinctly, it does not appear that the adoption of agriculture was *causal* to the construction of patriarchy—as we currently understand that term—to the same degree that it was in the establishment of other hierarchies of power within human communities, such as the stark division of labor between those who physically till and those who manage the stoop labor of others. That is to say, while hunter-gatherer bands "rarely have steep gender hierarchies," and while their "attitudes toward marital fidelity and premarital female virginity tend to be quite relaxed," it is still the case that "forager bands are male-dominated" (Morris 40). This, of course, does not mean that the birth of farming was not productive of many important gendered effects, since those who plow often have material objects of value (implements, specie, and, less frequently, the land itself) to pass down to inheritors, which means that issues of "legitimate" paternity come to the fore, birthing a myriad of knock-on effects, most of which are dire for women. This alone suggests a wide gap between collectors' and tillers' imaginations of gender, and, indeed, anthropologists have been attempting to clarify various Neolithic shifts in patterns of gendered power for a good while now (Sterling). There is much to engage with here, but I must plead both my own status as an ephebe in the field of anthropology and my sense of being an outrider amid the territory I am already surveying. Covering what ground I have—as you can see—has already resulted in an extensive book. So, as tantalizing and as potentially productive of helpful textual readings as the subject of gendered power within the forager/farmer conflict promises to be, I believe I have acted prudently in deferring such discussions to another day.

But, finally, even if these explanations are accepted, some might ask why one so cautious about speaking on topics quite familiar within his own discipline is nevertheless so bold as to deploy the theoretical concepts, material discoveries, and terms of art belonging to a discipline very much *not* his own. The fact is, I am a literary critic; I am not and never will be a proper anthropologist. Nevertheless, I always hope and often believe that I have put the smattering of anthropology (and archeology and ethnology) that I have learned to good and proper use in pursuit of my goals—goals that, in the end, are literary. I confess I was drawn toward anthropology by its practitioners' evolving view of the Neolithic and the implications that view might have for literary studies, rather than by the discipline's procedures and activities in a more general sense. Still, the more I have learned about how anthropologists go about their business, the more I have been impressed by their enthusiasms, their scruples, and their patience—this last a virtue that literary critics have little need for. And, as I have become familiar with their seemingly inescapable foundational texts, their staid orthodoxies and revisionist revolts, and the tensions between their general theories and their specific efforts of praxis (some conducted within literal trenches), I have come to see an intellectual landscape whose terrain is not so very different from that of my own professional homeland.

But, however comfortable I have become within the purviews of anthropology, it is the astoundingly *dis*comforting idea of the agricultural trap that is the genesis of, and that provides the sustaining energy for, my subsequent pages. What continues to fascinate me is the notion of an upheaval that can be seen from two distinct yet equally persuasive intellectual perspectives, a historical one in which it happened long ago (indeed, so long ago as to precede and to bring into being the historical record itself), and a paleoanthropological one in which it occurred only yesterday. Like one of those teasing "either-or" images, it is difficult to see this ambiguous and hypnotic object both ways at once. And if the chronological status of agriculture's triumph is disconcerting, its legacy is even more radically dichotomous, for it seems to have given us most of what we possess and cherish and yet to have robbed us of what we most essentially need and desire. Perhaps, then, it is the kind of thing that only literature can allow us to comprehend.

1

The Farm Implements of War

THERE IS a difficulty involved when we try to comprehend the grip that the practice of agriculture has long exercised over our deepest assumptions about what constitutes adequate recompense for toil, about who should possess the power to compel others, and about how much anxious aforethought is necessary to secure our tomorrows—in short, when we try to think about agriculture as productive of, and sustained by, an ideology. This difficulty in part stems from the very definitions of rigor we have developed for our various strands of materialist critique, for we tell ourselves to be sensitive to ever-shifting patterns of social power, to incremental technological advances, and—lately, where we can—even to the agency of obscure individuals in short-term historical frames. We value a comfort with nuance, a conviction of unrelenting change, a sharp eye for the uniqueness of local conditions. For all these sound reasons, then, we tend to balk at the notion that even an enterprise as basic and ubiquitous as agriculture could shape an ideology that persisted with little change from the rise of Mesopotamian Uruk in the fourth millennia BCE until the middle of the twentieth century. Nevertheless, a strong indication that we are justified in speaking of a continuous, coherent ideological discourse from the age of Sargon through the age of steam is the remarkably consistent presence and presentation of this ideology's necessary Other, the hunter-gatherer.

At myriad points across this vast expanse of time we can hear those inhabiting and reproducing a tiller's view of the world telling a familiar trio of stories about foragers, making of them figures to pity, to resent, and to fear, but never under any circumstances to envy, no matter how resistant our soils or how recalcitrant our crops. If these narratives all seem to harbor a kernel of contradiction at their core, that is all the more reason to feel in them the efforts of an ideology that is fully in harness and sweating hard, unconcerned with intellectual consistency. First, foragers are said to spend the vast majority of each day tediously hunting and collecting their food, only to hang from year to year on the brink of starvation. Second, while they wander about through rich landscapes potentially ripe for the plow and are therefore decidedly obstructing the designs of more industrious peoples, they are not really "using" that land in any legitimate sense of the word, and indeed they are hardly "there" at all. And, third, while they possess only the weakest sense of social cohesion, they countenance and practice the most atrociously unlawful intimacies amongst themselves—namely, cannibalism and incest. For millennia, it was in part this figure of the forest (or the steppe)—a weary starveling, an indolent loiterer, a perverse and man-eating isolato, the unnaturalness of whose food was a marker of the troglodytic way it was obtained—who kept shoulders straining against the plow and knees bent before the millstone.

One of the earliest agriculturalist depictions we have of such an unfortunate who, by ranging beyond the bountiful irrigated fields drags himself through existence in ignorance of the blessings of grain, is vividly carved on the causeway leading to the pyramid of the Pharaoh Unas, constructed toward the end of the third millennium BCE. These particular victims of a hunger brought on by their own stupidity suffer impossibly pinched waists and are caught as they pluck and gobble the vermin infesting their scalps while tottering against each other on bent, emaciated legs. Though we are not completely sure whether the reliefs depict foragers or nomadic pastoralists, they are clearly gypsies rather than plowboys, people literally beyond Pharaoh's supposedly protective pale (Wilkinson 89). This distinction, between those within the grain state's curtain wall of sovereignty who eat sufficiently and those outside it who starve, was baked into the language of Mediterranean antiquity. Richard Waswo, in his exhaustive account of Western agrarianism's eliminationist war on nonfarmers, reminds us that the Latin verb *colo*, which spawns our terms "culture" and "cultivation" (the latter in both a material and behavioral sense), originally meant "to dwell and to worship as well as to till the soil," delivering a good portion of what anthropologists would come to call the "Neolithic package" in a pair of syllables. Ever since, "civilized society" has been synonymous with "permanent settlements on cleared land reaping regular harvests, building their walls and towers skyward." Meanwhile, "the polar opposite of that picture, in language and in life, is the supposed savagery of forest-dwellers. Hunters and gatherers are as far beyond the pale of civilization as it is possible to be," and hence "people who roam forests and build no walls are not *quite* people" (6–9, Waswo's italics). Such uncultivated noncultivators could be represented in any number of ways consolatory to the tiller's mind, and, therefore, even when they were depicted as eating each other, they were never depicted as growing fat from the practice.

We must now undertake a large temporal leap, although the point of doing so will be to see how, ideologically, we have landed in much the same place. By the eighteenth century, a loose and impressionistic protoanthropology began to emerge in western Europe whose speculations concerning what early humanity *must* have looked and acted like (whether one's frame was biblical or secular) drew its energy from versions of John Locke's famous dictum that "in the beginning all the world was America" (29). The way many an Enlightenment thinker saw things, New World Indians were chronically short of food because hunting and gathering required so much more acreage than did agriculture to sustain a single individual. Thus, according to Richard Cantillon, even "a small Tribe of these Indians will have 40 square leagues for its hunting ground," and it is because of these extravagant requirements that "they wage regular and bitter wars over these [lands'] boundaries" and must (it is darkly but vaguely suggested) "always proportion their numbers to their means of support from the chase" (3–5). Likewise Montesquieu, who sadly opines that noncultivators "have need of an extensive country to furnish subsistence for a small number," especially if they live by hunting rather than pastoralism, such that they "can scarcely form a great nation" (275). If Amerindians are, furthermore, found to be a melancholy and peevish people, says the historian of early America Jedidiah Morse, such is not to be wondered over, given the metrics of nutrition noted above: "A people who are constantly employed in procuring the means of a precarious subsistence, who live by hunting the wild animals, and who are generally engaged in war with their neighbours, cannot be supposed to enjoy much gaiety of temper, or a high flow of spirits" (39).

When such eighteenth-century philosophers and social commentators shifted their focus from particular Amerindian nations to ancient man in general—which they did easily and often—what mainly interested them was the mechanism that, after eons of intellectual darkness, had driven peoples (historically successful peoples, that is) to abandon foraging for those "higher" means of procuring their sustenance: first pastoralism, conceived as a kind of biblically approved halfway house, and then on to agriculture, the foundational sine qua non of true civilization. For Helvétius, this mechanism is the lash of hunger, since, "after having, in part, destroyed the animals, when the peoples can no longer live by their hunting, the dearth of food will teach them the art of raising flocks and herds" (162). William Blackstone agrees, asserting that a preagricultural landscape "would not produce her fruits in sufficient quantities" to support anything but people living in "primaeval simplicity," and who walked an earth almost "bare of inhabitants" (7, 3), a theory that Lord Kames echoes by informing us that "want of food, occasioned by rapid population, bought on the shepherd-state in the old world" (*Sketches* 2, 362). Indeed, to read most protoanthropologists (or "speculative historians," as they were later happily dubbed) is to get the impression that Stone Age terrain is composed mostly of, well, stone—from which a few pebbles of nourishment had to be laboriously chipped by exhausted cave dwellers, as John Millar explains: "A savage who earns his food by hunting and fishing, or by gathering the spontaneous fruits of the earth, is incapable of attaining any considerable refinement in his pleasures. He finds so much difficulty, and is exposed to so many hardships in procuring mere necessaries, that he has no leisure or encouragement to aim at the luxuries and conveniences of life" (17–18).

These assumptions are taken up unaltered by those occasional eighteenth-century works of literature that explicitly attempt to envision primordial human beings, for in Henry James Pye's *The Progress of Refinement* (1783), we encounter the "selfish savage" who is "compell'd by chace his scanty food to gain," since only "a steril soil, and frowning heaven / Are to his race by ruthless Nature given" (ll. 27–33). Luckily, this chronic hunger compels Pye's hunter-forager to invent herding and then tilling, an ultimately fortunate deprivation that also temporarily plagues early man in Richard Payne Knight's *The Progress of Civil Society* (1796), in which

The hunter's labours less productive grew,
And pale-faced famine slowly rose to view . . .
   [Until] want inventive, and prospective thought,
More certain sources of nutrition sought. (Knight 1, ll. 39–40, 43–44)

What most such Enlightenment speculations about early peoples, poetic or prosaic, have in common is that they leave no room for a successful, sustained life of foraging. It is at best a kind of cultural infancy—a school of hard knocks—that punishes the troglodyte until, out of sheer desperation, they think up something better. If there are still people who hunt and gather today, then the inference must be that they have somehow stagnated or degenerated, a notion that pseudoscientists of the following century would attempt to expand into various racist taxonomies of cultures.

As anthropology evolved into a professional academic specialty over the course of the nineteenth century, the consensus about the dire ratio of primitive peoples' caloric intake to energy expended stayed pretty much where the eighteenth century had left it. If anything, the position was hardened by the intervention of Malthus, whose calculations about the inevitability of population increases only darkened the visions of starveling primitives whose catch always fell short of their hunger. Thus "the Malthusian savage lived in a Hobbesian world in which human rationality was constantly at the mercy of sexual instinct" and wherein "the inherent tension between human reason and human biology was reducible only by continuous suffering or recurrent disaster" (Stocking 220). As Malthus advised, population growth beyond the carrying capacity of any landscape might be theoretically curbed by sexual restraint and long-term planning, but if these could not be expected of the contemporary London poor, they were certainly not likely to have been found in the Paleolithic, whose denizens were presumed to follow what anthropologists would later term an "immediate return economy," which to the Victorians seemed a recipe for starvation:

> The savage has few other than material wants, and these he endeavours to satisfy only for the moment. To appease hunger for the day; when requisite, to protect his body against heat or cold; to prepare his lair for the night; to follow the instinct of propagation; and instinctively to guard and tend his offspring—this constitutes all his care, all his enjoyment. He thinks and acts only for the day which *is*, not for the day which is coming [and thus] he is compelled to fish and to hunt, or he must perish. (Nilsson lvii)

Interestingly, the sheer paucity of early *Homo sapiens*, controlled in Malthusian fashion by the stinginess of their hunting grounds, was also said to be limited by warfare, which was itself paradoxically *un*hindered by the small number of potential combatants even as it was *mandated* by the aforementioned scarcity of food. As a result, a primitive who "fed on wild fruits, or devoured raw fish," simultaneously "fought with his fellow, or with the brutes for the carcasses killed by them" for truly "his life was a continual state of warfare" (Westropp 4–5). Unsurprising, then, that at the place where intraspecies violence and chronic hunger converged, there lay in wait Victorians armed with potent shafts of pity and revulsion. Here, for instance, is John Lubbock, coiner of the terms "Paleolithic" and "Neolithic": "The true savage is neither free nor noble; he is a slave to his own wants, his own passions; imperfectly protected from the weather, he suffers from cold by night and the heat of the sun by day; ignorant of agriculture, living by the chase, and improvident in success, hunger always stares him in the face, and often drives him to the dreadful alternative of cannibalism or death" (586). At least the vision here is of "starvation cannibalism," a practice actually observable in the world at rare and dire moments, rather than the "gustatory" variety often alleged by early modern explorer-entrepreneurs—and, as we shall see, by their apologist Defoe.

The second traditional slander against hunter-gatherers is ineluctably bound up with the first, even as it seems in some ways to stand in contradiction to it—such hardy reinforcement in combination with supple flexibility constituting the paradoxical strength of many an enduring ideology. If primordial human beings found themselves eking out a miserable living on upon a biome that barely afforded them sustenance, this was no fault of the terrain's. Rather, the land only refused to freely give up its inherent bounty because it was being incompetently employed. The "poverty" of the hunter-gatherer cultures that many a conquistador claimed to see was therefore not due to the intrinsic barrenness of the forests, savannahs, or hills wherein they were dwelling, but to the fact that the people were foraging upon such lands rather than farming them. Again, Waswo clarifies the issue etymologically, noting that "the archaic word *gaste* (cognate with Eng. *waste*) was applied to any agriculturally unexploited territory, forest as well as desert" (61). In our contemporary world, where it is difficult to find a stretch of country that is not being exploited in some way for human ends of some kind, we tend to think of a "wasteland" as a place so barren or hostile that it is difficult even to imagine extractive industries making a go of it (if it is not extraction itself that has laid the country waste). Early modern settler-colonialists, however, labeled what to us would qualify as many a green and pleasant land as "waste" because, rather than being "worked" by farmers, it was merely "occupied" or "roamed over" by hunter-gatherers. Farming, or owning farmland, is how even the humblest European hoped to get rich in the New

World (barring gold mining and slave trading), and, since the Indians didn't farm, they were ontologically negligible (and hence might as well be enslaved). Of course, the Indians of, say, Virginia and Mesoamerica, did, in fact, practice hand-sowing and hoeing, but this is not plowing, so it doesn't count as genuine agriculture, just as Defoe's (cannibalistic) Caribs in actuality practiced a slash-and-burn horticulture that also doesn't qualify. In the words of one seventeenth-century priest engaged in a churchly debate about native land claims, the Indians practice "no careful agriculture" and thus aren't really using the land they occupy (Pluciennik 63). Or, as that historian of the Spanish conquest William Robertson observes in the late 1700s, such fitful poking at the soil "is neither extensive nor laborious" (this last a telling requirement, as we shall see), and, anyway, "as long as hunting continues to be the chief employment of man to which he trusts for subsistence, he can hardly be said to have occupied the earth" (2.117, 130). Any land innocent of the plow is thus figured as wasted land, as wasteland.

What, then, is to be done about such bad stewards of such vast tracts? Alas, a common answer has been some euphemistic version of Kurtz's scrawled addendum to his Benevolent Report. Any number of examples could be cited, from Julius Caesar to John Ford, and Waswo does just that, though his comprehensiveness does not prevent him from recognizing a synoptic epitome when he sees one. The diplomat Emer de Vattel's *Le Droit des genes* of 1758 he rightly calls "the grandest and most influential justification" for the removal of nonfarmers ever penned, one that owes much of its force to an "accessible style" that is "especially clear" (181–82) about its eliminationist intentions. For our purposes, then, we will let it function synecdochally for a chorus of apologists for Agriculture Militant:

> The cultivation of the soil is not only to be recommended by the government on account of the extraordinary advantages that flow from it; but from its being an obligation imposed by nature on mankind. The whole earth is appointed for the nourishment of its inhabitants: but it would be incapable of doing it, was it uncultivated. Every nation is then obliged by the law of nature to cultivate the ground that has fallen to its share.... Those people, like the antient Germans, and the modern Tartars, who having fertile countries, disdain to cultivate the earth, and chuse rather to live by rapine, are wanting to themselves, and deserve to be exterminated as savage and pernicious beasts. (1.7.81, quoted in Waswo 182)

De Vattel mentions the ancient Germans as one example of a people whose refusal to farm he redefines as a kind of haughty selfishness. He can do this because he does not see "the first ages of the world" as a place of scarcity, but rather as a place that even "without cultivation, produced more than was sufficient to feed its few inhabitants" (1.7.81). This, then, represents hunter-gatherers, past and present, not as incompetents but as purblind enemies of human flourishing, people, as he puts it, "wanting to themselves," unconscious self-harmers blind to the civilized beings they could have become had they only strapped themselves to a plow and team. Like *Robinson Crusoe*'s Amerindians, they are both ontologically thin and yet somehow a mortal, moral danger that must be defeated, the original Invisible Men.

A final prejudicial paradox involves the sociality of hunter-gatherers that, in its Enlightenment form, emerged once again from a process wherein observations of existing indigenous peoples (often scant, third-hand, and decidedly interested) formed the basis for rationalistic extrapolations about primordial humankind in general. Here we must begin with Rousseau, who—if he is uncannily prescient concerning our current notion of an "agricultural trap" that, once sprung, consigns human beings to drudgery, inequality, and endemic violence—is about as far off the modern mark as it is possible to be concerning the interpersonal relationships now thought to be enjoyed amid foraging bands. We will scrutinize Rousseau's theories more closely in chapter 2, but for now suffice it to say that he imagined early hunter-gatherers as so sparsely dispersed across the early landscape that they encountered each other only occasionally, whereupon they sometimes engaged in brief individual combats or sometimes copulated without initiating lasting pair-bonds. This pinballing existence, in which there were neither "Houses [n]or Huts or property of any kind," and in which "everyone bedded down at random and often for one night only" (*Discourse* 145), made for a kind of lonely *pax antiquae* that, in his mind, was idyllic precisely because it precluded the establishment of those incubators of human vice, hamlets, villages, towns, and cities. It was thus the radical apartness and seamless self-sufficiency of the hunter-gatherer that ensured his happiness.

A surprising number of later commentators kept intact this vision of foragers as beings experiencing weak or distant interpersonal bonds, though most of them reversed Rousseau's moral assessment of this state, seeing it as an exile to be endured rather than a freedom to be cherished. Thus we hear Robertson lamenting that "man existed as an individual before he became the member of a community," and that amid primitive peoples "their political union is so incomplete, their civil institutions and regulations so few, so simple, and of such small authority, that men in this state ought to be viewed rather as independent agents, than as members of a regular society. The character of a savage results almost entirely from his sentiments or feelings as an individual, and is but little influenced by his imperfect subjection to government and order" (2.59). It is this last phrase that explains the persistence of this vision of primordial social impoverishment among many who participated in, or were influenced by, the Scottish Enlightenment. The focus of such thinkers tends to be, first, property, and then, following on in due course, law as a system that regulates property. Since hunter-gatherers have few possessions (about this, at least, they were correct), their thinking was that such people had little need for laws or governments, which, in the speculative historians' top-down view of how sociality begins and grows, means that foragers also had fewer and weaker *personal* affections for one another than modern people, whose laws and governments are elaborate and mature. We can see this same genealogy of the passions operating a century later in Herbert Spencer, who claims that because savage societies "necessarily lived on wild food" and suffered a "wide dispersion of small numbers," they "were, on the one hand, not much habituated to associated life, and were, on the other hand, habituated to that uncontrolled following of immediate desires which goes along with separateness. So that while the attractive force was small the repulsive force was great. Only as primitive men were impelled into greater gregariousness by local conditions which furthered the maintenance of many individuals in a small area, could there come that increase of sociality required to check unrestrained action" (1, sec. 35). Thus, as does Rousseau, Spencer sees agriculture as bringing with it the end of the age of bachelorhood rampant, though for the latter this is no tragic curtailment.

Despite the fact that foragers were seen as living too far apart from each other, they were also, gastronomically and sexually, too close for Victorian comfort. We have already seen the nineteenth-century anthropologist John Lubbock envision Paleolithic mankind as a starveling frequently driven to cannibalism. Lubbock, like his fellows, arrived at this conclusion partly by extrapolating from what he thought he knew about extant foraging peoples (Mithen 131), and in part due to Locke's licensing notion of "America" preserving the Paleolithic in amber. Of course, it had been precisely the discovery of Amerindians living upon a continent coveted by Europeans that turned Herodotus's trickle of cannibal reports into the flood perpetrated by Columbus and subsequent conquistadores, since anthropophagy always justifies invasion and dispossession. By Lubbock's time this rubric—"if out there, then also back then"—was so thoroughly enshrined as an orthodoxy that "the nineteenth-century imagination view[ed] European civilization as an imperiled bastion hemmed in by both temporal and spatial borders across which were ogres" (Arens 120). As far back as Strabo, however, the notion that prehistoric people ate each other was often accompanied by, if you will, a sister charge—that of incest. As Walter Arens, the great skeptic of anthropophagy, asserts, "There are two reasons for this equation. First, like eating human flesh, incest is a striking indication of a lack of culture. As a result, cannibals were also accused of having no incest taboo. . . . Second, in many cultures, including ours, there is a symbolic equation between sex and eating." And, lest we think this linkage died out with high-buttoned shoes, it is worth remembering, as Arens does, that Freud also linked the two crimes in his myth of civilization's origin, requiring both of these dark urges to be repressed before savagery could be left behind (146–47). All of this suggests that Claude Lévi-Strauss was correct in describing cannibalism as "the alimentary form of incest" (*Naked* 141), a mental conjunction that for generations allowed the condescending delineators of prehistoric hunter-gatherers to have their cake and eat it, too.

Given the Old Story's vivid suppositions about the downsides of foraging, the question of just *why* so many cultures eventually developed agriculture and committed themselves to living by means of it was literally too obvious to need asking. Here is Jared Diamond, whose early education apparently mirrored my own regarding its characterization of the Neolithic:

> From the progressivist perspective on which I was brought up, to ask "Why did almost all our hunter-gatherer ancestors adopt agriculture?" is silly. Of course they adopted it because agriculture is an efficient way to get more food for less work. Planted crops yield far more tons per acre than roots and berries. Just imagine a band of savages, exhausted from searching for nuts or chasing wild animals, suddenly gazing for the first time at a fruit-laden orchard or a pasture full of sheep. How many milliseconds do you think it would take them to appreciate the advantages of agriculture? (64–65)

This assumption, that the agriculturalist's fortune was an inverted (or righted) image of the forager's misery, had prevailed almost unchallenged since the first tablets of self-aggrandizing rhetoric were promulgated by the first kings of Sumeria. Whether it was classical philosophers, medieval chroniclers, Renaissance historians, or modernist psychologists, all—excepting Rousseau, of course—were united in seeing the adoption of agriculture as the benign Rubicon of our species' cultural development, the climacteric that made possible all the arts of peace, all the sciences of plenty, and all the charters of civilized conduct and comfort. Next to such indubitable blessings, the negative, unintended effects of tilling (if indeed any could be identified) were as motes of dust amid the blaze of the sun. According to this pervasive narrative of human development, agriculture "replaced the savage, wild, primitive, lawless, and violent world of hunter-gatherers and nomads. Fixed-field crops, on the other hand, were the origin and guarantor of the settled life, of formal religion, of society, and of government by laws. Those who refused to take up agriculture did so out of ignorance or a refusal to adapt" (Scott 7). Under the influence of such a story, to oppose agriculture was to paint oneself as a throwback, a misanthrope, or a sentimental fantasist.

To feel keenly the historical persistence and thoroughgoing success of this triumphalist narrative concerning agriculture, we need only turn to that magisterial work of scholarly synthesis, Lewis Mumford's *The City in History*, published in 1961. Mumford is clear eyed about the nature of the first Mesopotamian grain states, likening them to the "totalitarian" regimes of the twentieth century (72, 83) and delineating the immiserated lives of their nonelites at some length. He notes, for instance, that "the early city" is "no longer a community of humble families living by mutual aid," but rather "a caste-managed society, organized for the satisfaction of a dominant minority" (38), wherein the ordinary field hand "must now work harder and practice self-denial to support a royal and priestly officialdom with a large surplus" (30). Such drudges might have carried the nominal title of "citizen," but they were essentially and unprecedentedly unfree, for it was "precisely in the new functions of the city that the truncheon and the whip—called politely 'the scepter'—made themselves felt" (51–52). Even when the granaries were full, these powerless many were now "compelled under threat of starvation to labor like slaves" (89), since the "artificial creation of scarcity in the midst of increasing natural abundance was one of the first characteristic triumphs of the new economy of civilized exploitation" (36). Indeed, Mumford is so candid as to admit that "perhaps the best definition for the inhabitants of an early city is that they are a permanently captive farm population," a regimented class of toilers from whom "repetitious labor" was demanded so relentlessly that it stamped upon both mind and culture "the structure of a compulsion neurosis." Thus "the ancient city, in its very constitution, tended to transmit a collective personality structure whose more extreme manifestations are now recognized in individuals as pathological" (46–47). Amid such a huddled and harried togetherness, even the lonely atomism of Rousseau's primordial hunters begins to seem attractive by comparison.

But was not this "contraction of personal life" (Mumford 102), these burdens of drudgery and servitude, amply compensated for by increased and more reliable calories for all? Seemingly not, for Mumford admits that city-states practicing fixed-field agriculture are fragile entities, since "the proto-urban community became increasingly dependent upon natural forces outside its control," until "a flood or a plague of locusts might cause widespread suffering or death in these inchoate urban centers too big to be easily evacuated or suppled with food from afar" (40). Nor was this the only road to famine, given that the nascent royal dynasty "measured its strength and divine favor by its capacities, not merely for creation but even more for pillage, destruction, and extermination" (51), the result of which was that "the many gains made through the wider associations and laborious co-operations of the city were duly offset by the negative economic activity of war," a "cyclic disorder . . . embedded in the very constitution of the ancient city" (43). Indeed, Mumford sums up his section on the early grain cities in a tone of melancholy futility that anticipates the voice of Coetzee's Magistrate: "Thus the most precious collective invention of civilization, the city, second only to language itself in the transmission of culture, became from the outset the container of disruptive internal forces, directed toward ceaseless destruction and extermination. . . . Each historic civilization . . . begins with a living urban core, the polis, and ends in a common graveyard of dust and bones, a Necropolis, or city of the dead: fire-scorched ruins, shattered buildings, empty workshops, heaps of meaningless refuse, the population massacred or driven into slavery" (53).

It seems a dire cultural transformation, this process that culminates in a walled city surrounded by irrigated fields of emmer. And *yet*—at no point in this otherwise unflinching depiction of the grain city can Mumford bring himself to grant the development of agriculture a *causal* role in the resultant social unfreedom and psychic diminishment. To say this is not to chastise him for not knowing what we, today, believe we know about the rise of tillage, but simply to take notice of the pattern within his thought that identifies him as someone operating within the Old Story about how and why foragers gave way to farmers during the Neolithic. To exculpate plowing, Mumford contrasts the walled city of Mesopotamia not with the forager encampment, but with what he terms the "Neolithic village," which he imagines—and this must be stressed—as a place *fully occupied with agriculture*, but in which all the vices he associates with early agrocities are absent and replaced by corresponding virtues. This idyllic hamlet is, for instance, characterized by a rough "democracy" of "face-to-face meeting[s]," during which "each member stood at eye level" and "only age established precedence and authority" (20). Amid this community that resembles a family, and for as long as "the chief ends of life" were "nutrition and reproduction, the pleasures of the belly and the genitals," then "Neolithic village culture met every requirement" (19). It is curious that although the denizens of Mumford's Neolithic village pursue precisely the same kind of field labor as their unfortunate descendants in Uruk and Lagash, we hear nary a word about the difficulty, drudgery, or crippling repetitiveness of *this* toil. And if one suspects that intervillage conflict must be in some way premonitory of later intercity warfare, we can at least rest assured that when small farming settlements clashed it did not entail, as it apparently did in the days of forager bands, "the singling out of a few live captives for ceremonial slaughter, and eventual serving up in a cannibal feast" (42). As we shall see, this last gambit is a tried and true element of the Old Story: to avoid thinking about how and what foragers actually eat, claim that they eat each other. It works every time. But the main point is that here, in the middle of the twentieth century, a justly respected voice demonstrates that what we are hearing is not the decline and attenuation of the Old Story about foraging and farming, but its continuing, vigorous reproduction.

If the success of any ideology can be measured by the degree to which it is ubiquitously accepted as common sense, by how long its baroque framing of the world can be mistaken for necessary structural elements, where could we hope to find a triumph equal to that enjoyed by the apologetics of agriculture? While it is a common enough figure of speech to refer to this or that ideological formation as having recourse to the optical illusions and sleights-of-hand employed by the professional illusionist, in this case one is tempted to explore the metaphor toward the frontiers of the literal. After all, it must be a simple matter of weight and volume that any given community's yearly harvest (provided the crop succeeds) produces an exponentially larger pile of food (once it is processed) than could the daily accumulation of any similar-sized community's hunting and gathering. Then, too, the land that must be dedicated to cereal production is, like the heaps of grain it produces, impressively capacious yet immediately comprehensible by a turn of the head, not dispersed over hundreds of square miles in discrete patches that do not so blatantly advertise their nutritional potential—though surely this last is itself an assumption of the forest-blind farmer. Still, one wonders, is there something about the visual surround necessitated by fixed-field tillage that has anciently beguiled the human sensorium, that has perpetrated such a masquerade of abundance that the arduous toil, the unequal laws, and the constant worry could simply not be seen as flowing from the same (intermittently) overflowing fountain? Surely the source of these miseries must lie elsewhere: in the inscrutable purposes of the gods, or in our sinful failure to comply with divine commands, or just in a run of very bad luck. At any rate, given the long arc of agriculturalist ideology briefly traced above, it is clear that ever since we abandoned the forests' abundance for the monocultures of our furrowed fields and furrowed brows, we have made a desert and repeatedly convinced ourselves to call it peace—a peace that we have maintained in part by fighting a forever war against the forager.

2

Sowing the Seeds of Our Discontent

Despite the ubiquity and tenacity of agriculturalist ideology across several millennia, this chapter concerns two distinct challenges to its hegemonic reign: first, Rousseau's brilliant, abstract, and eccentric speculations about how the advent of agriculture perverted the natural goodness of what he imagined as a race of happy hunter-gatherers; and, second, the broadly similar—though rigorously empirical—Neolithic transformation constructed by contemporary academics after lengthy immersions within still-extant forager communities. The former of these was, for all its oddities, a herald of the latter. Blazing forth in the mid-eighteenth century, Rousseau's lasting achievement was simply to engrave onto his culture's psychological map an alternative to the Old Story, no matter how marginal it long remained—to insist that a countervailing narrative could be imagined and an inverted assessment of civilization's beneficent "rise" articulated. Two hundred years later, when professional field anthropologists largely succeeded in toppling farming's triumphalist account of itself, they could do so in part because Rousseau had declared that such a paradigm shift was both intellectually possible and morally necessary. In taking these two interventions as the subject of this chapter, I am not claiming that they are the only moments of dissent worth looking at, for were I writing a full-on history of English literature's encounter with proto- and professional anthropology, I would be obligated to look at others as well. But my purposes are more focused; thus I will limit my discussions to Rousseau's notion of our tragic self-domestication and to modern academics' positing of the agricultural trap, and this because the former is imbued in the fabric of *Frankenstein* and *Wuthering Heights* and the latter in the early masterpieces of J. M. Coetzee. These fictions are all skeptical of agro-culture's apologetics and curious about what human beings might look, act, and feel like if the plow were suddenly banned from the Earth it has scarred, or if its effects could somehow be evaded, or if it had never been thought of in the first place. As we shall eventually see, they all pursue these speculations by resurrecting the figure of the hunter-gatherer and setting him scandalously, perilously afoot in the modern world.

Turning to Rousseau, it is first necessary to clarify the protoanthropological assumptions he shared with those Enlightenment thinkers whose views about agriculture he rebelled against, since Shelley and Brontë also accept that basic framework, even as they cast a sympathetic ear toward Rousseau's heresies concerning it. It is no exaggeration, then, to claim that from the rise of the philosophes to the advent of Darwin, educated opinion was nearly unanimous in believing that the early history of human beings could be divided into four distinct, successive, and progressive stages of development, each characterized by the particular activity by which people obtained their sustenance. First and primordially, it was claimed, humankind hunted and foraged; next, they practiced nomadic pastoralism; third and most fatefully, they took up agriculture; and finally they engaged in commerce. Ronald Meek, in *Social Science and the Ignoble Savage*, his encyclopedic account of myriad four-stage "conjectural histories," reveals that the list of intellectual figures who argued for, or simply assumed the validity of, this particular anthropological narrative is both broad and long. French adherents include Turgot, Helvétius, Goguet, Condorcet, alongside Rousseau himself (Meek 69–98, Stocking 14–15). Across the Channel, the leading figure promulgating the stadial theory is Adam Smith, who succinctly lays out its basic assumptions: "There are four distinct states which mankind pass thro:—1st, the Age of Hunters; 2dly, the Age of Shepherds; 3dly, the Age of Agriculture; and 4thly, the Age of Commerce" (Meek 117). Among other British proponents of this same speculative framework one finds Adam Ferguson, Lord Kames, John Millar, Edmund Burke, Edward Gibbon, William Falconer, William Russell, John Malthus, and John Stewart Mill.

Nor were writers of intellectual prose the only figures to promote and elaborate the four-stage vision: witness the aforementioned James Pye. According to this poet laureate (1790–1813), during the primordial age the hunter-forager was chronically famished until, with the passing of time and the slow accumulation of experience, "the expanding Mind perceives her latent powers," ushering in an era wherein "his grazing charge the gentle herdsman tends, / And o'er the vale his eye delighted bends." In Pye's imagination, this process of improvement evolves toward its predestined culmination in the final two stages of society named by Smith:

> Down the steep cliff, and o'er the craggy brow
> Strong Agriculture drives his laboring plow,
> And to the currents of the rising gale
> Adventurous Commerce trusts her swelling sail. (Pye, 1: ll. 48, 55–56, 193–96)

Roughly contemporaneous to Pye's *Progress of Refinement* is Knight's *Progress of Civil Society*, divided into sections which include "1: Of Hunting," "2: Of Pasturage," "3: Of Agriculture," and "4: Of Arts, Manufacture, and Commerce" (Meek 209–12). If these poems are little read today, it is also worth noting that Constantin-François Volney's *The Ruins: Or Meditation on the Revolutions of Empires and the Law of Nature* (1791)—that text that so signally contributes to the disillusionment of Mary Shelley's Creature in *Frankenstein* (1819)—is also (among its other priorities) a vehicle for the four-stage theory. Here, too, humankind is first found "wandering in the woods and on the banks of rivers in pursuit of game and fish," until, "instructed . . . by the experience of various and repeated accidents," we collectively ask ourselves, "Why not collect under our hands the animals that nourish us? why not apply our cares in multiplying and preserving them? We will feed on their increase, be clothed in their skins, and live exempt from the fatigues of the day and solicitude for the morrow." Once in possession of the relative leisure provided by perambulatory herding, and "having observed that certain seeds contained a wholesome nourishment in a small volume, convenient for transportation and preservation, they imitated the process of nature; they confided to the earth rice, barley, and corn, which multiplied to the full measure of their hope" (65–66). There exist, of course, unfortunate races that have remained stuck in one of the earlier stages (about whom more later), but, for those blessed by climate, temperament, Fortune, or God, the path toward civilization is both singular and clearly marked.

Testifying to the four-stage system's cultural entrenchment is the fact that—though it clearly displays the marks of its rationalist conception—there is almost no evidence of Romantic-era reactions against it. Rather than sweeping it aside, Romantic social critics for the most part kept the theory intact while employing it to reach more particularist conclusions within its long-fixed categories, "tempering universalism with respect for local cultures." What this frequently amounted to, as in the case of Herder, was an infusion of nationalist assertions into the philosophes' and the Scottish Enlightenment's grand, species-spanning framework, an insistence that that "each culture has its own nature and potential, which must be developed out of themselves according to their own internal principle of growth" (Palmieri 45), resulting in various national "expression[s] of the *Volksgeist*" (Stocking 20). Beyond such refinements, however, there was no paradigmatic revolution that threatened the dominance of the four-stage outlook until the publication of *The Origin of Species* (Levy 52–55), and even then it "persisted in altered but recognizable forms throughout the nineteenth century" (Palmieri 2). Therefore, "while the Enlightenment has traditionally been a fertile source of ancestors for anthropologists seeking to anchor their own ideas more deeply in time, the early nineteenth century has been a kind of 'dark age,' barren of [new] theoretical interest save for figures like August Comte" who nevertheless "kept the [established] developmental tradition alive" (Stocking 9). In Britain, for instance, economists and philosophers such as Ricardo and Mill, who were primarily focused on stage four and only ventured back into stages one and two to find embryonic evidence of what they were primarily interested in—property rights, or communal cooperation, or population trends—left the four-stage structure of the orthodox narrative of human advancement essentially unchanged (Stocking 32–41), their new wines flowing into old bottles.

In Britain, even the religious resurgence of the early nineteenth century percolated through rather than washing away the conventional stadial formulations, for there were ways of "accommodating progressive developmentalism to the reasserted claims of divine revelation" (Stocking 33–34). Most of these involved reconciling missionary reports concerning forager societies with Genesis 4:2—which describes Cain as "a tiller of the ground"—by claiming that after the Noahic Flood the survivors were dispersed across the face of the earth in such a parlous state that their knowledge of how to farm had been lost, sometimes along with the pastoral techniques acquired in stage two. A form of this theory had been articulated decades before by Turgot (Meek 73–74), but among nineteenth-century evangelicals it sometimes took on an ominous cast, for it was said that while some races possessed the innate genius to eventually reacquire agriculture, others suffered "cultural and physical degeneration in the wake of the Deluge," which confined them to hunting and gathering. The result of such biblical glosses was thus to "place the [currently extant] savage not at the foot of a single upward ladder of progress, but at the bottom of a diverging ladder of degeneration." Sadly, such racially bifurcated accounts soon became "the common currency of popular religious belief and the missionary movement" (Stocking 33–34). By these means did many an evangelical, who might have rejected a polygenic account of human origins on scriptural grounds, discover a simulacrum of it that conformed to the letter of the Pentateuch.

What is shared by almost all four-stage accounts of human development—be they religious or secular—is the assumption that of the three possible transitions between the four phases it is the one into agriculture that effects a truly fundamental change in the human condition, and that this change is thoroughly benign. As a typical example, Meek cites Cornelius de Pauw's *Recherches philosophiques sur les Américains* (1768–69): "And it is agriculture, says de Pauw, which has 'led men by the hand, step by step' from the uncivilised to the civilised state: 'Property and all the arts are ... born in the womb of agriculture.' Thus we may rank the different kinds of savages whom we find in the world in accordance with their greater or lesser distance from the state of 'moral perfection' towards which agriculture enables mankind to progress" (Meek 146). In Britain, this linkage between agriculture, private property, and the advent of true civilization was propounded by Locke (26–29), seconded by Sir William Hutcheson (4:147–48), and refined by Sir John Dalrymple, the last of whom makes a distinction between the movable property that might be owned by pastoralists and the more socially transformative immovable property that only comes into being with tillage (76–77; Meek 21, 29, 101). Thus, what keeps the troglodyte materially and culturally impoverished is his refusal to furrow the Earth into parcels of mine and thine.

Kames, for his part, opines that some forms of private ownership must have existed as far back as stage one and so credits the commencement of plowing with the rise of those other bellwethers of a civilized condition, laws and the state that enforces them:

> The shepherd life, in which societies are formed, by the conjunction of families for mutual defence, requires some sort of government; slight indeed in proportion to the slightness of the connection. But it was agriculture which first produced a regular system of government. The intimate union among a multitude of individuals, occasioned by agriculture, discovered a number of social duties, formerly unknown. These behoved to be ascertained by laws, the observance of which must be enforced by punishment. Such operations cannot be carried on otherwise than by lodging power in one or more persons, to direct

the resolutions, and apply the force of the whole society. (*Law Tracts* 1:57, footnote)

Indeed, according to Kames the agricultural revolution improved not only humankind's public institutions but also its private affections, since it is only "a man who has bestowed labour in preparing a field for the plough" who "forms in his mind a very intimate connection with it," and "a singular affection for a spot" to which he will "return with avidity" after any time away from it (1:104). Meanwhile, a waxing of the rational capacities of the mind are also credited to tillage by Sir William Temple, who associates the beginning of planting with all sustained forethought of longer than a day's-length (1:170–71; Meek 103–6, 26–27). It is pertinent to remember how vital to agriculturalist ideology this last position has always been. Farmers chronically assert that because agriculture is a "'delayed return' activity" in which the tiller must now "look far ahead in preparing a field for sowing, [and] then must weed and tend the crop as it matures, until (he hopes) it yields a crop," it follows that "the cultivator . . . is a qualitatively new person" distinct from the sorry run of his ancestors (and any neighboring foragers), who can now be portrayed as "improvident, spontaneous creature[s] of impulse" (Scott 65). If human beings are to rise from savagery to civilization, living for today must give way to anxious thoughts of tomorrow, and tomorrow, and tomorrow.

Was, then, the term "speculative historian" merely a euphemism for those who robustly theorized upon no anthropological evidence at all? Not entirely, for all of them could point to a vast laboratory across the Atlantic where the observation of living specimens offered (to their minds) strong proofs supporting their visions of how paleohistory surely unfolded. Indeed, Meek's main interest in the four-stage theorists is to show how marvelously influential was Locke's pronouncement that "in the beginning all the World was America" (29). Meek demonstrates how all stadial historians—both those many who viewed the stages as upward steps of progress, as well as those few, like Rousseau, who saw them as footprints heading off a moral cliff—pointed to Amerindians as evidence of what primordial human beings must have been like (either before the Patriarchs or after the Flood), "seeing" different Native American realities according to the requirements of their theory:

> On the one hand, those writers who were dissatisfied with certain aspects of European society—its over-refinement, for example, its

hypocrisy, or its system of ranks—could emphasise the simplicity, honesty, and equality of American society, holding the latter up (to a greater or lesser extent) as an ideal to be aimed at by Europe. On the other hand, those who admired contemporary European society—its diversity, the high level of its intellectual attainments, or its high material standard of living—could emphasise the dullness and uniformity of American life, the stupidity and cruelty of the savages, and their extremely low standard of living. (Meek 39)

Thus, with the (partial) exception of (some) primitivist versions akin to Rousseau's, most varieties of the four-stage theory could easily piggyback on the prevailing racist attitudes toward "savage" peoples—again, for the European theorists, these would be mostly but not exclusively Native Americans—who were currently occupying territory at the time those theories were penned. And, like the stadial conception itself, this notion of New World peoples as the conclusive dataset to be consulted was remarkably durable. So, if the Romantic nationalist could claim that rude nations persisting into the nineteenth century, being "fired with 'boiling passions' by the burning tropic sun, were permanently denied the 'finer intellect' of Europeans," the Victorian political economist could declare that such peoples practiced a form of commerce as yet unworthy of statistical study, while the religious missionary could explain their persistence in stages one or two by the fact that they had been deprived of that cultural accelerant, the Christian Word, or by casting them as a sinning nation preserved in historical amber to furnish a providential warning to more fortunate peoples (Stocking 36, 41–45). If our theorists rarely mentioned the race of the primordial hunter-gatherers they posited as living in distant ages, no one was shy about pointing out that the present-day inhabitants of stage one were not white—which brings us to Rousseau's great parting from that majority who would have perceived in the term "noble savage" only a laughable oxymoron.

Rousseau did in fact subscribe to many of the protoanthropological ideas outlined above: the progressive four-stage story of human culture, the outsized importance of farming's rise within that story, and the usefulness of Amerindians as a window unto the lives of ancient people generally. Where he differs, sharply and passionately, is in his view of the moral and spiritual consequences for humanity that the discovery of agriculture entailed, seeing it as a fatal transgression against the best qualities of our natural inheritance. According to Rousseau, primeval man existed in a state of nature, in which individuals were scattered very thinly indeed across the primordial landscape, each hunter-gatherer barely interacting with any other. Sometimes, it is true, these loners "attacked one another upon meeting," but, then again, "they rarely met," so that although in one sense "everywhere the state of war prevailed," from another perspective "the whole world was at peace" (*Essay* 269). This condition of primordial atomism also applied to relations between the sexes, since "males and females united fortuitously, according to chance encounters, opportunity, and desire . . . [and later] parted just as readily" (*Discourse* 145). What is perhaps most disconcerting about Rousseau's evocations of prehistoric life, though, is his tone, for he describes a primitive state in which the most deeply imbued social and individual desiderata of modernity—progress, purpose, family, sociability, eloquence—are absent, but evokes this subtractive landscape with a sigh of nostalgia:

> Let us conclude that, wandering in the forests without industry, without speech, without settled abode, without war, and without tie, without any need of others of his kind and without any desire to harm them, perhaps even without ever recognizing any one of them individually, subject to few passions and self-sufficient, Savage man had only the sentiments and the enlightenment suited to this state, that he sensed only his true needs, looked only at what he believed it to be in his interest to see, and that his intelligence made no more progress than his vanity. If by chance he made some discovery, he was all the less in a position to communicate it as he did not recognize even his Children. The art perished with the inventor; there was neither education nor progress, generations multiplied uselessly; and as each one of them always started at the same point, Centuries went by in all the crudeness of the first ages, the species had already grown old, and man remained ever a child. (157)

But, Rousseau asserts, at some point in time, perhaps because of a general increase in population, people began congregating together, congealing first into family groups and then subsequently into small villages, for he, like contemporary anthropologists, surmises that some form of sedentism must have existed before tillage could have begun in earnest, because "peoples that do not settle cannot possibly cultivate the soil" (*Essay* 269). But, since humans are inherently good, the baleful self-swindle of sowing and reaping could not take hold absent the unlucky imposition of outside forces (Ferrara 40–41). Rousseau nominates an outbreak of vulcanism, which at one blow suggested to people the possibility of smelting metals and—thanks to the resulting ash and other ejecta—killed off the game and left farming as the last, desperate, toilsome alternative by which to fend off starvation through furrowing the ground with metal implements. There is an obvious absurdity to this, but if we read it in the same spirit we do Freud's myths of the primal horde we can discern here, too, a literary confection that attempts to symbolically account for the origin of long-established cultural constants. By the time the skies cleared, however, mankind's moral prospects had become permanently shadowed, for all the ills and follies of our species' adulthood had already found their purchase: "The first man who, having enclosed a piece of ground, to whom it occurred to say *this is mine*, and found people sufficiently simple to believe him, was the true founder of civil society. How many crimes, wars, murders, how many miseries and horrors Mankind would have been spared by him who, pulling up the stakes or filling in the ditch, had cried out to his kind: Beware of listening to this imposter; You are lost if you forget that the fruits are everyone's and the Earth no one's" (*Discourse* 161).

This is truly a second Fall, which Rousseau does not hesitate to couch in the diction of Genesis: "As for agriculture, it . . . involves all the arts: it introduces property, government, laws, and gradually wretchedness and crimes, inseparable for our species from the knowledge of good and evil." And, if there is any doubt as to who plays the serpent's role in this recapitulative tragedy, he can be recognized by the infernal engine he has introduced into the world, for "Moses . . . appears to have disapproved of agriculture by attributing its invention to a wicked man and making God reject his offerings: the first tiller of the ground would seem to have proclaimed by his character the bad effects of his art" (*Essay* 272). Let us be clear: in Rousseau's mind, it is mankind's initial defection from sylvan freedom to communal bondage that first brought sin into the world, but even if this exodus slightly pre-dated tillage, farming is nevertheless the supremely poisoned fruit of sedentism's poisoned tree because it not only *results* from the founding of settlements but also *amplifies* that process, necessitating the establishment, continuation, and expansion of various soul-warping social institutions. So, when Rousseau casts his eye on the eras subsequent to our species' stumble into agriculture, he conjures a vision that might be that of Walter Benjamin's despairing Angel of History: "With this slight motion I see the face of the earth change and the vocation of mankind settled: I hear, far off, the joyous cries of a heedless multitude; I see Palaces and Cities raised; I see the birth of the arts, laws, commerce; I see peoples forming, expanding, dissolving, succeeding one another like the waves of the sea: I see men clustered in a few points of their habitation in order there to devour one another, turning the remainder of the world into a dreadful desert" (273). Still speaking in a biblical cadence and describing what we postmoderns might recognize as habitat loss, Rousseau depicts a deluded host that goes smiling to perdition and laments "vast forests changed into smiling Fields that had to be watered with the sweat of men, . . . where slavery and misery were soon seen to sprout and grow together with the harvests" (*Discourse* 167). Rousseau may speak of all of this more in sorrow than in anger, but he can forgive our ancestors only because they knew not what they did.

If Rousseau's primordial atomism is worlds away from modern anthropology's recognition of the close communal bonds enjoyed amid extant hunter-gatherer groups, more prescient is his understanding of agroculture's mystified imperative that we domesticate ourselves alongside the cereal grasses and animals we presume to control. We will soon see what contemporary anthropologists have to say about the difficulty of distinguishing rider from ridden on any given domus, but, for his part, Rousseau can only deplore the sorry state of all species found in the vicinity of a sheepfold or a barn:

> The Horse, the Cat, the Bull, even the Ass are, most of them larger in size, all of them have a sturdier constitution, greater vigor, force, and courage in the forests than in our homes; they lose half of these advantages when they are Domesticated, and it would seem that all our care to treat and to feed these animals well only succeeds in bastardizing them. The same is true of man himself: As he becomes sociable and a Slave, he becomes weak, timorous, groveling, and his soft and effeminate way of life completes the enervation of both his strength and his courage. (*Discourse* 138–39)

This view, though never until recently the majority report concerning agriculture's consequences, did find its occasional adherents among Rousseau's immediate successors, as we can see in the following from Herder:

> Generally speaking, no mode of life has effected so much alteration in the minds of men, as agriculture, combined with the enclosure of land. While it produced arts and trades, villages and towns, and, in

consequence, government and laws; it necessarily paved the way for that frightful despotism, which, from confining every man to his field, gradually proceeded to prescribe to him, what alone he should do on it, what alone he should be. The ground now ceased to belong to man, but man became the appurtenance of the ground.... Hence it is, that, throughout the whole World, the dweller in a tent considers the inhabitant of a hut as a shackled beast of burden, as a degenerate and sequestrated variety of the species. (57; see Meek 192–97)

But Rousseau is most impressively prophetic of our present moment in his attempt to describe what in modern parlance might be termed the mentalité of agro-culture, and in his insistence that it is not our species' transhistorical default setting but, rather, the product of an historical transformation in the way we feed ourselves. Agriculture's cultural fallout, to employ a phrase from *Wuthering Heights*, has "gone through and through [us], like wine through water, and altered the color of [our] mind" (Brontë 62). Arthur Melzer concisely sums up Rousseau's conception:

> Part of the evil of this condition is the resulting fatigue and frustration. But the primary evil is the loss of unity over time, the loss of "repose" and of the plenitude of existence found in it. Man's constant needs and desires, projecting him into the future and away from his present self, make him say: tomorrow I will *live*, today I will *prepare* to live. Spending his life thus "on the way," he is never "there" and at rest. He never knows a moment when he possesses all that he wants and thus possesses himself; never a moment when he embraces his present existence and says: let this moment last forever. Continually postponing his existence, he dies without ever having lived. (66–67)

Contemporary anthropologists have gone some way toward filling in the observable particulars of this diagnosis, examining early grain states and iterating the psychic costs of "delayed return economies," often finding that this delay (long valorized as the hallmark of civilization) also implies many denials, some self-imposed, many imposed from above. As Rousseau proclaimed, the spiritual price of grain is higher than advertised, and the boundaries of the tiller's imaginary more straitened than they first appear.

Many an explicator of Rousseau gives short shrift to the philosophe's account of agriculture's rise and the responsibility it shoulders for our subsequent ills, as if there were something embarrassingly uncommonsensical about it, like the one unsavory conspiracy theory adhered to by an otherwise amiable relative. Perhaps it was the volcanoes. At any rate, many such commentators are eager to push on and engage with Rousseau's political prescriptions for our modern cultural condition, never mind how he says we got here. And engage they have, for Rousseau's propositions about how extant polities might be reformed have, over the span of 250 years, remained central to the question of "what is to be done," whether it be posed by academics, professional politicians, or revolutionaries. And the answers emanating from the left and the right still betray, respectively, an ongoing and almost instinctive attraction to, or loathing of, Rousseau's assertions about his own present moment and his desired future. But about his conception of the distant past it was long possible for even an enthusiastic admirer to know little. Indeed, a mid-twentieth-century reader generally informed about the contents the *Confessions*, of *Émile*, and even of the *Discourse on Inequality*, could put down a copy of Lewis Mumford's *The City in History* and not understand that the portrait of farming's rise put forward in that politically progressive account of urbanism stands utterly at odds with the one articulated by the very fountainhead of progressive politics. Farming, it could still appear to such a reader, succeeded foraging simply because it had to, because our species always gravitates toward the better alternative, the more efficient method, the easier means to a desired end—that's simply human nature.

Then, on or about April 1966, human nature changed—or at least a long-dominant view of it began to crumble. This pivot point was the Man the Hunter conference that took place at the University of Chicago. It was designed, said its organizers, to consider and promulgate "substantial amounts of new data on hunter-gatherers" that were "rapidly changing our concept" of how foragers actually lived, data that would mandate a thoroughgoing reappraisal of "the basic concepts of descent, filiation, residence, and group structure" among such peoples. Poignantly, the conveners also recognized a deadline imposed by history: "Hunting and gathering, as a way of life, is rapidly disappearing and it was hoped that the symposium would serve to stimulate further research while there were still viable groups to study" (Lee and DeVore vii). The Man the Hunter conference is generally acknowledged to have both inaugurated the anthropological subfield of hunter-gatherer studies and to have initiated a gradual shift in popular attitudes concerning foragers that has, in this century, manifested itself in a fascination with things—and especially foodways—conceived to be "paleo." Many contributors to Man the Hunter went on to transform our view of prehistory, but, fairly or unfairly, it was Marshall Sahlins, a nonspecialist responder to one of the panels, who produced the conference's most influential paper. Eventually republished as "The First Affluent Society" in his 1972 volume *Stone Age Economics*, Sahlins's oft-assigned essay can be fairly credited with giving an initial shove to the process whereby what had hitherto been known as the "agricultural revolution" began its transformation into the "agricultural trap."

"The First Affluent Society" takes aim at the received outlook that hunter-gatherers are, and always have been, required to work without respite from sunup to sundown in order to glean a minimum of calories from a parsimonious landscape. Sahlins reviews a sampling of textbooks purporting to describe the life of foragers and finds that "the specter of starvation stalks the stalker through these pages. His technical incompetence is said to enjoin continuous work just to survive, affording him neither respite nor surplus, hence not even the 'leisure' to 'build culture.' Even so, for all his efforts, the hunter pulls the lowest grades in thermodynamics—less energy/capita/year than any other mode of production. And in treatises on economic development he is condemned to play the role of bad example: the so-called 'subsistence economy'" (1). Sahlins attacks this conventional story, however, by drawing evidence from recent ethnographies focusing upon hunter-gatherer communities such as the Ju/'hoansi of Namibia, aboriginal groups in Australia, and the Hadza in Tanzania. Among the material presented, he directs our attention to what such foragers actually report about how they spend a typical day. After adding up and averaging their self-assessments of how many hours they devote to gathering, hunting, and preparing sufficient food, as well as of how many they give over to visiting friends, napping, and recreating, Sahlins puts forward his central contention: "A good case can be made that hunters and gatherers work less than we do," and, rather than constituting a "continuous travail, the food quest is intermittent," just one quite manageable task amid a much more varied life in which "leisure [is] abundant, and there is a greater amount of sleep in the daytime per capita per year than in any other condition of society" (14). He then provocatively summarizes by asserting that "hunters keep banker's hours, notably less than modern industrialized workers ([even those who are] unionized), who would surely settle for a 21–25 hour week" (34–35). One implication of Sahlins's reassessment goes beyond the needed correction of an ethnological metric, for "The First Affluent Society" suggests that the conventional story repeated among farming cultures—that as hard as tillage is, farm laborers are at least better off than the thin and weary people who must unceasingly wander the forest—is in fact an ideological construction, socially useful to those who direct the hoeing rather than wield the implements themselves.

Of course, the title of Sahlins's article is meant to evoke John Kenneth Galbraith's secular bible of economic theory, and perhaps the most important work Sahlins's essay accomplishes is to challenge the Galbraithian notion of what constitutes basic categories of affluence and poverty by suggesting that foraging peoples may possess alternative conceptions of these things that are just as valid as ours. The problem, says Sahlins, is that the Galbraithian definition of affluence is bound up with the accumulation of material goods, and that therefore hunter-gatherers, because they own few possessions, automatically become the objects of our pity for inhabiting that most despised of conditions, that of being chronically "poor." But, he points out, "there are two possible routes to affluence," since "wants may be 'easily satisfied' either by producing much or desiring little." And if the Galbraithian view (i.e., that of modern economics generally) argues that "man's wants are great, not to say infinite, whereas his means are limited," the hunter-gatherers seem to reply that, from their perspective, "human material wants are finite and few, and [the] technical means [of achieving them are] unchanging but on the whole adequate" (1–2). As imaginatively challenging as this alternative schema may be, one could still ask whether Sahlins is implying that the Ju/'hoansi and other such cultures are merely following Thomas Carlyle's chilling advice to the Victorian poor that, when it comes to achieving their optimum fraction of perfect happiness, they should attempt to lower their hedonic denominator. It becomes clear, however, that for Sahlins it is not just that we have been "equip[ing] the hunter with bourgeois impulses and paleolithic tools," such that "we [have] judge[d] his situation hopeless in advance" (4). Rather, our problem is one involving our baseline assumptions about causality and mobility. We tell ourselves that *because* hunter-gatherers must be so frequently moving on, they can't possibly accumulate the things they would naturally desire, when in fact the mobile imperative of their lives makes the accumulation of material things a matter of indifference to them: in other words, "we are inclined to think of hunters and gatherers as *poor* because they don't have anything; perhaps better to think of them for that reason as *free*" (14, Sahlins's italics)—free not merely of material burdens, but of a conception of the world itself as defined by that foundation of modern economics, scarcity. Millennia of sedentism have indoctrinated us into the assumption that to move about in order to feed ourselves is to be driven over the landscape by the goad of want, the whip of fear, whereas the foragers Sahlins scrutinizes express "a trust in the abundance of nature's resources rather than despair at the inadequacy of human means": "Certainly, hunters quit camp because food resources have given out in the vicinity. But to see in this nomadism merely a flight from starvation only perceives the half of it; one ignores the possibility that the people's expectations of greener pastures elsewhere are not usually disappointed. Consequently their wanderings, rather than anxious, take on all the qualities of a picnic outing on the Thames" (29–30).

What Sahlins is implying here is a cultural version of the psychological theory that says that, given differing sets of infantile experience, children can emerge as adults who either express a trusting curiosity about the world or, alternatively, who harbor a suspicious anxiety about each new person and encounter. When looked at in this way, the assumption of scarcity and the necessity of anxiety seem to be baked into the enterprise of fixed-field tillage. After all, between the farmer and the forager, who is it who keeps an angst-ridden eye upon the weather, who worries if the same patch of soil will produce year after year, who frets that vermin will eat his hard-earned store? It is here that Sahlins's argument neatly loops back into his debunking of the notion that hunter-gatherers are always working hard and always hungry, for, historically, such is a description of the plowman rather than the forest nomad. As Stephen Mithin puts it in his survey of global prehistory, *After the Ice*, what differentiates hunter-gatherers from agriculturalists is that, "for them, the key to a full stomach [is] knowledge, not labor" (165). Thus, as difficult a mental reversal as it represents, we must entertain the notion that our species once habitually moved from place to place because we *trusted* the ability of the earth to reliably provide, and that our fear, distrust, and belief in natural scarcity was not the *reason* we stopped moving, but a *consequence* of that decision. Sahlins's debunking of the core assumptions that for so long allowed tillers to pity and condescend to nonplowing peoples suggested that perhaps envy was the more appropriate response.

In the years following the publication of *Stone Age Economics*, the Neolithic transition from foraging to farming came under further revisionary scrutiny that eventually inverted many of the assumptions about human health and well-being that had once undergirded the benign, optimistic view of an agricultural revolution. One of these was the issue of nutrition. Anyone who has attempted, during a visit to a museum or historic house, to explain to a child why a suit of armor looks so small or a doorjamb so low by whispering that "people were shorter then because their food wasn't as nutritious as ours" has probably inculcated the canard that there is a steady, inverse correlation between the number of years before the present and average human height. This is an error that remains widespread. However, just as the skeletal remains of domesticated animals can in part be distinguished from those of their wild cousins by the reduced length of major bones, so, too, does this shrinkage afflict the *Homo sapien* who has domesticated himself by ceasing to forage and beginning to till fixed fields round about a domus:

> The bones of "domiciled" Homo sapiens compared with those of hunter-gatherers are also distinctive: they are smaller; the bones and teeth often bear the signature of nutritional distress, in particular, an iron-deficiency anemia marked above all in women of reproductive age whose diets consist increasingly of grains.... Sedentism, crowding, and a diet increasingly dominated by cereals were revolutionary changes that left an immediate and legible mark on the archaeological record. (Scott 84–85)

Nor was a decrease in stature the only physical effect undergone by people who traded the forest for the farm, and the hunt for the pastorage of sheep, goats, pigs, and cattle. In the first place, the unprecedented crowding together of human beings required to pursue agriculture, and the sedentary life of those who dwell amid the fields they must constantly tend, brought with them sanitary challenges that hunter-gatherers, whose populations are more dispersed and who seldom linger for long in one spot, did not have to reckon with on the same scale. Thus in early farming communities we see archeological evidence of fecal-borne maladies such as cholera and typhoid. But illnesses created by rubbing shoulders with our fellow humans are overshadowed by the diseases that arise from sharing close quarters with domesticated animals and the vermin that feed upon stored grain, maladies such as smallpox, influenza, measles, and the plague. Indeed, "a list of diseases and conditions evident in skeletal and fecal remains of early farmers but absent among hunter-gatherers" include "malnutrition, osteomyelitis and periostitis (bone infections), intestinal parasites, yaws, syphilis, leprosy, tuberculosis, anemia (from poor diet as well as from hookworms), rickets in children, osteomalacia in adults, retarded childhood growth, and short stature in adults" (Manning 37). Across the decades after Man the Hunter, it became increasingly clear that the real winners in the Neolithic period had been the microbes to which humans were vulnerable, who had never had it so good as when hunter-gatherers began to live by farming.

One reason put forward as to why the adoption of agriculture meant a general decline in nutrition is that, as the Neolithic progressed, and even as it spread geographically, the sheer number of different foods that people consumed shrank dramatically. The domestication of plants that began approximately twelve thousand years ago was nothing less than a "profound economic transformation" that "resulted in a relentless loss of plant biodiversity, as an ever-expanding human population became increasingly reliant on a food supply drawn from fewer and fewer staples" (Jordan and Cummings, "Innovations" 599). The plants that agriculturalists favor are those that are amenable (naturally and through domestication) to harvesting and storage, which limits the spectrum of nutrients they can offer human beings. Moreover, "the health risks of eating only a few types of food are particularly high when cereal grains provide the bulk of calories" (Gremillion 110). Compared to the thousands of species of fruits, nuts, legumes, grasses, and herbs usually available to foraging bands, the farmer eats from a narrow and nutritionally rickety table. (A similar, though less drastic diminishment occurs when forest hunting gives way to pastoralism.) And, of course, the perfected form of malnutrition is starvation, which also becomes a more frequent occurrence as the range of available foods narrows. Whereas any number of plants and animals can, for various reasons, disappear from the range of hunter-gatherers without triggering a famine, tilled fields that tend closer and closer to being monocultural create much more suffering when weather, insects, or blights cause them to fail. We are accustomed to think of complex systems liable to catastrophic failure as being a modern hallmark—chemical factories, nuclear reactors, oil tankers—but it is sobering to think that the pattern for such "all in" gambles on survival or extinction was first laid down millennia ago.

It seems also to be the case that when a foraging band does occasionally suffer from hunger, the great majority of its members suffer to a similar degree. This is because, among most hunter-gatherer cultures, figures of authority tend to be temporary and situational, their powers limited within familial lines or to other particularized cohorts, and rarely carry with them the power of life and death. Because members of (extant) foraging societies can move rather freely between affiliated but physically separated bands, and because, unlike in agricultural settlements, "individuals are not bound to fixed areas, to fixed assets or to fixed resources," they are empowered to "move away without difficulty and at a moment's notice from constraint which others may seek to impose on them." This ability to vote against would-be tyrants with one's feet "is a powerful levelling mechanism, positively valued like other levelling mechanisms in these societies" (Woodburn 92). Thus it is not a question of hunter-gatherers being, as individuals, somehow innocent of social ambition; rather, it is that such ambitions are actively checked at the level of the community: "People [in foraging bands] are well aware of the possibility that individuals or groups within their own egalitarian societies may try to acquire more wealth, to assert more power or claim more status than other people, and are vigilant in seeking to prevent or to limit this. The verbal rhetoric of equality may or may not be elaborated but actions speak loudly: equality is repeatedly acted out, publicly demonstrated, in opposition to possible inequality" (Woodburn 88). Hence the situation that repeatedly occurred on the western frontier of the United States, where impatient or indifferent Indian agents believed themselves to be negotiating (or bilking) the "chief" of an entire "tribe," only to find that other members of the indigenous nation recognized no such person possessed of any rights to order them about, much less surrender their ancestral grounds.

Such egalitarianism, however, was clearly not evident in even the earliest agricultural settlements of Mesopotamia, where social stratification and a marked division of labor is detectable from the beginning of the archaeological record (Zerzan, *People's History* 86–87). Indeed, inequality seems reliably to grow up alongside field crops, as if it were itself a variety of cereal grain, for wherever grasses begin to be domesticated there soon arrives evidence of a distinction between the many who perform the stoop labor of fixed-field tillage and those few who oversee it from a canopied platform. Such disparities in life experiences, which are spawned by even the earliest farming communities, only intensified with the growth of urban centers such as Uruk or Akkad, for while the bones of kings and hierophants may share the signs of malnutrition that mark those of their underlings, repetitive-motion injuries from bending, milling, and hauling disfigure only the latter. Thus, though "human bondage was undoubtedly known in the ancient Middle East before the appearance of the first state," the region's earliest grain cities "elaborated and scaled up the institution of slavery" as eagerly as they did the "sedentism and the domestication of grain" that made these oppressions possible in the first place, such that "it would be almost impossible to exaggerate the centrality of bondage, in one form or another, in the development of the state" (Scott 155). And there seems little in the ancient Near East to differentiate the lot of the enslaved person, the subject of corvée labor, or the peasant tethered to the land—unfreedom and a lifetime spent between sun and furrow was their unfortunate and ubiquitous lot. Thus, while my use of the word "farmer" as a generic term will be occasionally required, it should always be kept in mind that the term most properly refers to the *owner* of a farm, while in point of fact *farm laborers* have always vastly outnumbered those who either manage fields in the name of the temple or crown, or who occasionally own the land outright. Unlike when something happens to a band of hunter-gatherers, when something happens to a settlement of agriculturalists it always happens unequally.

If, as Walter Benjamin asserts, there is no document of civilization that is not at the same time a document of barbarism, let us now consider any farming settlement's defensive wall as a text and read what it says to us about the correlation between the rise of agriculture and the increase of organized violence. It certainly appears as if ramparts sprang up about the same time as domesticated cereal grains, for "there was a sufficient threat of warfare to stimulate the investment in massive defensive constructions as early as the Pre-Pottery Neolithic A community at Jericho"—that is, between 10,000 and 8,800 BCE, at the very dawn of fixed-field tillage (Redman 320). Without romanticizing foragers as people wholly innocent of interpersonal and intergroup violence, such self-encircling barriers speak of something new under the sun. Given the fact that hunter-gatherer communities do not *hold* territory, attacks between hunter-gatherer communities for territorial gain are a nonsequitur, and it also makes little sense for one band of foragers to mount a plundering raid on another, for there will be no cache of food and few status objects to carry off. By contrast, the very laboriousness of agriculture makes the stored harvest (provided the harvest has succeeded) an attractive object of theft while the social stratification endemic to farming settlements assures that the royal and priestly compounds will contain some luxuries worth looting. Indeed, one of the first recognizable divisions of labor in the earliest agrocities was a separate warrior class: "This process reached maturity during the second half of the Early Dynastic period [Mesopotamia between 2650 and 2300 BCE] for which there is widespread evidence for organized warfare and an elite whose primary purpose was to conduct armed campaigns. Archeological and written evidence indicates that militarism played a major role in the formation of early cities and states. The king lists show a preoccupation with war, many of the important monuments of the Early Dynastic period being portrayals of military campaigns" (Redman 321). And while an elite warrior class might *conduct* incessant military adventures, it was the mass of unfree laborers who were drafted into fighting them. If, within foraging bands, by contrast, the power of any individual to coerce others into battle is severely capped by everyone's mobility, then the ease and abundance of the foraging life serves as an additional check upon military strongmen, for, notwithstanding the intimate social bonding that characterizes such communities, "adults of either sex can readily, if they choose, obtain enough food to feed themselves adequately and are . . . *potentially autonomous*" (Woodburn 95, italics mine). Within such "fission-fusion" societies, the man who would be king can simply find little traction for his ambitions, martial or otherwise.

What can contemporary anthropology say about the social bonds within ancient foraging communities, and the contrast such affective ties might present to those that were operative within early farming towns like Çatalhöyük or early grain cities such as Uruk? Perhaps the most that one can confidently affirm is that recent ethnological observers (until very lately all of them visitors from agriculturalist societies) are consistently struck by the intimacy and intensity of social bonds in surviving hunter-gatherer bands and can point to a number of social practices designed to tamp down resentments and foster communal harmony. For instance, according to Lorna Marshall, who performed fieldwork among the Ju/'hoansi, such aids to communal harmony include frequent gift-giving, elaborate rituals of politeness, and nonaggressive ways of expressing dissatisfaction. Most important among these, however, is clearly the expectation, consistently satisfied, that all food will be communally shared:

> The custom of sharing meat helps to keep stress and hostility over food at a low intensity. The practical value of using up the meat when it is fresh is obvious to all, and the !Kung [i.e., Ju/'hoansi] are fully aware of the enormous social value of the sharing custom. The fear of hunger is mitigated: the person with whom one shares will share in turn when he gets meat; people are sustained by a web of mutual obligation. If there is hunger, it is commonly shared. There are no distinct haves and have-nots. One is not alone. (71–72)

If this is at all typical of Paleolithic societies—a question that is rightly and continually at issue (Cannon 93–98; Jordan 904–6)—the archeological record can at least offer a contrast in food distribution once the agricultural regimes of Mesopotamia come into full blossom. While the surviving pottery of Sumerian Ubaid culture (6500–4000 BCE) are often finely wrought and intricately decorated, by about 3800 BCE a marked change can be observed: "While Ubaid potsherds show delicate patterns and thin profiles, the most conspicuous Uruk [period] pot, found in huge numbers at any Uruk site, is a misshapen and lumpish clay bowl, a throw-away mass-produced container known as the so-called beveled-rim bowl. Archaic signs associate this bowl with food and it has been argued that grain rations, or perhaps some cooked food, were handed out to workers" (Leick 35–36)—handed out, that is, as payment for field labor. To view this contrast is to instantly understand that the bevel-rimmed bowl was "produced on something approaching an industrial level" (Van de Mieroop 177), and that such vessels' deliberate ugliness was designed to visually underscore the existence of "distinct haves and have nots" every bit as much as to fulfill its practical purpose: "In the subsequent Uruk period, the ubiquitous beveled-rim bowls were crude, mass-produced containers of rations. . . . [Thus] the common experiences of eating and drinking, which [had been] . . . vehicles for artistic expression and thus a way to know the world, were transformed into the bureaucratic management of the food supply, so that the everyday acts of production and consumption (in work gangs) were altered by the new state's desire to simplify and shape the universe that it was intending to create" (Yoffee 101). In other words, the bevel-rimmed bowl of porridge was every bit as dull and demeaning as the day of stoop labor that earned it, and, far from being a vehicle for the communal sharing of natural bounty, it was a penurious ceramic paystub.

But, in the end, perhaps we must return to Sahlins's "bankers' hours" to get at the heart of the affective differences between foragers and farmers. If the Ju/'hoansi among whom Lorna Marshall lived do indeed enjoy what we would call long daily stretches of leisure time, she reports that they fill it up with a ceaseless stream of talk:

> The [Ju/'hoansi] are the most loquacious people I know. Conversation in a [Ju/'hoansi] encampment is a constant sound like the sound of a brook, and as low and lapping, except for shrieks of laughter. People cluster together in little groups during the day, talking, perhaps making

artifacts at the same time. At night, families talk late by their fires, or visit at other family fires with their children between their knees or in their arms if the wind is cold.

There always seems to be plenty to talk about. People tell about events with much detail and repetition and discuss the comings and goings of their relatives and friends and make plans. Their greatest preoccupation and the subject they talk about most often, I think, is food. (67)

What I am suggesting here is that the closest we are going to come to something empirical will be to let duration stand as a proxy for intensity. Just as it is true that among Marshall's subjects access to physical resources such as waterholes is dependent upon their membership in a band, "they are also extremely dependent emotionally on the sense of belonging and on companionship. Separation and loneliness are unendurable to them. . . . Security and comfort for them lie in their belonging to the group, free from the threat of rejection and hostility" (65–66). We know from the archaeological record that the unfree denizens of Lagash worked much longer and harder than the Ju/'hoansi, which makes it likely that they also had, in some absolute sense, less to say to each other, which in turn reflects a diminished sociality whose root cause is the turn to agriculture. Among the Ju/'hoansi, by contrast, and by implication among hunter-gatherers more generally, the talking cure is interminable, and thus spiritually efficacious.

One way in which the employment of a scholarly, and therefore supposedly neutral, term of art has continued to subtly valorize farming at the expense of foraging consists in labeling the former a "delayed-return activity," whereupon hunting and gathering becomes an "immediate-return activity." No one who has encountered the two terms juxtaposed can help but hear the rustle of virtues sidling over toward the tiller, for she is thus required to plan carefully, to delay gratification, to engage in abstract thought, and to employ mathematics, while the forager supposedly is not. There are two problems with this, the first of which is, according to James Scott, that the distinction results in "a caricature of hunter-gatherers," which suggests by its "implied contrast" that "the hunter-gatherer is an improvident, spontaneous creature of impulse, coursing the landscape in hope of stumbling on game or finding something good to pluck from a bush or tree" (65). The truth, of course, is that getting one's subsistence through a deep understanding of one's environment involves the construction of such things as weirs, nets, traps, and chutes for animal capture, as well as facilities for "smoking, drying, or salting of the catch," and that all these are "delayed-return activities par excellence," even though they require a fraction of the toil demanded if one is instead trying to bring fixed fields of cereals to successful harvest (65–66).

The second problem is that a colorless phrase such as "delayed-return activity" washes out something that is ineluctably at the center of the delay: chronic anxiety. As Scott points out, "from field clearing . . . to sowing, to weeding, to watering, to constant vigilance as the crop ripens, the dominant cultivar organizes much of our timetable," tying farmers to "meticulous, demanding, interlocked, and mandatory annual and daily routines" (90–91), routines that are remarkably unforgiving of error, negligence, or even leisure. Moreover, the enemies of farmers are everywhere in the environmental surround—in thunderclouds, rodent warrens, a hundred species of weeds, and mold spores invisible to the naked eye, such that even if all the mandatory tasks are accomplished, survival is still largely in the hands of laughing Chance. Thus, adopting a tiller's mindset means "accepting the relentless need to remake" the landscape rather than gathering what it offers, and to "setting pleasure at the far end, the distant terminus, of a journey of hardship" (Brody 83), a hardship that is psychic as much as it is physical. By contrast, one of the responders to Sahlins's positive reassessment of foragers at the Man the Hunter conference drew attention to his argument that such peoples enjoy "confidence in the yield of the morrow" (Helm 89), and Sahlins himself declares that "rather than despair at the inadequacy of human means," hunter-gatherers feel "a confidence which is the reasonable human attribute of a generally successful economy" (29). The point is that here, as in Einsteinian physics, space and time cannot be separated—to trust that the land is sufficiently abundant is to trust in tomorrow, and that trust is by definition the opposite of anxiety. The first affluent society was also the last one not to sicken its mind with worry.

To not fret about tomorrow is also to refuse anxiety concerning the coming decade, or the next century, which moves our argument into the realm of history, or, rather, the absence of our familiar conception of such. It always sounds a bit odd to describe a negative state, but if we are truly to compare the lives of foragers and agriculturalists, we should be as clear as we can about what the lack of an historical consciousness might entail. As I have just unwittingly demonstrated, the words "negative" and "lack" arise almost inevitably, but we can also access an utterance where this supposed cypher is given a name, so that its positive attributes might be spoken. Here is Coetzee's Magistrate from *Waiting for the Barbarians*:

> What has made it impossible for us to live in time like fish in water, like birds in the air, like children? It is the fault of Empire! Empire has created the time of history. Empire has located its existence not in the smooth recurrent spinning time of the cycle of the seasons, but in the jagged time of rise and fall, of beginning and end, of catastrophe. Empire dooms itself to live in history and to plot against history. One thought alone preoccupies the submerged mind of Empire: how not to end, how not to die, how to prolong its era. (154)

The Magistrate's "time of the cycle of the seasons," his longed-for alternative to that civilized chronicle of barbaric acts we call "history," is not experienced as an absence but as an abundance, not as a stasis but as a process. His vision seems congruent with much that extant hunter-gatherers have told anthropologists about their intellectual conceptions and lived experience of change over time, which are ineluctably bound up with their expectations about the generous and reliable bounty of the landscapes through which they move:

> To foragers, change was immanent in the environment—it happened all the time, when the wind blew, the rain fell, or an elephant cleared a new path. But change was always constrained by a deeper sense of confidence in the continuity and predictability of the world around them. Every season was different from those that preceded it, yet these differences always fell within a range of predictable changes....
>   To produce food [by means of agriculture, however,] requires that you live at once in the past, present, and future. Almost every task on a farm is focused on achieving a future goal or managing a future risk based on past experience. (Suzman 236)

Coetzee's Magistrate, though himself an anthropologist on the brink of escaping his own and his settlement's agro-culture, cannot quite bring himself to credit nonfarmers with something he can call "civilization," even though he is clearly no longer content with his own. Perhaps it is true, then, that it is exclusively "the non-domesticated [who] know that only the present can be total," who "live life with incomparably greater immediacy, density and passion than we do"—we who, in Percy Shelley's words, "look before and after.... And sigh for what is not" (Zerzan, "Future Primitive" 265). For now, the point is to recognize that what we commonly call "a sense of history" is merely at base a farmer's mindset that reactively fears the years to come on the good authority of the bitter disappointments of years gone by. And when such a mindset feeds on hopes, it often becomes, in a phrase with appropriately laborious connotations, "an errand through time," a vision of a polity's destiny set by "priests [and] sky gods [for] a chosen people" (Martin 42), whose timetable may be every bit as uncompromising as that of the yearly agricultural calendar.

Another question that has, in recent decades, been thoroughly rethought, if not yet conclusively answered, is how intrinsically aggressive prehistoric agriculturalists tended to be when encountering huntergatherers whose foraging territories they coveted for plowing. But this is bound up with a prior question, since "the real problem ... is not to explain why some people were slow to adopt agriculture but why anybody took it up at all when it was so obviously beastly" (Tudge 3). What seems beyond dispute is that there was a long ramp-up to what we would today immediately recognize as fixed-field agriculture. Paleolithic huntergatherers opportunistically tended naturally occurring patches of wild cereals, selecting those that were the easiest to exploit and discarding the rest, thus spreading the seeds of those chosen in localities close to camping sites, furthering this process of unconscious plant domestication over millennia until at some point it became an intentional strategy (Jordan and Cummings, "Innovations" 599–603; David Harris 735–40). Why, though, full-fledged tilling cultures came into independent existence in such places as Mesopotamia, the Nile Valley, Northern India, the Yangtze Delta, and Mesoamerica is still debated, with the "takeoff" usually attributed to some combination of climate change, demographic increase, evolutionary imperatives, cultural tensions, or—given a recent interest in individual agency—entrepreneurial individuals (Suzman 180, 205; Hayden 658). There are even those who maintain that some kind of religio-ideological development took place that made the cosmologies of key Paleolithic peoples more amenable to planting, both of cereal grains and of themselves (Cauvin).

However, if there is anything that unites most of these theories—the majority of them carefully hedged and tentatively asserted—it is the idea of *crisis*. That is to say, the one idea that gets no hearing at all anymore is the traditional one that agriculture was such an obvious improvement upon foraging that once a genius invented it or a people stumbled onto it, it was immediately adopted by general acclimation. This cannot have happened, since existent "hunter-collectors often display all the skills and techniques necessary for practicing agriculture minus the step of deliberate planting" (Marvin Harris 12). In the famous remark of a Ju/'hoansi forager, whose people had long, extensive, and often unhappy experience with the farming cultures that surrounded them, including a vivid sense of how hard their tilling neighbors toiled: "Why should we plant, when there are so many mongongo nuts in the world?" (Lee 47). Hence, the needed addition of some kind of emergency, or at least some kind of chronic, increasing unpleasure, to the recipe. For a good many centuries the development of agriculture was thought to be the inevitable development of robust people who were either realizing God's plan or leveraging their innate intelligence—a moment of peak eudaemonia, in other words. Now, by contrast, it appears as the dubious, perhaps desperate expedient of people under duress. Volcanoes, anyone?

Once agriculture was established in its geographical cradles, how was it exported? To articulate the two extreme possibilities, did the *idea* of tilling spread as foraging peoples perceived its clear advantages and began mimicking their neighbors by taking up the plow and the grindstone? Or did agriculturalists, pressured by swelling numbers (since farming does allow faster population growth than hunting and gathering) and hungry for evermore land to plant upon, push aside or exterminate the nonfarmers who were still employing the land in a Paleolithic fashion? Of late, much of this debate has centered around the still relatively new field of paleogenetics, which employs the genomes of human remains to reconstruct (to the layman's eyes) surprisingly detailed maps of human migrations across thousands of miles and thousands of years. Between the soft and hard versions of agriculture's spread into Europe, the geneticists seem to lean toward the latter, for into a continent entirely occupied by foragers,

> came the first farmers, who lived between about eighty-eight hundred and forty-five hundred years ago in Germany, Spain, Hungary, and Anatolia. Ancient farmers from all these places were genetically similar to present-day Sardinians, showing that a pioneer farmer population had landed in Greece probably from Anatolia, and then spread to Iberia in the west and Germany in the north, retaining at least 90 percent of their DNA from that immigrant source, which meant that they mixed minimally with the hunter-gatherers they encountered along

the way. Further investigation, though, showed that it was not quite so simple. . . .

[Still, by 4000–3000 BCE,] Europe had reached a new equilibrium. The unmixed hunter-gatherers were disappearing, persisting only in isolated pockets like the islands off southern Sweden. In southeastern Europe, a settled farmer population had developed the most socially stratified societies known up until that time. (Reich 105–6)

This note of caution from the scientists about the language spoken by prehistoric DNA—"It was not quite so simple"—has not prevented others from looking at the historical record of more recent epochs and drawing strong conclusions. As Richard Manning puts it, "We have no clear examples of colonized hunter-gatherers who willingly, peacefully converted to farming. Most went as slaves; most were dragged kicking and screaming, or just plain died" (41). And yet most contemporary paleoanthropologists seem eager to emphasize exceptions and complications, some pointing to Neolithic communities that appear to have farmed while also practicing a good deal of hunting and gathering (Raemaekers 819–20), and others noting the persistence, especially in lands deemed only marginally workable by tillers, of a patchwork of farming and foraging communities who clearly traded rather than raided for each others' products (Damm and Forsberg 849–51). Still, to express the majority opinion in the cool diction of social science, during the Neolithic period farming spread into lands occupied by foragers through a process that featured decidedly more "displacement" than "co-option." Apparently the first dual-use implement was a sickle.

The preponderance of evidence showing farming cultures to have been chronically aggressive toward the hunter-gatherers outside their city walls is only bolstered by the scholarship suggesting that urban ramparts, and even the Great Wall of China itself, served a different function than that promulgated by the cultural elites who ordered them built. The view now is that they were intended mainly to keep unfree agricultural laborers *in* rather than nomadic barbarians *out*, that their primary purpose was the control of a workforce that was unfree and who had good reason to suppose the open steppe offered an easier life than the cordoned field (Scott 30, 138, 233). Thus, while the "wall may have defended the city from attack or conquest at certain points in its life . . . its most important daily function was to regulate passage into and out of the city" (Oles 51). One implication of this is that the traditional notion that walls are erected to keep "primitives" from trespassing into "civilized" gardens is one of the first and most enduringly important pieces of agriculturalist ideology. Here, as in the risky dependence on error-prone technology that characterizes the agricultural gambit itself, there is something strikingly modern about the bad faith of ancient Mesopotamian kings. An implacable enemy is designated, a nation's coffers are drained to erect a towering infrastructure in the name of "defense," and yet the actual victims of the resulting surveillance and martial capabilities turn out to be the citizens of the supposedly besieged bastion itself. It appears that many aspects of the way we live now first began to be fashioned alongside the bevel-rimmed bowl.

One aspect of agriculture that has received little attention generally, but that we will take up at some length later in this book, is the way in which agriculture has visually and physically fragmented our world. If, as touched on above, the Great Wall of China, as well as those which surrounded grain cities from Gilgamesh's Uruk onward, were fulfilling functions other than those trumpeted by their polities' ideologies, they were always palpable objects in the visual field: looming, blocking, overlooking, shadowing. One of the first consequences of agriculture—of markedly, permanently changing the landscape through human effort as a way of securing subsistence—is to physically and mentally bifurcate the environmental surround in a way that foraging does not require one to do: "Thus farming societies routinely divided the landscape around them into cultural and natural spaces. Spaces that they successfully rendered productive through their labor, such as farmhouses, yards, granaries, barns, villages, gardens, pastures, and fields, were domesticated, cultural spaces, whereas those outside of their immediate control they considered wild, natural spaces. And, critically, the boundaries between these spaces were often demarcated by fences, gates, walls, ditches, and hedgerows" (Suzman 238–39).

If agriculture always plants, nurtures, and propagates ramparts alongside its cereals, it simultaneously throws up bastions within the mind that segregate "our" domain from the rest of nature, creating a habit of thought that is alien to the forager's sense of a fluid and pervasive sacredness, in which, even among different species "a chain of life join[s] every individual creature and thing, so that continuous transition or metamorphosis of one being into another appears both possible and necessary" (Sandars 65). Another way to conceive of the difference between the foraging and the agricultural mind would be to say that in the former well-being is predicated on the continuous and unimpeded flow of energies between and among disparate entities, while in the latter it is precisely the blockage of such flow that is crucial to satisfactions, since "walls exist primarily not to *differentiate*, but to *segregate*," segregation denoting not just that one understands the difference between two things but that one intends to prevent an exchange between them (Oles 15). Therefore the consequences of such rearings stretch far beyond the mechanics of agronomy, for, "like the rest of the things people make, walls both reflect and create values" (xix). As late as the mid-twentieth century, social critics sometimes articulated a nostalgia for an era (Classical Greece, the Middle Ages, the Renaissance) when human communities and psyches were supposedly less kaleidoscopic than those fractured under the blows of modernity. It is now understood, of course, that such voices underestimated the complexity of and contention within the past ages they pined for. But, if we expand our view from historical to anthropological time frames, we can perhaps perceive a more genuine object of desire, a lost unity of psychology, landscape, and cosmology that came to an end when the products of our species' ingenuity became so fragile as to require their—and our—walling off from the wider world.

And if the first Enclosure Acts were written during the Neolithic, this brings us to yet another unsettling fact about the birth of farming. Consider for a moment all the commonplaces, all the unremarked givens of our lives, whose beginnings we can now plausibly trace to our species' agricultural turn. That fateful cultural swerve divided up the physical world into parcels that eventually were fitted with the labels of "theirs" and "ours." It led to long-term planning, which, as we have seen, is another way of phrasing chronic worry. It created the first bosses and the first underlings, the first genuine juxtapositions of material wealth and poverty. And, perhaps most portentously, it made labor into something it had never been before—a virtue. This last occurred because of the radical precarity of farming, since, unlike the long line of hunter-gatherers who preceded them, the first tillers walked a daily knife's-edge of survival at the mercy of a multitude of factors they could not control. The one factor they *could* control, within the limits of human exhaustion, was how hard they worked, so they worked all the harder, and then harder still, making a fetish of their sweat (Tudge 35, 49; Suzman 225). And, once their numbers increased and the foragers' arts were lost or rendered moot, then the trap had snapped shut and there was no going back. Which meant in turn that there was no solution but to hope for the ever-upward line upon the graph, the good weather due to arrive next season, the larger yield next year, the "progress" that would surely deliver them from penury. Could it thus be that capitalism—that other hyperobject so overawing, so seemingly immovable, so invisibly pervasive—is itself, ultimately, just another epiphenomenon of agriculture, albeit its most momentous?

If there is any truth to this, what follows? I believe that a keener awareness of capitalism's genealogy need not prompt us to absolve it of any of the sins we are used to attributing to it—that, indeed, seeing capitalism as a belated but formidable progeny of the plow might contain an occasional clarifying surprise. Think, for example, about the modern supermarket, which metastasized from a lone Piggly Wiggly in 1916 to a world-enveloping template that now dictates how everyone fiscally situated between the destitute and the megarich physically obtains their daily bread (Green 114). The fact that urbanites from Hoboken to Hanoi know how to navigate a cart down a grocery aisle is usually explained in the language of economies of scale, reduced labor costs, and just-in-time supply chains. But could it also be the case that every trip to the supermarket activates some response within us that coalesced over the 95 percent of our species' existence wherein we were all of us hunter-gatherers? After all, what the megastore offers is a version of daily foraging in which—provided one has the money for checkout—every expedition meets with abounding success. The question then becomes, how hard or softly need we scratch the capitalist consumer's brittle surface before the hunter-gatherer beneath can be sensed?

Or, to put it another way, how thorough, how irreversible has been our Great Forgetting? If the chapters that follow are at all convincing, then the answer must be that somewhere deep within our minds remain pathways that still resemble the crookedness of the forest trail rather than the linearity of the furrowed field. If this were not the case, then the narrow spectrum of emotions that a farmer is authorized to feel when glimpsing a forager (i.e., pity and fear) should be the sum of it. But there is often a disquieting remainder. If there is not, why do the "monstrous" Creature and Heathcliff, declared to be the nomadic enemies of sedentary civilization, claim our sympathies despite their supposed physical and moral ugliness? How do Coetzee's foragers, who have seemingly been forced away from their spiritual wellsprings, still possess an innate dignity and reticent wisdom that their scythe-wielding oppressors can only envy and attempt to ignore or destroy? Why are Prospero and Crusoe not only quick to libel hunter-gatherers as cannibals but also forced by their mere proximity to perform anxious caricatures of the clearing, planting, and hoarding that are supposedly the very markers of their own superior rationality? And why do the walls rising from both Crusoe's and Cruso's islands, as well as the ramparts surrounding both Frankenstein's Geneva and Thrushcross Grange, seem to promote a curious confusion about whether they defend or incarcerate those within them? Are we really so content to continue reaping what we have been sowing for so long, or are we haunted by the feeling that, as the saying goes, we have somehow chosen a very hard row to hoe?

3

Shelley's and Brontë's Solitary Walkers

IF ROUSSEAU'S notion that vulcanism might have sparked the birth of agriculture puts some of his readers off, it is nevertheless the case that one particular volcano played a part in the genesis of that very Rousseauean narrative *Frankenstein* (1818). Many of Mary Shelley's readers have heard that the eruption of Mount Tambora in April 1815, which blanketed the earth in a persistent veil of stratospheric particulates, was responsible for the extraordinarily cold and rainy summer of 1816, which in turn led the frustrated tourists at the Villa Diodati to make the best of things by devising a story-writing competition on a Gothic theme. What is less remembered, however, is that the same geologic event that ruined The Year without Summer's high season also blighted the ensuing harvest. Indeed, the "the subsistence crisis of 1816–17 was the worst European famine since 1709–10 and probably amounted to the most severe scarcity since the seventeenth century," meaning that across western Europe "the shortfall of cereal production ... drove bread prices beyond the reach even of the majority who were employed at customary wage levels." This widespread food insecurity and regional famine "set on foot the last great wave of European grain riots," whose violent manifestations "ranged from time-sanctioned demonstrations in grain markets or in front of bakers' shops to looting, rioting, and arson. Rural misery in some regions spawned a rebellious upsurge of pillage and rioting and, on occasion, ravaging vagrant bands attacked farms and even markets" (Post 27, 36, 68). Thus, if Mary Shelley was already inclined to utilize her novel as a vehicle for promoting Rousseau's ideas concerning education, it may be that the hollowed faces and outstretched hands she encountered every day in the London streets also increased her susceptibility to his theories about the happiness enjoyed by foragers and the sorrows inaugurated by the plow. Perhaps this is why, at the text's midpoint, in the midst of his confession to Victor, the Creature bemoans his own fate in words that might well stand as Rousseau's own lament for the anthropological tragedy of humankind: "Oh, that I had forever remained in my native wood, nor known nor felt beyond the sensations of hunger, thirst, and heat!" (92). At any rate, Shelley's novel suggests that Victor's Creature, himself an ontological mistake, might have somewhat mitigated that error by never stepping forth from the forest where, in his precocious "youth," he was quickly mastering the forager's art and enjoying his closest approach to happiness.

But, of course, there is one plank in Rousseau's primitivist platform that Shelley refuses to endorse, for the lack of companionship that perfects the happiness of the philosophe's hunter-gatherer is precisely what immiserates the Creature. An essay on Rousseau that Shelley wrote two decades after the novel clearly delineates where, anthropologically, she will follow him, and where she will (and always did) balk. On the one hand, she appears to grant the hedonic and moral advantages of the foraging life compared to that on offer from agro-culture:

> The scroll of society unrolled itself before him, such as he found it, blotted and tainted.... And beside it he placed a picture of pristine innocence, of man enjoying the full development of his physical powers; living for the day as it rose, untouched by care, unbewildered by intellectual speculations, by vanity, emulation, or pride; man liberated from the control of opinion and the tyranny of his own unreasonable desires. ("Rousseau" 134)

On the other hand, Rousseau's vision of the Paleolithic as an era of atomistic self-sufficiency neither attracts nor convinces her. Thus, while

> much may be granted to the strength that human beings enjoy in savage life[, and] much to the little needed by the inhabitants of those happy isles where food grows beneath their feet; [it is nevertheless a fact that] man has ever been found (except in one or two cases, where the human animal descends below brutes,) the protector of women, and the source of his children's subsistence; and among all societies, however barbarously constituted, the gentler and nobler individuals among them have loved their wives and their offspring with constant and self-sacrificing

passion. Let us advance civilisation to its highest pitch, or retrograde to its origin, and let both bring freedom from political and social slavery; but in all let us hold fast by the affections: the cultivation of these ought to be the scope of every teacher of morality, every well-wisher to the improvement of the human race. (134–35)

And so, while the Creature speaks Rousseauean orthodoxy when he asserts that he was born "benevolent," and that his "soul glowed with love and humanity" until, encountering the corrupted hearts of others, "misery made [him] a fiend," he deviates markedly by claiming that the source this chronic and deforming unhappiness is the fact that he is "alone, miserably alone" (75)—ergo his un-Rousseauean request to Victor for a mate whose name he will presumably know and whose children (Victor fears) he will help to rear.

Maximillian Novak offers an important generalization about most of the stadial historians discussed in chapter 2, including Rousseau, noting that "in the seventeenth and eighteenth centuries, discussions of the primitive state of man almost always commenced with the image of an isolated being, abstracted from society." Defoe's Crusoe, for instance, is an example of this, and we know that Shelley read *Robinson Crusoe* just prior to commencing work on *Frankenstein*. These Enlightenment isolatos, Novak goes on, could be figured in at least three ways: "as able to achieve and enjoy roughly the same happiness and freedom as modern peoples, as luckily possessed of Golden Age virtues and powers that have deteriorated or disappeared in the modern era," or as "insecure, and so far from being happy" that they drag out their existence "in constant fear of death" (*Defoe* 23). Crusoe himself is interesting in this regard, as he is surprisingly untroubled by his isolation until, after seeing the alien footprint, he begins to fear being "murther'd" and "devour'd" on an hourly basis. But, for all the texts that appear on the Creature's syllabus, Defoe's novel is absent. Instead, the one speculative historian who is explicitly name-checked is Volney, whose view of early man seems to identify primitive felicity with primitive community, and who informs us that ancient foragers immediately "associated to secure their existence, to augment their powers, to protect their enjoyments," "succor[ing]" each other and "shar[ing]" the means of subsistence (chap. 7). Shelley's Creature is thus doubly unfortunate since, living as a hunter-gatherer, he obtains his food in a way that should, in theory, allow him to exercise and retain Novak's "Golden Age virtues and powers," but does so only while simultaneously lacking the primordial community that, in Shelley's view, would not merely sustain them but also in large part *constitute* them. If, as Melzer claims, Rousseau is a figure who garners vehement admirers but yet possesses "no disciples" (ix), we must count *Frankenstein* as offering yet another proof of this.

These necessary distinctions having been made, we can proceed to the details of how Shelley figures her Creature as a stage-one hunter-gatherer, and what his identity as such implies about the novel's tentative longings for a world innocent of the plow. To begin with, Victor's creation is a composite human constructed from resurrected portions of the dead. This means that the Creature is, in his very conception, both a revivification of the human past and a single figure who, because he is made of many others, becomes (if only in an ironic and Gothic key) a representative figure, a singleton who stands in for a posited but unnamed group of others. He therefore resembles nothing so much as that staple figure of Rousseau and his fellow stadial theorists, "man in the state of nature"—even *before* he himself is rudely thrust out into nature by Victor's criminal neglect. Furthermore, while Frankenstein brags of birthing "a new species" (Shelley 36), he creates a being who is unmistakably human, making his project not so much the creation of biological novelty as a re-creation of our own species, a second Genesis that sets the cosmic clock back to dawn and lets a more or less familiar story of human development begin rerunning itself before our eyes. Even Victor's first horrified description of his animated handiwork evokes a biblical-era past, since, according to him, "a mummy again endued with animation could not be so hideous as that wretch" (40). Then, of course, once the Creature comes to full consciousness of his own situation—and absorbs *Paradise Lost*—he perceives himself as an amalgam of Miltonic first man and Enlightenment monad: "Like Adam, I was apparently united by no link to any other being in existence" (101). Thus, while on one level the Creature is undoubtedly something new under the sun, the newness he radiates suggests at every moment a paradoxical primality, a time long past when our species as a whole was but newly created.

It is a critical commonplace that the Creature's recounting of his earliest days, when he wandered about the forest and "saw, felt, heard, and smelt at the same time" because he could not as yet "distinguish between the operations of [his] various senses" (77), represents "a striking description of what in Lacanian terms would constitute the early stages of the Imaginary order" (Kotze 45). Helplessly subject to hunger and cold, but also delighting in birdsong and moonlight, he encounters "a shapeless mass of disordered perceptions and needs" while enjoying—because he is as yet a "non-subject" inhabiting a "non-linguistic state"—exemption from adult anxiety, frustration, and self-division (Kotze 56; see also Brooks "Monster" 92; Comitini 193–94). Throughout his adulthood and even in his last moments he persists—as Lacan insists we all shall—as "an eternally desiring subject" (Braunstein 110) longing to relive his lost idyll of infancy: "Some years ago, when the images which this world affords first opened upon me, when I felt the cheering warmth of summer and heard the rustling of the leaves and the warbling of the birds, and these were all to me, I should have wept to die; now it is my only consolation" (180).

    This is all convincing, but central to our concerns is the fact that while the Creature enjoys this Edenic psychological state he also lives in a manner reminiscent of the hunting-and-foraging stage posited by the conjectural historians. He wanders about the forest eating a diet of "berries[,] . . . nuts and roots," as well as that staple of the Golden Age, "acorns," while quickly learning to "distinguis[h] the insect from the herb, and by degrees one herb from another." Throughout these (in a double sense) early days, he "rambles" and "travels" while the sun shines, and then makes his bed "on the ground, and s[inks] into sleep" (77–80). Not that there seems anything wrong, in Shelley's mind, with the edibles of later stages, for when the Creature innocently pilfers a shepherd's lunch, he tastes "bread, cheese, milk, and wine" (80), rejecting only the last. Later on, though, while the DeLaceys consume "the vegetables of their garden and the milk of one cow," he continues to "satisfy [him]self with berries, nuts, and roots" (84–85). Amplifying this difference in diet, there seems to exist a natural antipathy between himself and those inhabiting later cultural stages, since the shepherd flees him in terror, "village[rs]" stone him (80), a "rustic" shoots him (111), and his hopeful approaches to the farm-laboring DeLaceys end in debacle (a domus for them, a forager's lean-to for him). Thus it is interesting that in drawing a distinction between his own reaction to the advancing seasons and that of everyone else, he seems to recapitulate a cultural evolution that is unavailable to himself: "Men, who before this change seemed to have been hid in caves, dispersed themselves, and were employed in various arts of cultivation" (88). A nonparticipant in this stadial progress, he remains throughout the novel an inhabitant of caverns and ravines, emerging only in reaction to Victor's provocations and procrastinations.

    If, during his habitation within the imaginary order, the Creature can be said to have had foraging thrust upon him, once he enters the symbolic order, he appears to remain a hunter-gatherer by choice. As he declares during his attempt to persuade Victor to build the female, he conceives of his own and his mate's futurity as constituting a permanent commitment to stage-one existence and seems to think himself the ethical superior of pastoralists and farmers for undertaking such a resolution: "If you consent, neither you nor any other human being shall ever see us again: I will go to the vast wilds of South America. My food is not that of man; I do not destroy the lamb and the kid to glut my appetite; acorns and berries afford me sufficient nourishment. My companion will be of the same nature as myself, and will be content with the same fare. We shall make our bed of dried leaves; the sun will shine on us as on man, and will ripen our food" (115). It might be objected here that the real point is the Creature's vegetarianism, but of course Victor learns to his cost that the Creature is a hunter par excellence, since he himself is stalked by his monster from the environs of Geneva all the way to Scotland. But the Creature will kill animals, too, if only to make a sarcastic point to Victor, as in the note he leaves his creator north of Archangel: "I seek the everlasting ices of the north, where you will feel the misery of cold and frost, to which I am impassive. You will find near this place, if you follow not too tardily, a dead hare; eat and be refreshed" (166). We can hear in this as well a confirmation of what was only hinted at earlier—that the Creature accepts, as a point of pride, the farmer's envious and fearful attribution to the nomadic barbarian of a hypertrophied musculature: "I was more agile than they and could subsist upon coarser diet; I bore the extremes of heat and cold with less injury to my frame; my stature far exceeded theirs" (123). Of course agricultural ideology just as often insists that the physiques of the starveling wanderers are *inferior* to that of those who work the fields (the insistence on *some* kind of difference being the requirement), but here, too, the Creature precisely fits the stereotype, for who possesses a more defective body than he (Youngquist 345–46)? And, concerning his ambiguous appearance, one wonders whether Shelley might have had in mind that previous "monstrous" hunter-gatherer, Caliban. After all, the Creature, like Caliban, is a log-hauler (though he performs this labor in a spirit of charity), and he, too, claims that language has only taught him how to curse his own condition—though, again, like Shakespeare's islander, he is capable of magnificent bouts of eloquence, and, finally, he, like Prospero's "thing of darkness," is prevented from fulfilling his fervent desire to reproduce.

But if *Frankenstein* seems to be at least forager-curious, Frankenstein is violently forager-phobic. Where the Creature intends his promise of relocating to "South America" as proof that he will inhabit an environment that will both keep him clear of humanity and permanently sustain his hunting and gathering, the same location, to judge by Victor's tone, seems to suggest only incest and cannibalism (those ubiquitous libels against hunter-gatherers): "Even if they were to leave Europe, and inhabit the deserts of the new world, yet one of the first results of those sympathies for which the daemon thirsted would be children, and a race of devils would be propagated upon the earth, who might make the very existence of the species of man a condition precarious and full of terror. Had I a right, for my own benefit, to inflict this curse upon everlasting generations?" (132). Since the logical absurdities of Victor's fear are evident (i.e., he could render the female sterile, and then why wouldn't their children emerge perfectly normal?), we are thrown all the more strongly on other motivations for them. The Creature is incestuous, of course, in that he and his mate would share a "father," however negligent (Gilbert and Gubar 228). And cannibalism seems the subtext throughout Victor's fevered imagining that the female might "become ten thousand times more malignant than her mate, and delight, for its own sake, in murder and wretchedness," causing "future ages" to "curse [Victor] as their pest" (132). The breaking point comes for Frankenstein when he spies the Creature "at the casement," emphasizing his perpetually unhoused condition, where Victor claims "a ghastly grin wrinkled his lips" (132)—exposing, one presumes, "his teeth of pearly whiteness" (39), of which we were informed on the night of creation, and that help explain little William's accusation: "You wish to eat me and tear me to pieces" (112). The Creature, by contrast, says of their proposed future, "Our lives will not be happy, but they will be harmless" (115), and he has already figured such an exile to the forests as a return to his primordial, "natural" environment: his "*native* wood," as we have already heard (92, my italics). But Victor's hears only the Creature's vow—made in the heat of his rejection by the DeLaceys—to wage "everlasting war against the species" (107), for the scientist's hyperbolic insistence that allowing the pair to forage together would endanger "the existence of the whole human race" (132) recalls nothing so much as *Robinson Crusoe*'s final vision of a never-ending combat between plantation owners and cannibal armies emerging from the jungle. Like a farmer sighting a "homeless" barbarian, Frankenstein loathes the Creature at the first sight of him exiting the woods (55). Victor's mind, unlike that of *his* creator's, seems imbued with the agriculturalist assumption that what begins with nuts and berries must end with human hearts and livers.

In light of Victor's desire to see his foraging creation as a member of another species altogether, his own syllabus may be as relevant as the

Creature's, for it seems no accident that Paracelsus was one of the intellectual heroes of his youth. Paracelsus was among that cadre of early modern figures who reacted to European discoveries of New World hunter-gatherer cultures by positing a polygenic origin for the various races of the earth, and this despite the notion's heretical divergence from the Mosaic account accepted as orthodox—and, indeed, as theologically central—by Catholic and Protestant authorities alike. Thus, because there was no mention of Amerindians in the Bible, explorers' reports of them prompted Paracelsus to square Genesis with Columbus by declaring that God must have filled the primordial earth with various strains of pre-Adamic hominids through a series of separate creations: "The children of Adam did not inhabit the whole world. That is why some hidden countries have not been populated by Adam's children, but through another creature, created like men outside of Adam's creation. For God did not intend to leave them empty, but had populated the miraculously hidden countries with other men" (quoted in Slotkin 42). Such polygenic theories, though first employed by anxious theologians, persisted into the decades following *Frankenstein*'s publication as the go-to conjecture undergirding various strands of secular, "scientific" racism. Once matriculated at Ingolstadt, Frankenstein supposedly accepts his father's assessment of Paracelsus and his ilk as peddlers of "sad trash" (23), and yet this particular racial alchemist chimes in with Victor's later desire to see his foraging enemy as "nothing in [a] human shape" (55).

But if Victor's willful disbelief in the Creature's humanity can draw on Paracelsus's tomes for support, *Frankenstein* itself eventually tells against him on this matter. By the conclusion of the novel the cumulative weight of the Creature's tragic Weltanschauung, his complete mastery of several literary registers, his balanced eulogy over Victor's corpse, and above all the agonistic intensity of his own guilt and regret, has put the question to rest. Indeed, the only palpable difference between the novel's primordial and modern antagonists is that the former appears, in an almost Darwinian sense, *fitter* than the latter, for as the Creature leads Victor on an epic chase through various climactic regimes stretching from "the wilds of Tartary" (164) to the Arctic, his energy and resilience appear steadily to wax, while those of his pursuer wither. It would seem that, just as Rousseau asserted, the "wild" version of the species is larger, healthier, and more robust than the domesticated breed (*Discourse* 138–39). And so, by the time the Creature mounts his funeral pyre, the catalog of Victor's blindnesses toward what—or, rather, whom—he has created is lengthy and damning. But Frankenstein's lack of insight extends farther still, for when the novel is viewed in the light of Rousseau's beliefs about foraging and farming, he can be perceived as misunderstanding not just his nemesis, but his own vocation as well. Far from creating "a new species" (36), he has resurrected an older, or alternative, version of his own, and one for whom a different, nearly extirpated way of living seems for a moment imaginable, almost graspable. It is not for the physiologist to revive the dead and return to them the power to speak—that is the office of the anthropologist.

SINCE THE middle of the twentieth century, successive generations of critics have shown that *Wuthering Heights* possesses intellectual components that its first commentators—a nervously defensive Charlotte most notable among them—overlooked by representing the novel as something too spontaneous to pause for thought, too primal to form a coherent opinion on controversies of the day, too autochthonous to comprehend a respectable philosophical position. And so, as the decades passed, Brontë's fiction was successively discovered to put forward a self-consistent religious vision, to evidence a compelling theory of human psychology, to possess a progressive politics, to mount a gendered protest, to be cognizant of matters of race. Why, then, should we hesitate to assume that it also possesses a conjectural anthropology, especially since a popular version of one (albeit often multivalent and sometimes conflicted in its specifics) was ready to hand? After all, the novel's very structure resembles that of a modern-day anthropological monograph, first introducing us to seemingly exotic people who follow apparently savage customs, then gradually revealing the alternative cultural coherence such customs construct. Furthermore, critics following approaches far different from mine have found within her novel "a fascination in the question of origins" and a "myth of how culture came about, and specifically of how nineteenth-century society occurred, [a] tale of where tea-tables, sofas, crinolines, and parsonages like the one at Haworth came from" (Gilbert and Gubar, 251, 257). If Mr. Lockwood is an incompetent though persistent field ethnologist who never quite comprehends the gestalt of the "surly *indigenae*" (27, Brontë's italics) he professes to study, the novel that ironizes him communicates its thick description of their unfamiliar lifeways with conviction and authority.

All that has been discovered concerning Emily Brontë's intellectual milieu—at Haworth and, briefly, at Brussels—combined with the consistent testimony concerning her intense intellectual curiosity by those who knew her, suggests a mind both sure to encounter the ubiquitous four-stage theories of human development and likely to imaginatively transform them according to the needs of her art. Sandra Gilbert and Susan Gubar, for instance, remind us that Reverend Brontë authored "several books of poetry, a novel, and a collection of sermons," and that "it was the habit of the Brontë family, [no less than] in the Wollstonecraft-Godwin-Shelley family, to approach reality through the mediating agency of books" (250). At the Haworth parsonage, the mental atmosphere was intellectual but not avant-garde, multilingual but not cosmopolitan, broadly informed but not scholarly, religiously devout but not narrowly sectarian. Thus Emily seems perfectly placed to receive and consider anthropological ideas that were, by the 1840s, of long and respectable pedigree, cumulatively abundant in their circulation, and that were not yet under attack by new paradigms. Furthermore, we have ample evidence that the abstract structure of the stadial systems was likely to attract her interest precisely because it was daringly "conjectural." We know, for instance, from Charlotte's report, that Emily "work[ed] like a horse" during her schooling at Brussels (which was conducted in French), and from her tutor there that she possessed "a head for logic" and a "powerful reason," an assessment seconded by Charlotte, who claimed that Emily was indeed "something of a theorist." Noting Mrs. Gaskell's suggestion that Emily taught herself to read German, Stevie Davies posits an "avid bookworm" whose lifelong autodidacticism was as voracious and as eclectic as William Blake's, since, "while she refused 'influence' with contumely and fled the 'palaces of instruction' (that is, the education system) as indoctrination centres, her mind was bathed in the light of others' understandings all her life" (46–47, 48–49). And, while documentation of the specific books she read is largely absent, we know that *Blackwood's* and *Fraser's* offered her regular exposure to digests of academic opinion and "metaphysical reading of a highly intellectual kind." Therefore, as Lucasta Miller warns, any "limiting [of] our view of Emily's reading to the precise books to which we know for certain she had access" is the quickest way to radically underestimate the scope of her cultural engagements (192–94, 233, 249).

One promulgator of the four-stage system whose influence on Brontë has been firmly established is Walter Scott (Hewish 35, 62), a pupil of the stadial theorist Adam Ferguson at Edinburgh University and a friend of the lecturer's son. It is worth noting, then, that Scott's Waverley novels hinge upon a conflict between peoples at different stages of development in the sense promulgated by our conjectural historians, juxtaposing as they do the pastoral (and raiding) Scottish Highlanders with representatives of the lowland, commercial Hanoverian regime (Irvine 37). Furthermore, executing a maneuver undertaken by several of the figures mentioned in the previous chapter, Scott "identifies the Highlanders with two other instances of this stage of society: the North American Indians and the archaic Greeks depicted in the Homeric epics." In doing this, Scott expresses "a deep ambivalence toward narratives of progress, a condemnation of the new, modern order," and a partial, wavering "commitment to the values of the earlier, less civilized stage" (Palmeri 226), all of which are sentiments recognizable in *Wuthering Heights*. If Heathcliff is not, politically or ethnically, a Scottish Highlander, he is nevertheless a small-h highlander, since it is geographical elevation that constitutes the most physically palpable and symbolically synoptic difference between his realm atop the moors and the sheltered valley location of Thrushcross Grange. More will be said about Heathcliff's resemblances to Native Americans shortly, but for now we can note that the influence of Scott might further be tracible in Brontë's ambivalent "resolution" of her own novel's stadial conflicts through the love story of Hareton and young Cathy. If it is true that the Waverley novels move "toward qualified comic resolutions involving marriages that bring together representatives of the contending historical forces"—marriages that "often involve some contraction of desire or reduction of aspirations" (231, 247)—then such finales seem to provide a template for the uncomfortable combination of structural inevitability and emotional deflation that troubles the final chapters of Brontë's text.

That Emily Brontë knew the works of Rousseau also seems beyond question. As early as 1840 there exists a letter from Charlotte Brontë to Hartley Coleridge that mentions Rousseau, and in Charlotte's novel *Shirley* (1849) he is a topic of conversation among the characters (Lodge 148; Redondo). This is significant because we are on almost as firm a ground inferring Emily's reading list from Charlotte's as we are deriving Mary Shelley's from Percy's (or vice versa). Then, too, the intrinsic evidence from *Wuthering Heights* is difficult to ignore. Consider, for instance, Melzer's account of Rousseau's various prescriptions for effecting the spiritual healing of people corrupted by modern, stage-four societies—prescriptions that, unsurprisingly, serve to nudge them toward a closer resemblance to the contented hunter-gatherers of his own peculiar version of stage one. In a patient cured by Rousseau's physic, "spontaneity replaces strength of self-control," and "sincerity replaces wisdom, for [the individual's] task is not to choose rationally" among his polity's competing conceptions of the good, "but only to embrace what genuinely comes from himself" while "reject[ing] what comes from society, which is alien and divisive" (22). There is a kind of moral aspiration still available to this free-thinking being, but "the ultimate object of self-love . . . is not some perfected form high above one, but [rather] the deepest thing within one," and, indeed, "whatever is most one's own" (42). Given that Rousseau posits a "natural intractability of man" (46) that opposes all social pressures to conform, happiness resides in preserving a "free and wild" version of ourselves (42), in practicing a "benign indifference to others" and in seeking "oneness with our natural, bodily selves" (44). He who does these things will "exist fully, undiminished by division or conflict, with nothing held back and nothing left out" (45). I would suggest that the attributes above, when taken together, constitute an almost mathematical formula whose solution is Heathcliff, and that this is the same back-of-the-envelope answer arrived at by Lockwood: "They [at the Heights] *do* live more in earnest, more in themselves, and less in surface change, and frivolous external things" (49). If Heathcliff is a Byronic hero, he is equally a Rousseauean one.

But is Brontë also among that minority of Rousseau's admirers, such as Mary Shelley, who lend a sympathetic ear to his denunciations of the plow? Is she willing to grant, along with him, that humankind's abandonment of foraging for farming constituted a self-domestication whose legacy is an enfeeblement of body and spirit? En route to answering these questions I shall be revisiting several long-canonical readings of *Wuthering Heights* (Terry Eagleton's, Gilbert and Gubar's, Margaret Homans's) in order to reexamine their arguments through an anthropological lens. What will be revealed, I believe, is not just evidence that Brontë has absorbed the stadial theories of human social development, including Rousseau's, but that—as one might expect from a radically open yet fiercely independent mind such as hers—she has transformed and refined them into a unique and compelling vision of her own. And yet, at the same time, this idiosyncratic conception will be recognized as newly familiar and newly relevant to ourselves in its view that sedentism and agriculture have sown moral decline and hedonic diminishment in their wake. The language of *Wuthering Heights* has often been likened to that of a prophetic utterance, and one of the things it foretells is that, when at last viewed from a sufficiently clarifying height, our long-standing contract with Cain will be revealed as something of a devil's bargain.

We can begin with the loneliness of Wuthering Heights, considered for the moment as a terrain or landscape, rather than as the specific edifice within it. This loneliness is, after all, the first thing brought to our attention as Mr. Lockwood exclaims over the "solitary neighbour that [he] shall be troubled with" and remarks that he "do[es] not believe that [he] could have fixed on a situation so completely removed from the stir of society," and that therefore the precincts compose "a perfect misanthropist's Heaven" (3). However deluded and unreliable Lockwood is about the denizens of the Heights and even about his own motivations, there is never any question that the environs are indeed sparsely settled. This is relevant because many of our stadial protoanthropologists see human crowding as the engine which pushes the species from one stage into the next. Rousseau himself in the *Discourse on Inequality* asks us to suppose that at first happy hunter-foragers were spread parsimoniously across the face of the earth, but that eventually they "multiplied so much that natural produce no longer sufficed to feed them" (143), which eventually led to the collective disaster of agriculture. For Helvétius, though the process is more benign, the dynamo is the same, for when population "increase[s] enormously, and a given area of land cannot provide for the subsistence of a greater number of inhabitants without being made fertile through human labour, then the pastoral peoples ... disappear and give place to agricultural peoples" (Meek 95). Likewise for Lord Kames, for whom "want of food, occasioned by rapid population" is the "built-in mechanism" (159) that turns foragers into shepherds and then shepherds into tillers. Knight, too, in the midst of his *Progress of Civil Society* informs us that

> As growing numbers claim'd increase of food,
> In smaller herds the cattle browse the wood:
> The hunter's labours less productive grew,
> And pale-faced famine slowly rose to view. (2: ll. 37–40)

Finally, and most famously, Malthus saw "human development as a progress from savagery to civilization, in which the pressure of population provided the dynamic force" (Stocking 34). With these examples in mind, we can see that Brontë's "Empty Quarter" of Yorkshire is the kind of place that lends itself to the depiction of some remnant or recrudescence of humanity's earlier stages of being. Brontë's moorland, because it is "so stripped of neighboring civilization, [and] of related social and historical events," allows readers to imagine they are "experiencing the rudimentary process of civilization itself" (Reed 211–12). The Heights can therefore function as a setting in which Brontë can depict a struggle between peoples at different stages of development without transgressing the outer boundaries of nineteenth-century realism. It is a territory in which something akin to Rousseau's primordial atomism can—in a physical sense, at least—be permitted to persist.

If the landscape surrounding the Heights is denuded enough to mimic that imagined as primordial by the conjectural historians, the characters placed upon it seem to restlessly traverse it in a manner consistent with how those historians viewed the movements of stage-one peoples. The ghostly Catherine who disturbs Lockwood has been "walking the earth these twenty years" (22), while Catherine and Heathcliff's childhood delight is "to run away to the moors in the morning and remain there all day" (37). In her last delirium Catherine recalls the lapwings "wheeling over our heads in the middle of the moor" and longs to be rambling "under Penistone Crag" once again (95–96). She declares, "I wish I were out of doors—I wish I were a girl again, half-savage, and hearty, and free" (98) and even demands to be buried "not among the Lintons, mind, under the chapel roof; but in the open air" (99). Heathcliff, of course, is an inveterate walker of the hillsides, "go[ing] out onto the moors frequently" during the "shooting season" (181) and, as his very name suggests, is most at home out of doors. As the novel nears its end, he takes to rambling not just during large stretches of the day, but at all hours, leaving the house in the evening and remaining abroad such that "in the morning," Nelly finds him "still away" (246). This leads Lockwood to conclude that "night-walking amuses him, then" (247), and Nelly affirms that her employer soon "plotted another midnight excursion" (249). Even after death, Nelly recounts that "the country folks, if you asked them, would swear on their Bible that he *walks*" (254, Brontë's italics).

Among the subsequent generation, Catherine's penchant for wandering is inherited by her daughter, who, according to an apprehensive Nelly, "took such a taste for this solitary rambling that she often contrived to remain out from breakfast till tea" (147). Intriguingly, on one such excursion young Cathy imagines herself as a houseless nomad: "Catherine came to me, one morning, at eight o'clock, and said she was that day an Arabian merchant, going to cross the Desert with his caravan" (147). When Nelly attempts to supervise and curtail her steps, "'Oh, a little further—only a little further, Ellen,' was her answer, continually" (163). Nelly herself cannot help but associate Wuthering Heights with perambulation, for when asked by young Linton Heathcliff what the place is like, she can only assure him that he "will have such nice rambles on the moors!" (158). But, of course, young Linton's unfitness for life at the Heights, in the wider sense of that place-name, is precisely his houseboundedness, his hypersedentism, not so much an agoraphobia as an ancraophobia—that is, a fear of winds. Declaring that "to walk four miles would kill [him]," Linton instead suggests even in the teeth of his father's threats that they should remain indoors.

> "Have you nothing to show your cousin, anywhere about; not even a rabbit, or a weasel's nest? Take her into the garden, before you change your shoes; and into the stable to see your horse."
> "Wouldn't you rather sit here?" asked Linton, addressing Cathy in a tone which expressed reluctance to move again.
> "I don't know," she replied, casting a longing look to the door, and evidently eager to be active.
> He kept his seat, and shrank closer to the fire. (166)

Nelly and Cathy call again only to find him "not fit for enjoying a ramble" (197), while yet another visit prompts Cathy to declare it "folly dragging [him] from the hearthstone" and Nelly to exclaim that "instead of rambling with his sweetheart on the hills, he ought to be in bed, under the hands of a doctor" (202–3). In contrast to Linton's cloistered sallowness that day, Nelly notes that Cathy's "countenance was just like the landscape—shadows and sunshine flitting over it, in rapid succession" (201). Thus, the more closely Linton shelters within Wuthering Heights the edifice, the less he seems fitted to exist amid Wuthering Heights the territory.

If the isolation of the neighborhood is straightforwardly insisted upon, when we come to consider the stone-and-mortar building itself, we are immediately confronted with ambiguities. "Wuthering Heights" may be the name of a structure, but the present participle of its meteorological first term, combined with the plural of its geographical second term, suggest a place that is contiguous with the weather and landscape, rather than lording it over either. The building is a place open to the moors and the winds, and Lockwood remarks that "pure, bracing ventilation they must have up there at all times" (4). Catherine, longing for her girlhood home, confirms that the house, though stoutly constructed of stone, is yet permeable to the breezes:

> "Oh, if I were but in my own bed in the old house!" she went on bitterly, wringing her hands. "And that wind sounding in the firs by the

lattice. Do let me feel it—it comes straight down the moor—do let me have one breath!"

To pacify her, I held the casement ajar, a few seconds. A cold blast rushed through, I closed it, and returned to my post. (97)

Nelly is the book's designated closer of windows (Gilbert and Gubar 292)—witness her "ejaculation of discontent" and her "shutting [of] the casements, one after another" (249), which Heathcliff has opened in order to further the reverie of his final days. Thus Steven Vine, reading out the meaning of the dialect-word "wuther" (according the OED, both a physical blow and the swaying or trembling caused by such a punch), argues that the house is "an architectural torsion wuthering between stability and instability," and that "the 'height' of the house . . . suggests the limit of the habitable; as if, in such sublime extremes, the domestic were always about to pass into the 'atmospheric.'" As a result, "there can be no stable distinction between the inside and outside of Heathcliff's dwelling," since "the exterior enters in and the within comes to share the properties of the without" (340–41). Or, as one critic succinctly phrased it some decades before, Wuthering Heights "seems to be the home of all those natural forces, death-dealing or life-giving, which it is built to withstand" (Goodridge 69).

Whether, for individual characters, the structure is death dealing or life giving seems to depend on where in the novel he or she calls home—in an emotional and spiritual sense—for, as Laura Berry has pointed out, the list of those who are involuntarily detained or literally imprisoned at the Heights includes Lockwood, Isabella, Nelly, and young Cathy (211). All of these prisoners are emotional denizens of the Grange (even Cathy, ultimately), and if Heathcliff prevents them from leaving the premises, in one sense it seems as if he is merely fulfilling the detainees' expectations of what a building is *for*. A "grange" is, after all, by definition an enclosed farm, and we discover that Brontë's valley establishment is indeed entirely bounded by a fieldstone wall. At times this perimeter is mentioned merely in passing, as Nelly nevertheless overdetermines when she notes "a labourer working at a fence round a plantation on the borders of the grounds" (148), but at times its solidity and impermeability are insisted upon, as when Cathy and Ellen accidently find themselves on opposite sides of it:

But the return was no such easy matter; the stones were smooth and neatly cemented, and the rosebushes and blackberry stragglers could yield no assistance in re-ascending. I, like a fool, didn't recollect that till I heard her laughing, and exclaiming—

"Ellen! You'll have to fetch the key, or else I must run around to the porter's lodge. I can't scale the ramparts on this side!"

"Stay where you are," I answered, "I have my bundle of keys in my pocket; perhaps I may manage to open it, if not, I'll go." (177)

Because the Grange features walls that—like those described by anthropologists of the early agrarian city-states—are primarily designed to keep its unfree subjects *in* rather than its roaming enemies out (Scott 30, 138, 233), it is tempting to figure the Grange as a kind of grain state in miniature, or at least to explore how far the similitude can be carried. True to form, its ruler, Edgar Linton, jealously attempts to prevent communication between his subjects and the houseless nomads up at the Heights out of a justified fear of defections. We are told that "till she reached the age of thirteen, [Cathy] had not once been beyond the range of the park by herself. Mr Linton would take her with him, a mile or so outside, on rare occasions; but he trusted her to no one else," a carceral program that ensures that "Wuthering Heights and Mr. Heathcliff did not exist for her; she was a perfect recluse" (146). (Interesting here that "recluse"—a term Lockwood wishes to apply to Heathcliff—actually describes a denizen of the Grange.) Edgar's fears that any knowledge of Heathcliff's abode will tend to draw his subjects thither prompts him to declare that Cathy "cannot associate with [Linton] hereafter; and it is better for her to remain in ignorance of his proximity, lest she should be restless, and anxious to visit the Heights" (156). Hence his "reiterated orders that she must not wander out of the park, even under [Nelly's] escort" (147). According to anthropologic precedent, however, Edgar's efforts seem doomed to fail. As James Scott declares in regard to the early agro-city, "Do what it might to discourage and punish flight—and the earliest legal codes are filled with such injunctions—the archaic state lacked the means to prevent a certain degree of leakage under normal circumstances" (153). In fact, young Cathy does manage to clandestinely visit the Heights in the teeth of all parental prohibitions, leading Nelly to scold that "Mr. Linton charged me to keep you in" (149). Soon enough the adults' hopes that Cathy might remain "perfectly contented" (146) with her captivity of ignorance are extinguished: "'I can get over the wall,' she said, laughing. 'The Grange is not a prison, Ellen, and you are not my jailer'" (184).

This figuring of the walled farm as a prison is something else young Cathy shares with her mother, as we can see from the latter's deathbed confession at the Grange: "And ... the thing that irks me most is this shattered prison, after all. I'm tired, tired of being enclosed here. I'm wearying to escape into that glorious world, and to be always there; not seeing it dimly through tears, and yearning for it through the walls of an aching heart; but really with it, and in it" (124–25). It might be objected here that Catherine is merely employing a familiar Christian metaphor, but we must not forget that the text has already licensed us to translate spiritual terrain into geographical: "I was only going to say that heaven did not seem to be my home; and I broke my heart with weeping to come back to earth; and the angels were so angry that they flung me out, into the middle of the heath on the top of Wuthering Heights; where I awoke sobbing for joy" (63). The Grange's walls are made of stone, but they seem meant to wall out a contrasting mode of being, a different possibility of culture, an antithetical notion of human beings' relationship to space, a threatening-because-liberating homelessness. It is little wonder, then, that Catherine predicts a "fight to the death" (77) between the Grange and the Heights.

Those who might balk at seeing Thrushcross Grange as a grain state in miniature should recall that the Grange is the only locale where something like the diseases of crowding manifest themselves, since the elder Earnshaws are carried off "within a few days of each other" (70) by an unspecified but clearly communicable malady, while Edgar catches his fatal infection from "walk[ing] out among the reapers" during a late harvest (175). Heathcliff, on the other hand, grows up "taller and twice as broad across the shoulders" as Edgar (45) and, upon his return to the Heights, is reported by Dr. Kenneth to "loo[k] blooming" and to be "rapidly regaining flesh" (143). Even toward the novel's end, as Catherine's otherworldly solicitations grow stronger, Heathcliff predicts a long life for himself: "With my hard constitution, and temperate mode of living, and unperilous occupations, I ought to, and probably *shall*, remain above ground, till there is scarcely a black hair on my head" (246, Brontë's italics).

But what *are* Heathcliff's "unperilous occupations"? How do people at the Heights procure their subsistence, and how is it described? Margaret Homans remarks that "although it creates the impression of taking place in the presence of the Yorkshire moors, very few [of the novel's] scenes are actually set out doors" (69), an observation that Henry Staten reinforces by noting that, with the exception of Nelly and Joseph [and, briefly, Zillah], "we never actually see any household servants or farm labourers" (135). Indeed, readers are left to infer what passes for toil at the Heights from a surprisingly meager set of references scattered across three hundred pages and that are not once strung together into a scene or even a sustained description of people at work. At various moments, Nelly refers to the eponymous structure itself as a "farmhouse" (152) and to Heathcliff's holdings generally as a "farm" (14, 29, 37, 84) whose main crop appears to be hay (29, 32, 159) raised as supplemental fodder for grazing sheep (12)—animals who are sometimes referred to generically as "cattle" (204, 236), and who are at certain seasons confined in a "[sheep]fold" (65)—or, as Joseph would have it, "t'fowld" (8). Joseph also mentions "corn" (66), though this, too, is probably a generic term meant to refer to any cereal, since Lockwood finds "oatcakes" (4) set out on his first awkward visit. There is a "barn" (8, 65), likely the same structure elsewhere referred to as a "stable" (44), which shelters horses (159, 166) and a cow, since Zillah milks one (191) and complains elsewhere that Linton must have "always milk, milk for ever" (162). Finally, the adult Heathcliff once wields a "pitchfork" (8), and Joseph gathers lime as a fertilizer (54), while Isabella complains of the "porridge" for dinner and of the rooms "smelling strong of malt and grain" (111). And that is the extent of, as Terry Eagleton puts it, "the terse economy of the Heights" (*Myths* 106). But why such reticence about the fact that Wuthering Heights is an upland sheep farm, quite common at the time of the novel's writing (and, indeed, still today) amid the Yorkshire moors? Because, I would argue, Brontë is pursuing two agendas that are—at these isolated moments in the text—in tension with each other. She wishes, along with many a nineteenth-century realist, to give a verisimilar account of her fictional locale's agroeconomic practices, but she also seems bent upon depicting the denizens of the Heights as *not engaged in agriculture at all*. If Homans is correct that Brontë somehow writes an indoor novel that feels as though it takes place outdoors, she also manages to depict a sheep farm that (at least when Heathcliff is master of it) requires surprisingly little labor to run. As Sahlins might put it, people at the Heights apparently need only clock in for the "bankers' hours" required of hunter-gatherers.

Of course, the question of farm labor and who performs it is at the heart of Eagleton's reading of the novel as a theater of nineteenth-century class relations. For him, the salient difference between the Grange and the Heights is that the former is inhabited by the gentry while the latter is occupied by yeomen:

> The delicate spiritless Lintons in their crimson-carpeted drawing-room are radically severed from the labor which sustains them; gentility

grows from the production of others, detaches itself from that work (as the Grange is separate from the Heights), and then comes to dominate the labor on which it is parasitic. In doing so, it becomes a form of self-bondage; if work is servitude, so in a subtler sense is civilization. To some extent, these polarities are held together in the yeoman-farming structure of the Heights. Here labor and culture, freedom and necessity, Nature and society are roughly complementary. The Earnshaws are gentlemen yet they work the land; they enjoy the freedom of being their own masters, but that freedom moves within the tough disciple of labor. (*Myths* 105)

Eagleton is convincing from a Marxist point of view, though it is worth noting that Staten takes him to task for not recognizing that the Heights' Earnshaws are *also* members of the gentry, pointing to the fact that Heathcliff is described by Nelly as being "a cruel hard landlord to his tenants" (152; see also 52)—though Staten concedes that, here, too, we *never see* these tenants or the slightest trace of the rental land they presumably work (134–36). But, instead of joining this quarrel about differing modes of agricultural work and ownership, let us push further down the track we have been pursuing and attempt to see the signal difference between Grange and Heights not as differing modes of tillage but as a contrast between farming and a preagricultural existence. We must remain aware, though, that here the same ambiguity that applies to the house applies to its master—that is, when we ask whether Heathcliff is a farmer, the answer is not simple. On the novel's verisimilar plane, yes, of course (maybe as a yeoman, maybe as one of the gentry), but on the plane of suggestion and implication, perhaps not. Nelly—echoing Iago's description of Othello as "an extravagant and wheeling stranger / Of here and everywhere" (1.1.130–31)—casts him as the opponent of such: "Were I in your place, I would frame high notions of my birth, and the thoughts of what I was should give me courage and dignity to support the oppressions of a little farmer!" (46). Eagleton appears at moments to affirm the primordial, not just the class-defined alien-ness of Heathcliff that I am attempting to articulate, affirming that he enters the family "as both gift and threat," providing the Earnshaws with a "chance to transcend the constructions of their self-enclosed social structure and gather him in." I would agree, but within a wider historical frame than the critic here intends. Heathcliff may be, upon arrival, "proletarian in appearance," but Eagleton also admits that "the obscurity of his origins also frees him of any exact social role" (*Myths* 102). Perhaps Heathcliff is a dynamo of disruption not because he represents a lower economic class but because he is the representative of an earlier anthropological stage.

Certainly the epithets leveled by denizens of the Grange toward those at the Heights are among those that have traditionally been aimed by agriculturalists at foragers, frequently emphasizing their lack of a fixed address. Early in the novel, Old Earnshaw's wife deplores the arrival of Heathcliff, whom she calls a "gypsy brat" (30), at her house, while her son Hindley banishes the "vagabond" from his table (18). When a young Heathcliff and an as-yet-un-"civilized" Catherine are captured down at the Grange, their intrusion is perceived among the Lintons as a raid by thieving nomads against the domus, with Heathcliff, even when recognized, being described as a "gypsy" who is "quite unfit for a decent house" (40). What follows is a remarkable inversion of a North American "captivity narrative," in which it is the farmers who capture a hunter-gatherer and turn her against her previous culture, for when she returns to the Heights, her former foraging companion—with whom she once "scamper[ed] on the moors" (18)—now appears to her as the "dirty" savage whose "dusky" fingers might defile her newly refined clothing, a novel contrast between them that Heathcliff embraces: "I shall be as dirty as I please, and I like to be dirty, and I will be dirty" (43). If this is indeed a topsy-turvy version of an Indian captivity narrative, Heathcliff will, once he gets the chance, script more orthodox examples of the genre for Isabella, Nelly, and Cathy. And if we begin to suspect that Locke's pronouncement that "in the Beginning all the World was America" (29), which was taken as gospel by so many stadial historians, may be operative in *Wuthering Heights*, then we may come to suspect that such resemblances might be more than accidental.

Furthermore, if we maintain an ear for words appertaining to agriculture, it seems significant that Catherine describes Heathcliff to an infatuated Isabella as "an *unreclaimed* creature, without refinement—without *cultivation*; an arid *wilderness* of furze and whinstone," and that she goes on to call him "a fierce, pitiless, wolfish man" (80, italics mine; see Reed 219). For dwellers within the planters' pale, it is, of course, the wolf that epitomizes the as-yet-unsubdued lands beyond the wall, a metaphor developed soon after by Nelly: "His visits were a continual nightmare to me; and, I suspected, to my master also. His abode at the Heights was an oppression past explaining. I felt that God had forsaken the stray sheep there to its own wicked wanderings, and an evil beast prowled between it and the fold, waiting his time to spring and destroy" (84). This suggestion is reiterated by Nelly when, during Heathcliff's deathbed encounter with Catherine, he "gnashe[s] at [her], and foam[s] like a mad dog" until she "d[oes] not feel as if [she] were in the company of a creature of [her] own species" (125). Little wonder, then, that Isabella later asks her with serious intent, "Is Mr. Heathcliff a man?" (106), though Heathcliff would seemingly own the hard impeachment, bragging as he does that he has "taught [Hareton] to scorn everything extra-animal as silly and weak" (168). A wolf, then—though there is an even more ubiquitous slander that cultivators aim at foragers, and Heathcliff does not escape it, for Isabella attributes to him a set of "sharp cannibal teeth" (136). But, again, at the end of it all Heathcliff acknowledges without shame his status as one dwelling outside, and intending harm to, the social shelter of the domus: "'I believe you think me a fiend!' he said with his dismal laugh, 'something too horrible to live under a decent roof'" (253), echoing old Mrs. Linton's initial assessment.

For Eagleton, Heathcliff's tragedy is that, in exacting revenge upon the dwellers at the Grange, he becomes all too like them: "He is, then, a force which springs out of the Heights yet subverts it, breaking beyond its constrictions into a new, voracious acquisitiveness. His capitalist brutality is an extension as well as a negation of the Heights world he knew as a child.... Heathcliff is subjectively a Heights figure opposing the Grange, and objectively a Grange figure undermining the Heights.... His rise to power symbolizes at once the triumph of the oppressed over capitalism and the triumph of capitalism over the oppressed" (*Myths* 112). Again, if one focuses on the realm of class relations, this is a gloss that explains much, but I am offering an alternative reading of Heathcliff's trajectory, one that stretches beyond the capitalist era to include an even wider sweep of human history. If the Grange is associated with the agricultural production of stages three and four, if it is carceral and disease-ridden like a miniature grain state, if its denizens slander Heathcliff with the usual epithets hurled against foragers, then it is less surprising that Wuthering Heights's verisimilar status as a farm "wuthers" in the same way Vine claims the physical edifice does. From this perspective, Heathcliff's transformation is not from proletarian to capitalist but from "plow-boy" (74) to uncultivated and uncultiva*ting* barbarian. Here it is Hindley's consignment of Heathcliff to field work (a punishment described only through its effects upon the latter) that eventually turns him into the extra-agrarian nomad whose revenge menaces the Grange. It is worth noting in this regard how clear eyed Brontë is concerning the dire mental and physical effects of stoop labor:

Continual hard work, begun soon and concluded late, had extinguished any curiosity he once possessed in pursuit of knowledge, and any love for books or learning. His childhood's sense of superiority, instilled into him by the favours of old Mr Earnshaw, was faded away. He struggled long to keep up an equality with Catherine in her studies and yielded with poignant though silent regret: but, he yielded completely; and there was no prevailing on him to take a step in the way of moving upward, when he found he must, necessarily, sink beneath his former level. Then personal appearance sympathized with mental deterioration; he acquired a slouching gait, and ignoble look; his naturally reserved disposition was exaggerated into an almost idiotic excess of unsociable moroseness; and he took a grim pleasure, apparently, in exciting the aversion rather than the esteem of his few acquaintance. (53–54)

However, far from turning him—as Hindley intends—into someone whose mentality is narrowed to the benumbing boundaries of a monoculture field, this consignment to agricultural labor is apparently what eventually motivates Heathcliff, when he returns and appropriates the Heights, to transform it into a realm in which stoop work is not only difficult to discern but in which agro-culture tout court is also disdained. Under such a view, for instance, the frequently noted fact that books are read at the Grange but merely hurled about as projectiles at the Heights can now be seen as Heathcliff's rejection of literacy as the handmaidenly bookkeeper of "little farmer[s]." Anthropologists have speculated that since writing emerged as "an artifact of state building, concentration of population, and scale," that hunter-gatherers' well-documented resistance to it was due to its "indelible association with the state and taxes, just as ploughing was long resisted because of its indelible association with drudgery" (Scott 148–49). But let us confine ourselves to the stadial historians—even for them, there was nothing specifically precapitalist (or, to use their own vocabulary, precommercial) about illiteracy, though there *was* definitely something pre*agricultural* about it. After all, Native Americans, those living exemplars of stage-one humanity, possessed no written language. Heathcliff can thus be refigured as agriculture's enlightened escapee—one who knows the evils of tillage because he was subjected to them, and who redeems the site of his former bondage by letting it revert to heath. So, while it is true to say that the sources of Heathcliff's continued prosperity at the Heights are as mystified as the means by which he initially becomes prosperous, they are so through a conflation of categories that are perhaps larger and of longer historical reach than even those of classical Marxism.

And as with writing, so with the conception of time. Lockwood complains that "time stagnates" at the Heights (23), and for him this is a genuine objection, since, as a representative of agrocommercial culture, he is wholly invested in diachrony, wherein each unique moment succeeds the next in an orderly, arrow-like, progressive narrative of before and after, detailing humanity's evolution from idiocy to enlightenment. This is underscored when, upon first approaching Wuthering Heights, his attention is captured by an inscribed date that prompts his desire to hear a quintessential diachronic story: "I detected the date '1500,' and the name 'Hareton Earnshaw.' I would have made a few comments, and requested a short *history* of the place from the surly owner" (4, italics mine). However, the inability of a diachronic perspective to make sense of the Heights is quickly shown, both by the fact that there is a Hareton Earnshaw living there at the present moment, and by the fact that the trio of names that Catherine has written after her own in her diary only befogs him, though she will in fact be an Earnshaw, a Heathcliff, and a Linton before the novel is through. The text's own chronology, of course, is ironclad, and yet almost entirely opaque from a readerly perspective, legible only after scholarly labor (Daley 357–61), as if Brontë were attempting to prove that conventional historical accounts are always possible but not always germane—at least not at the Heights. Indeed, when Catherine describes her differing relationships with Edgar and with Heathcliff, it is the former that is likened to phases pertinent to the yearly agricultural calendar, to "the foliage in the woods," and the "changes" worked by "winter ... in the trees," while the latter is depicted as existing on a geological timescale, resembling as it does "the eternal rocks beneath" (64).

This is all to suggest that there is an affinity between Heathcliff and Catherine's experienced relationship to time and the desire of Coetzee's Magistrate's for his people to "live in time like fish in water, like birds in air, like children," outside the tragic, diachronic purview of "the time of history" mandated by "Empire" (153). One of the oldest libels against hunter-gatherers lodged by imperialists, after all, is that they are a people who have not yet entered history, not yet created a diachronic story that they can tell about themselves, wandering as they supposedly do through a life composed of numbing, daily repetitions. Most stadial theorists also consigned foragers to a kind of ahistorical Limbo, for while even the most ancient pastoralists and tillers of Genesis insisted, by means of the genealogy or the king list, on the dateable and thus scriptable and providential nature of their lives, the years of nineteenth-century "savages" remained unnumbered and therefore unredeemed. Given the Heights' wholesale lack of interest in writing, by contrast, one is tempted to see Brontë's novel redefining history itself as the *contamination* of time's passing by the written word.

Eagleton observes that Heathcliff's "adult protests against Grange values" are complicated and compromised by the fact that he uses "Grange weapons" to further them (*Myths* 112), and in Eagleton's eyes this makes Heathcliff a tragic self-undoer. But it is also possible to see him as resembling what James Scott refers to as a "late barbarian"—that is, as a "nonstate pe[rson]" who operates in the interstices between grain states and who can thus "participate fully in the new opportunities for trade," as well as running "raiding and protection rackets … without becoming a subject of the state." For Scott, while there are some "deeply melancholy aspects of [this] golden age of barbarians," its overall prospects are not tragic:

> The life of "late barbarians" would, on balance, have been rather good. Their subsistence was still spread across several food webs; being dispersed, they would have been less vulnerable to the failure of a single food source. They were more likely to be healthier—especially if they were female. More advantageous trade made for more leisure, thus further widening the leisure-drudgery ratio between forages and farmers. Finally, and by no means trivial, barbarians were not subordinated or domesticated to the hierarchical social order of sedentary agriculture and the state. They were in almost every respect freer than the celebrated yeoman farmer. This is not a bad balance sheet for a class of barbarians over whom the waves of history were supposed to have rolled a long time ago. (255)

Thus, again, in widening the historical frame, one can remain in agreement with Eagleton's more general stipulations that Heathcliff represents "a past more brutal but also more heroic than the present" (*Myths* 114), that he is both "progressive and outdated," and that he embodies at once a "caricature of and traditionalist protest against the agrarian capitalist forces of Thrushcross Grange." One can further agree that the Heights does indeed seem to represent a "superseded world," such that Heathcliff's "death and the closing-up of the house seem logically related"

(112–13)—or that, as Thomas Joudrey would have it, at novel's end "the farmhouse seems poised to collapse into history, joining the lonely graves of Heathcliff and Catherine nestled within the nearby moors" (186). One can concede all this and still, from our perspective, see Heathcliff not as a tragic figure but as a wily survivor whose principled reversion to stage-one conditions is wrought by bitter experience amid the soul-narrowing furrows of stage three. Late in the novel he talks of his "wild endeavors to *hold*" a charged and ambivalent catalog of emotions—"my right, my degradation, my pride, my happiness, and my anguish" (245, italics mine). Indeed, from our perspective Heathcliff persists not so much as a tragic *sellout*, but, rather, as an ambivalently heroic *holdout*.

Eagleton appears quite open to supplementing his Marxist reading of *Wuthering Heights* with a psychoanalytical one, conceding that "the Heathcliff-Catherine relationship is a classic case of the Lacanian 'imaginary,' an utter merging of identities in which the existence of each is wholly dependent on the existence of the other, to the exclusion of the world about them" (*Heathcliff* 18). But, of course, the most thoroughgoing Lacanian account of the novel remains Margaret Homans's gendered analysis in *Bearing the Word: Language and Female Experience in Nineteenth-Century Women's Writing*. In articulating the different trajectories of Catherine and Cathy away from the imaginary order and into the symbolic, Homans emphasizes that while the former enjoys free run of the moors, the latter suffers confinement by the walls of the Grange:

> The difference between [Catherine's] transition into the symbolic order and the second Cathy's may be due in part to the fact that although they both as children love nature more than language, for the second Cathy, nature is bounded within the walls of Thrushcross Park and within her father's prohibition against going out too far unaccompanied. Whereas the first Cathy and Heathcliff run wherever they wish on the moors, and run to the Grange if they like, the second Cathy does not even know of the existence of Wuthering Heights or of her mother's favorite haunts until the age of thirteen. (77; see also Stoneman 523)

We can profitably reaccent Homans's insights by (as we did with Eagleton's) reading them sympathetically but within a larger, anthropological frame. What I am proposing here will be amplified in later chapters, but, for now, is it not the case that when one superimposes Lacan's imaginary order—an episode in the life of each individual—upon the hunting-and-gathering stage (as understood today) of our species' cultural arc, that suggestive similarities emerge? For instance, they are both idyllic, primordial states in which the bonding of individuals to each other displays an intimacy and intensity that, in later life, is secretly mourned and pursued but that can never successfully be recreated. They are both theaters of being in which "adult" anxieties about competition with others and about the uncertainties of future days are nonexistent. They are both conditions in which a sufficiency of sustenance is simply provided and never needs to be onerously procured. They are both realms in which writing is as yet unknown and unnecessary. And, finally, they exist as early idylls that dissolve before we know what manner of Eden we possess, an earthly paradise whose gates are forever closed to our reentry. Homans, speaking specifically of the situation of women in nineteenth-century Western culture, asserts that "the symbolic order is founded, not merely on the regrettable loss of the mother, but rather on her active and overt murder" (11). Has not a similar matricide also been effected at the anthropological level again and again by centuries of a vituperative agriculturalist ideology aimed at foragers, denigrating them as barbarians, vagabonds, cannibals, impulsives, infants, imbeciles, starvelings, unfortunates? As we have seen, most four-stage conjectural historians were progressivists, thoroughly imbued with such anti-forager assumptions, though a few, like Rousseau, were not. Clearly, Brontë is a primitivist, for the very fact that her stage-one mode of living, as embodied by Catherine and Heathcliff, can be plausibly spoken of as a lived imaginary order alerts us that her fictional explorations are, at base, Rousseauean in nature. And the fact that her protagonists can be convincingly described as "ferociously hungry children who, in their perennially primitive state, never stop devouring" (Berry 47) underscores the fact that they inhabit a presymbolic space that is simultaneously personal and anthropological. In what follows, I will further delineate two crucial aspects of this stage-one imaginary of *Wuthering Heights*: its sustenance and its sociality.

For the stadial theorists, it was the manner in which people obtained their nutrition that determined which level of development they inhabited, and thus it is suggestive that Gilbert and Gubar, in their own gendered reading of *Wuthering Heights*, see fit to differentiate the two houses with terminology relating to food: "Where Wuthering Heights . . . is close to being naked or 'raw' in Lévi-Strauss' sense—its floors uncarpeted, most of its inhabitants barely literate, even the meat on its shelves open to inspection—Thrushcross Grange is clothed and 'cooked': carpeted in crimson, bookish, feeding on cakes and tea and negus" (273–74). Thus, that "pale ... daughter of culture and Thrushcross Grange," Isabella, cannot survive at the Heights because "she is unable to stomach the rough food of nature (or [according to agriculturalists,] hell) just as Catherine cannot swallow the food of culture (or heaven)" (287–88). Nelly, guardian of the Grange's values, becomes, according to this view, "Milton's cook" (292), while "Heathcliff incarnates that unregenerate natural world which must be metaphorically cooked or spiritualized" (294), such that by the end of the novel he "can no longer eat the carefully cooked human food that Nelly offers him" (301–2). To this I would add that Heathcliff's strange last days are not merely characterized by a refusal to feed but also by *joy* in a way that strikingly anticipates Michael K's near-foodless reverie in the South African mountains, for here, too, Heathcliff's locomotion over the countryside becomes attended by an apparently painless fasting. Toward the end of his life, he perambulates day and night, dining, according to Nelly, only "once in twenty-four hours" (246). She says to him, "You must be hungry, rambling about all night," to which he answers, "No, I'm not hungry," insisting that such walks give him "the greatest pleasure" (247). Indeed, to the housekeeper's alarm, the more he wanders, the less he eats, as she "vainly remind[s] him of his protracted abstinence from food" and complain[s] that "if he stretched his hand out to get a piece of bread, his fingers clenched before they reached it, and remained on the table, forgetful of their aim" (251). So, yes, he is starving himself, and yet he invokes the same word later employed by Michael K amid his own unsettling indifference to hunger: "My soul's bliss kills my body." What "bliss" can this be that—here, as in Coetzee's novel—seems thrown up by the protagonist's vanished need to *care* about food? Again, one might be tempted to read it as some manner of Christian denial of the flesh, but Heathcliff disallows such a reading: "I tell you, I have nearly attained *my* heaven; and that of others is altogether unvalued and uncoveted by me!" (252). Tellingly, when the doctor arrives to examine his corpse, Nelly "conceal[s] the fact of his having swallowed nothing for four days" because she is "persuaded he did not abstain on purpose; it was the consequence of his strange illness, not the cause" (254). Whatever it is during his end times that Heathcliff is becoming, like Michael K amid a different continent's heights, he too has somehow transcended food insecurity, *refusing* to be hungry.

Thus it is all to the point that when Lockwood attempts to come to terms with the vivifying passions that are endemic to the Heights but sadly lacking in his own life, he employs a complicated metaphor involving food:

> They *do* live more in earnest, more in themselves, and less in surface change, and frivolous external things. I could fancy a love for life here almost possible; and I was a fixed unbeliever in any love of a year's standing—one state resembles setting a hungry man down to a single dish on which he may concentrate his entire appetite, and do it justice—the other, introducing him to a table laid out by French cooks; he can perhaps extract as much enjoyment from the whole, but each part is a mere atom in his regard and remembrance. (49, Brontë's italics)

There is, perhaps, an anthropological irony at work in this "gustatory parable" (J. Hillis Miller 54), in that Brontë may be repeating the erroneous belief of her day that the diet of foragers is monotonous when compared to that of farmers, even as she allows that "single dish" to represent a way of being that is more holistically integrated and more keenly experienced within the present moment than that to which inmates of the Grange have consigned themselves. At any rate, it is by such means that Lockwood points us toward the central advantage that the roaming denizens of the Heights enjoy over the sedentists of the Grange: an intenser, more fulfilling mode of sociality, exemplified by the uncanny and indissoluble bond between Heathcliff and Catherine.

But how to characterize that bond? Since it bears a number of superficial resemblances to, and engages enough stock atmospherics of, erotic love, there has always been a temptation to declare or assume it just *is* such and move on.[1] What my line of argument suggests, however, is that instead of trying to diagnose their tie as some hypertrophied or deviant mode of modern, romantic attraction, we instead view them as constituting a primal tribe of two. That is, if we cease to think of them as a titanic couple and instead see them as a concentrated community, their bond's contrast with the species of companionate marriage readily available (and fully depicted as happening) at the Grange is put into a richer relief. After all, some of the foundational, midcentury formalist and Marxist engagements with *Wuthering Heights* were already urging us to see something other than a frustrated love affair. Dorothy Van Ghent, for instance, found something too "anthropologically rudimentary" (159) about Heathcliff and Catherine to imagine them as the principals in a marriage, while Arnold Kettle insisted they represent "something beyond the individualist dream of two soul-mates finding full realization in one another" (214), a notion seconded by Raymond Williams, who sees emanating from them "not desire *for* another but desire *in* another" (66). Nelly recalls that during Catherine's childhood "the greatest punishment we could invent for her was to keep her separate from [Heathcliff]" (34), and this childlike covenant matures into—as Catherine herself famously articulates—a durable yet apparently nonsexual consonance of mentalities that is unavailable at the Grange: "My love for [Edgar] Linton is like the foliage in the woods. Time will change it, I'm well aware, as winter changes the trees—my love for Heathcliff resembles the eternal rocks beneath—a source of little visible delight, but necessary. Nelly, I *am* Heathcliff—he's always, always in my mind—not as a pleasure, any more than I am always a pleasure to myself—but, as my own being—so, don't talk of our separation again—it is impracticable" (64–65).

Heathcliff may on occasion sound like a spurned and jealous lover—or readerly habit can lull us into casting him as such—but even his bitterest upbraidings of Catherine can be taken as dismay at her betrayal of a precious group bond for the *merely* individualistic motivation of marrying well: "You loved me—then what *right* had you to leave me? What right—answer me—for the poor fancy you felt for Linton?" (125, Brontë's italics). Heathcliff and Catherine's community, like that of hunter-gatherers, is materially communitarian, for as the former exclaims concerning the Linton children's tussle over a puppy: "When would you catch me wishing to have what Catherine wanted?" (39). Nor does this aspect of their sociality disappear with the interventions of puberty and class that arrive after Catherine's captivity by, and eventual marriage into, the Grange:

> "Abstract your mind from the subject, at present—you are too prone to covet your neighbour's goods: remember *this* neighbour's goods are mine."
> "If they were *mine*, they would be none the less that," said Heathcliff. (84, Brontë's italics)

Granted, the two have little opportunity to hold physical objects in common, but the intention—or, more rightly, the assumption—that they would naturally and happily do so is strongly expressed. Thus their communal egalitarianism is more a spirit proposed than a praxis enacted, a kind of conjectural condition, if you will, for if Tom Winnifrith can rightly claim that "the contrast between Thrushcross Grange and Wuthering

Heights is in part a contrast between the hierarchical society and a classless society[,].... between a society that works for its living and a society that relies on the work of others" (192), then Gilbert and Gubar are willing to spiritualize this notion by affirming that the "inhabitants of Wuthering Heights seem to live in chaos without the structuring principle of heaven's hierarchical chain of being" (262). Put another way, Catherine and Heathcliff practice (or yearn to practice, yearn to revive) what Marx might have recognized as something akin to "primitive communism." Interestingly, this stage-one community they would constitute is the polar opposite of Rousseau's atomic primordialism, proving that when it comes to articulating her own version of the stadial anthropology, Brontë will invent her own system rather than be co-opted by that of another.

A further contrast with Rousseau involves Heathcliff's unrelenting vindictiveness and his willingness to employ coercion and violence whenever it suits his purposes, for these proclivities raise a question: If Brontë follows Rousseau in her general approval of stage-one *existence,* why present such an ethically mixed portrait of a stage-one *character?* Winnifrith is alert to this quandary, admitting that "it may seem to be a flaw in the novel that the life which has produced [Catherine and Heathcliff] should be so recommended," though he ends up applauding the moral complexity of the text for "showing us the attractive way of life in spite of the unattractive features of those who live this life, and the unpleasantness of another way of life in spite of the superficially pleasant nature of the characters enjoying it" (193). Whether one agrees with this or not, Heathcliff's "unattractive features" certainly refute Rousseau's insistence that stage-one people possess a "natural pity," a notion he vigorously articulates in the *Discourse on Inequality* in order to counter Hobbes's unflattering portrait of early man.[2] This sentiment, says the philosophe, is a "pure movement of nature prior to all reflection" that "contributes to the mutual preservation of the entire species," and though it has come to be expressed only "weak[ly] in Civil Man," it is still "lively in Savage Man" (*Discourse* 152–54). Heathcliff, however, seems adamant that such assertions do not apply to him: "I have no pity! I have no pity! The more the worms writhe, the more I yearn to crush out their entrails! It is a moral teething, and I grind with greater energy, in proportion to the increase of pain" (118). Later, in reference to Hareton and young Cathy, he declares: "Had I been born where laws are less strict, and tastes less dainty, I should treat myself to a slow vivisection of those two, as an evening's amusement" (204).

An answer as to why this should be the case is bound up with a speculative gesture—it can be no more—toward identifying Heathcliff's race.

But even such a foray, destined to end well short of certainty, seems sanctioned by Eagleton's invocation of "the hermeneutical riddle which haunts every page of *Wuthering Heights*: Who is Heathcliff? What is he? What does he want?" (*Heathcliff* 21). As we have seen from our discussion of the stadial historians, most of them took as a given Locke's pronouncement that "in the beginning all the World was America" (29). Adam Ferguson (foremost compeer of Adam Smith in the Scottish Enlightenment), to take but one example among many, declares that when scrutinizing Native Americans, Europeans "behold, as in a mirrour, the features of our progenitors" (133). Recall that Heathcliff is found homeless and speaking a foreign language on the Liverpool docks, and that, tantalizingly, Nelly implies that though his skin is noticeably darker than everyone else's in the neighborhood (other characters confirm this), he is not "a regular black" (45; see Dellamore 545–47; Von Sneidern). So, what kind of nonwhite person *is* Heathcliff? If Brontë follows the lead of the stadial thinkers in looking to Native Americans as living remnants of stage-one humanity, then the possibility that Heathcliff is meant to be an American Indian gains at least a patina of plausibility. One could go on to cite any number of instances of popular interest in Native Americans among the British press during the 1840s, including the arrival of successive groups of them at Liverpool to participate in George Catlin's popular and often-reviewed show of Indian artifacts (Flint 54–65).

However, the real question is Heathcliff's reprehensible behavior, and here is where the casual racism of British representations of Native Americans comes into play, for if there were literary gushings aplenty about the doomed nobility and poignant fidelity of Indians, it was also the case that "the Native American whom the nineteenth century inherited was a far more ambiguously coded figure, one who could, most certainly, be regarded as embodying a number of positive values, but who could also be presented as cruel, vengeful, and 'uncivilized'" (Flint 42). This image, shaped and hardened by British experience of warfare both against and in alliance with Indians on North American battlefields, "focused obsessively on torture, on scalping, on cannibalism and it was always in tension with the idealistic picture" presented by earlier renderings of the "noble savage." (The word "torture," by the way, appears half a dozen times in *Wuthering Heights*, and in all but one case Heathcliff is either performing or suffering it.) "Indians, consequently, became fascinating to Britons for their apparent contradictoriness, for their irresolvable mixture of nobility and ignobility, heroism and brutality, dignity and savagery" (Fulford 41–42). Is it not plausible, then, that if Brontë's depiction of Heathcliff is meant to represent a stage-one throwback, and, if it was a common practice to point to American Indians as being just such throwbacks, that she has constructed an ambivalent vision from ambivalent materials?

Wordsworth appears to have done exactly this in "Ruth," a poem included in the second, 1800 edition of *Lyrical Ballads* (Fulford 179–81). Here, the titular maid, living in England, is wooed by a white youth who was born in North America and has spent years in close company with Native Americans. He speaks ardently to her of the New World landscape and beguiles her with a vision of how, if she will accompany him there, they will live a preagricultural life such as his Indian acquaintances follow:

> "How pleasant," then he said, "it were
> A fisher or a hunter there,
> In sunshine or in shade
> To wander with an easy mind;
> And build a household fire, and find
> A home in every glade!" (ll. 73–78)

However, after convincing Ruth to return across the Atlantic with him, he cruelly deserts her just as they are about to take ship, spoiling the remainder of her life. The only explanation the poem provides for the young man's unexpected villainy is that, despite the fact that his vigorous praise of Indian ways of living seems to be fully endorsed by the speaker, he has been corrupted by spending too much time *with the Indians themselves*, who are ethically primitive:

> But ill he lived, much evil saw
> With men to whom no better law
> Nor better life was known;
> Deliberately, and undeceivied,
> Those wild men's vices he received,
> And gave them back his own. (ll. 145–50)

In both "Ruth" and *Wuthering Heights*, then, there appears a disconcerting tendency to laud the primitive life while at the same time expressing fear and moral condemnation of the "primitives" themselves—an odd inversion of the Christian directive to hate the sin but love the sinner. At any rate, while the life Heathcliff leads and the satisfactions he enjoys seem to have their origin in the primitivist wing of stadial anthropology and thus to be strongly positive, the personal traits he exhibits to all those outside his tribe of two bear traces of the unflattering depictions of Native Americans endemic in the periodicals and novels available to Brontë at the Haworth parsonage, which reiterated "a standard collection of motifs: torture, death-songs, cannibalism, adoption of the surviving captive" (Fulford 107). As to this last, for instance, cannot Hareton and young Linton be seen as adoptive captives of Heathcliff, one thriving and the other succumbing under what "civilized" people would describe as the "barbarous" regimen he imposes upon them? Indeed, given all the resemblances between Brontë's moors and the North American prairie of journalistic report, one is tempted to nickname the Grange "Fort Thrushcross."

It only remains to reiterate how prophetic is *Wuthering Heights*'s vision of the spiritual and bodily costs of agriculture when seen from the standpoint of modern-day anthropology. If the denizens of the Grange appear to be physically puny and fragile in contrast with Heathcliff, Catherine, and Hareton, in the eyes of the novel their greatest tragedy is the straitened limits they have imposed upon their imaginations, their audacity, and their ability to fully inhabit the experiential moment. Now according to twenty-first-century articulations of the agricultural trap, we *Homo sapiens* "are as much a product of self-domestication in both intended and unintended ways as other species of the *domus* are products of our domestication" (Scott 83). And so, if we know that we have wrought upon our captive animals an "emotional dampening," by bestowing on them the dubious luxury of needing to be "less intently alert to [their] immediate surroundings than [their] cousins in the wild" (81), a question arises: Have we also—simultaneously, unwittingly—dampened some of our own responses and capabilities? Scott will only suggest as much: "Is it the case, for example, that like their domesticates, sedentary, grain-planting, domus-sheltered people have experienced a comparable decline in emotional reactivity and are less intently alert to their immediate surroundings? If so, is it related, as in domestic animals, to changes in the limbic system, which governs fear, aggression, and flight responses? I know of no evidence bearing directly on this question, nor is it easy to imagine how the question could be addressed in an objective way" (86).

This caution in a social scientist is admirable, but, of course, the making flesh of implications we strongly suspect but cannot quite prove is one of the offices of literature, and one that, in a prescient manner, *Wuthering Heights* appears to fulfill. Certainly if, as seems to be the case, Rousseau was among the four-stage protoanthropologists toward whom Brontë was sympathetic, she could, as we have already seen, have found a similar idea about the degenerative effects of domestication upon both beast and man stoutly proclaimed in the *Discourse on Inequality*. And it is in that same remarkable text that Rousseau points his accusing finger at sedentism as the original sin that inaugurates this great and tragic self-domestication that we please to term our enlightenment. What is paradoxical about the Heights, though, is that it is a domus one can only possesses by walking, by roaming, by rambling, and, whatever Lockwood may want to believe about the supposed "sleepers in that quiet earth" (256), not even the grave can render Heathcliff sedentary. No: in *Wuthering Heights* the Grange is the only *working* farm we see, and Brontë seems to argue that settling in such a place—in a geographical, anthropological sense—has also meant settling in an aspirational sense. And settling for far too little, at that.

4

Coetzee's Carcer[e]al State

I F IT is true that within contemporary academic anthropology "agriculturalists ... have never looked so bad—in terms of their diet, their health, and their leisure," while, on the other hand, "hunters and gathers have ... never looked so good" in terms of these vital metrics (Scott 10), then the same holds true within, respectively, J. M. Coetzee's *Waiting for the Barbarians* (1980) and his subsequent novel, *Life & Times of Michael K* (1983). Coetzee, an academic himself at the time he was composing these novels, would have been aware of the revisionist thinking concerning our Neolithic adoption of farming that had its origin in the Man the Hunter conference (1966), and that was steadily replacing the agricultural revolution's comic narrative with the more tragic and ironic conception of the agricultural trap. Indeed, the trajectories of the Magistrate and Michael K—that troubled townsman and that contented hunter-gatherer—reveal that this new paradigm, even prior to its full articulation within the academy, provides Coetzee with a potent and comprehensive origin story for the chronic inequities, cruelties, and incomprehensions of the modern condition. As we shall see, *Waiting for the Barbarians* and *Life & Times*, when considered together, make an implicit argument about the genesis of inequality and unhappiness that is Rousseauean rather than Marxist, anthropological rather than historical, painting capitalist exploitation, racist oppression, and rampant militarism as epiphenomena of agriculture, as the spoil we have produced in our ancient and persistent rage to plow.

Much could be said about the Magistrate as Coetzee's figure for postwar anthropology itself, and specifically for that discipline's agonistic recognition of both its former complicity with racist, imperial, and colonialist projects, and its postmodernist realization that personal agendas will always contaminate the supposed objectivity of that oxymoronic figure, the participant-observer. Rather than iterate the rich particulars of what would become a digression, however, I will only point out that by the end of his narrative, the Magistrate has confessed to both his unnerving similarities to that policeman of Empire, Colonel Joll, and acknowledged that his program of amateur ethnology has been fatally compromised by his overdetermined feelings for the Barbarian Girl. But if he knows that he and Joll are, in one sense, "two sides of imperial rule, no more no less" (156), and if he understands that his "ang[er] at [him]self for wanting and not wanting" the Girl (37) has murdered his prospective monograph on the barbarians in its cradle (while further harming the Girl), he has not yet bested the Sphinx. We know this because he tells us so, declaring, in the novel's final moments, that there remains "something staring [him] in the face" that he "still [does not] see" (179). But what exactly is this third hard truth with which he has yet to come to grips? I would nominate the Magistrate's unconscious adherence to an agriculturalist ideology, which both implicates him in Joll's imperial aggressions and prevents him from grasping the profound cultural alternative that the Barbarian Girl and her people present to the Empire. For, despite his anthropologist's knowledge that his own imperial outpost will soon be buried in the sand, and despite his desperate attempt to understand what combinations of shame and desire his sole human subject inspires within him, we can see the Magistrate, in his final, baffled utterance, as Coetzee's figure for agro-culture itself: an entity that "lost [its] way long ago but presses on along a road that may lead nowhere" (180). To what extent, then, are both his guilt over being a man of Empire and his frustration at being unable to adequately imagine that Empire's Other caused by the long-plowed furrows that delimit his tiller's consciousness?

First, Coetzee strongly implies that what lies at the root of Empire's reflexive violence against the barbarians is the sheer precariousness of the agriculture that feeds (or fails to feed) the former. Although the author clearly takes pains to make the physical setting of the novel geographically and historically generic (Gallagher "Torture" 281), there are aspects that suggest something more specific on both counts. The Magistrate is in charge of a "walled town" (27) that lives beneath the shadow of "ramparts" (22), surrounded by "communal lands" (9) dedicated to fixed-field agriculture whose harvests are dependent upon a dam and a network of canals: "We have been here more than a hundred years, we have reclaimed land from the desert and built irrigation works and planted fields and built solid homes and put a wall around our town, but they [i.e., the barbarians] still think of us as visitors, transients" (58). Yes, the locale might be anywhere, but its texture is distinctly Mesopotamian, and the town is subject to the same pressures as the agrocities of the ancient Tigris-Euphrates plain, though the Magistrate is in a state of denial about this. For instance, while admitting that the barbarians think they "will outlast" the settlement because "every year the lake-water grows a little more salty," he assures us that "there is a simple explanation" for the deterioration, but that we should "never mind what it is" (58). An odd and uncharacteristic evasion, this. In actual fact, the gradual, inevitable salinization of soils fed by irrigation trenches is a well-understood process, one that plagued ancient Sumer. Furthermore, it can be accelerated by the clearing of trees, which Joll, supposedly in order to repress an insurgency, accomplishes by means of fire—the original Agent Orange—along the banks of the river that feeds the impounded lake. Thus, when returning the Girl to her people, the Magistrate and his party must risk their lives crossing brutal alkali flats, while the beam he has uncovered from the ruins displays "faded carvings of dolphins and waves" (116). Desertward the course of agro-Empire takes its way.

Furthermore, the town's dependence on their dam demonstrates how in Coetzee all agriculturalists exist within "a world where vast power [implies] infinite vulnerability" (Eckstein 197), and why they must therefore turn a blind eye to their own precarity while simultaneously blaming it on the supposed aggressions of an Other who lurks beyond the wall. Just as a rapist is "recognized ... as a barbarian by his ugliness" (142), so the breaching of the dam, according to the townsmen, must be the work of "barbarians," though "no one saw them" (114). As Lance Olsen declares, "The barbarians remain only a gap that Empire fills with its own panic" (49–50). But whether the cut was caused by sabotage or structural failure, agriculture's radical fragility is exposed in any event, for "almost the whole of the intricate system of channels and gates that distributes the water around the fields has been washed away," and "the crop is ruined and it is too late to plant again." The Magistrate himself laments, "At any moment [the farmers'] work can be brought to nothing by a few men armed with spades! How can we win such a war? What is the use of textbook military operations, sweeps and punitive raids into the enemy's heartland, when we can be bled to death at home?" (114–15). As Shen-Yen Yu comments, "Agriculture seems to be held accountable for triggering a vicious environmental circle that ... presages an apocalyptical end to the outpost of the empire" (87). Fleeing this Armageddon might be an option, but the one time he tries escaping into the countryside, the lifelong townsman winds up quickly admitting that "there is nothing for [him] outside the walls but to starve" (116). But, of course, it is not long before hunger penetrates within the ramparts as well, with the fleeing garrison carrying off "sacks of seed grain" (162), and the Magistrate imagining townsmen "fighting with pitchforks" (164) now that the walls are manned against the barbarians only by "armed dummies" (177). The few fields left unflooded are hurriedly harvested, but "the yield is less than four cups a day for each family," and so he urges his gaunt neighbors "to cultivate their kitchen gardens, to plant root vegetables that will withstand the winter frosts" (167). However, by the time the looting, the evacuations, and the desperate gleaning are finally over, the only agricultural products available in the market square are the "bread mould and milkroot" (173) the Magistrate purchases in order to stifle his erections.

If hunger doesn't lead him to doubt the wisdom of tillage, our narrator's bafflement about his own incarceration within the agricultural trap is odder still, given his surety concerning just what *kind* of ruins he has been digging up in the desert. In point of fact, there has been a surprising amount of confusion about this issue among critics, a number of whom have asserted that it is the ancestors of the barbarians who built the buried city (Moses 117; Head 87; Attwell, *Politics* 76–77; Meskell and Weiss 92). But the Magistrate only refers to the runic slips as being of barbarian provenance when he is unwillingly performing in the presence of Joll. Elsewhere in his accounts, he is in no doubt that those who peopled his buried city also wore the uniform of an empire that plowed: "Perhaps in bygone days criminals, slaves, soldiers trekked the twelve miles to the river, and cut down poplar trees, and sawed and planed them, and transported the timbers back to this barren place in carts, and built houses, and a fort too, for all I know, and in the course of time died, so that their masters, their prefects and magistrates and captains, could climb the roofs and towers morning and evening to scan the world from horizon to horizon for signs of the barbarians" (17). To casually assume, as Joll and some commentators have, that civilizations built on agriculture always endure, and that if something is buried under shifting dunes it is more likely to be the relic of nomads rather than of planters, is itself a prime example of agriculturalist assumptions in action—assumptions that the heaped earthen tells of Mesopotamia can quickly refute. The Magistrate, by contrast, possesses an "ironic view that comes from . . . his archaeological digs" (Ashcroft 107), a cognizance "that this particular empire of which he is a part is merely one phase in a much longer span of time ... during which empires rise and fall" (Rich 382)—and a knowledge that therefore *should* allow him to "negate Empire's *raison d'etre* as the upholder of 'civilized' values in the face of the 'barbarian' onslaught" (Dovey 255). To a certain extent, he does perform this act of negation, insisting that the "real" barbarians are the hardmen of the Third Bureau, so well instructed in "the new science of degradation" (124).

Yet he never does quite get to the heart of the matter, as we can see when, late in the novel, he first reminisces about his life as a frontier citizen before Joll arrived on the scene and then attempts to predict the future of the barbarians. As to the former, it is prefaced by his yearning for an Eden somehow outside the psychic, ethical, and imaginative walls of Empire: "What has made it impossible for us to live in time like fish in water, like birds in air, like children?" It is, he says, the fault of Empire itself, which, instead of locating its existence "in the smooth recurrent spinning time of the cycle of the seasons," has "created the time of history" and thus recognizes only "the jagged time of rise and fall, of beginning and end, of catastrophe" (153–54). Now, when he begins to write his abortive "record of settlement," he appears to momentarily entertain the idea that there did exist an era when the time of seasons was a reality for himself and his fellow townsmen—only to suddenly and angrily reject the notion:

> "No one who paid a visit to this oasis," I write, "failed to be struck by the charm of life here. We lived in the time of the seasons, of the harvests, of the migrations of the waterbirds. We lived with nothing between us and the stars. We would have made any concession, had we only known what, to go on living here. This was paradise on earth."
>
> For a long while I stare at the plea I have written. It would be disappointing to know that the poplar slips I have spent so much time on contain a message as devious, as equivocal, as reprehensible as this. (178)

What is puzzling about this passage is that the prompt of his bitter language ("devious," "equivocal," "reprehensible") remains unclear. It appears the walled town was *not* a paradise before Joll arrived—indeed, was never such—but *why* was it not? Because there was poverty and ignorance? Because he dispensed unequal justice and then read out pat sermons to the prisoners? Perhaps—or perhaps there was always some other roadblock athwart the entrance to Eden, one that he even yet does not clearly perceive.

He next turns his eyes to the barbarians and wonders about their fate over anthropological timescales. Previously he has uttered a stadial historian's caricature of the nomads, associating them with "intellectual torpor, slovenliness, [the] tolerance of disease and death" (59). However, just as the fisherfolk have been "seduced utterly by the free and plentiful food" available inside the city gates, "above all by the bread" (20), so, too, he predicts, will the pastoralists find themselves helpless before the baker's art: "But when the barbarians taste bread, new bread and mulberry jam, bread and gooseberry jam, they will be won over to our ways. They will find that they are unable to live without the skills of men who know how to rear the pacific grains, without the arts of women who know how to use the benign fruits" (179). What he imagines here is that the barbarians will live out a stadial comedy of upward development, enjoying the kind of win-win agricultural revolution (more food, less labor) that modern anthropology has overturned by positing the agricultural trap. The Magistrate has had to forget much to utter this prediction. He has apparently forgotten that Joll's torture sessions occurred in the town granary, that this storehouse of the harvest is "a massive building with heavy doors and tiny windows" like a prison, that it "lies beyond the abattoir and the mill" (5), and that it shares a wall with the military barracks. By invoking "pacific grains," then, the Magistrate unknowingly coins an oxymoron. But Joll's choice of the granary as the place to begin his "working with people" (145) is appropriate, given agro-culture's visceral fear of those who wander rather than plow, those who feed themselves by means of knowledge rather than labor, those who, in Coetzee's own metaphor, choose to live like the grasshopper rather than the ant (*White Writing* 19). Can it therefore be mere coincidence that Joll injures the eyes and feet of the Barbarian Girl, those same bodily assets that Friday will later draw to illustrate his own life before he was put to work leveling fields for cereals and rearing the walls of Cruso's ziggurat?

When asked in an interview about his narrator's mixture of blindness and insight, Coetzee strikes an ambiguous note: "The magistrate . . . makes an effort, but who is to say that the effort goes far enough." Then, referring to his early protagonists generally, he muses that "perhaps they are trapped in their situation but they don't resign themselves to being trapped in their situation. But whether they get out of it in their lifetime, that is another question" (Rhedin 7–8). So it may be that enlightenment is not entirely out of the Magistrate's reach, though it may as yet offer itself only through the tenuous medium of his subconscious. In his series of interlocking dreams, the hooded figure of the Girl stands in the town square busied in "building a fort of snow, a walled town which [he] recognize[s] in every detail: the battlements with the four watchtowers, the gate with the porter's hut beside it, the streets and houses, the great square with the barracks compound in one corner." But immediately he is disturbed by the forlornness of the miniature, for "the square is empty, the whole town is white and mute and empty. I point to the middle of the square. 'You must put people there!' I want to say." This dream recurs on subsequent nights, "reconfirming each time that the town she is building is empty of life" (60). Some weeks later he again seems to encounter her in the frozen agora, and this time attempts to sooth her torture-twisted feet, only to find them represented as "two huge potatoes" and to awake "with aching gums and blood in [his] mouth" (100–101). The most detailed dream, however, is the next one, which centers upon a gift of bread.

> It is the girl. She is kneeling with her back to me before the snowcastle or sandcastle she has built. She wears a dark blue robe. As I approach I see that she is digging away in the bowels of the castle.
> She becomes aware of me and turns. I am mistaken, it is not a castle she has built but a clay oven. Smoke curls up from the vent at the back. She holds out her hands to me offering me something, a shapeless lump which I peer at unwillingly through a mist. Though I shake my head my vision will not clear....
> Also now I can see that what she is holding out to me is a loaf of bread, still hot, with a coarse steaming broken crust. A surge of gratitude sweeps through me. "Where did a child like you learn to bake so well in the desert?" I want to say. I open my arms to embrace her, and come to myself with tears stinging the wound on my cheek. Though I scrabble back at once into the burrow of sleep I cannot re-enter the dream or taste the bread that has made my saliva run. (126).

The dream series is closed by a final rapture in which he seems propelled through the square by great winds, hurtling directly at the figure of the Girl:

> I am already tensing myself for the impact, when she turns and sees me. For an instant I have a vision of her face, the face of a child, glowing, healthy, smiling on me without alarm, before we collide. Her head strikes me in the belly; then I am gone, carried by the wind. The bump is as faint as the stroke of a moth. I am flooded with relief. "Then I need

not have been anxious after all!" I think. I try to look back, but all is lost from sight in the whiteness of the snow. (157).

Whatever authority the text lends these dreams seems in part to lie in their traditional role as prophesies. What the Girl appears to be foretelling, in her making of a snow fort, is the fate of the walled town that the Magistrate once governed, though on two distinct timescales. In the near term, the emptiness of the structure seems to presage the settlement's looming abandonment in the face of war and famine (Head 91), which is accomplished by the end of the novel. But, simultaneously, the fact that its defensive walls are made from flakes that will evanesce in the sun appears to prophesy its fate across the historical eons that are the province of anthropology and archeology. The melting of the town ramparts into the rubble of yet another site for future antiquarians to investigate was implied by the Magistrate's own musings about the antiquities he himself has unearthed. Now, if there is any consolation for him in this confirmation that even the "jagged time[s] of rise and fall" instigated by empires will be swallowed up in cycles much larger, here he receives it from a source he trusts more than himself. Then, too, the dream performs another traditional office—that of wish fulfillment, for the Girl appears to him unharmed and happy, perhaps a vision of what she might have looked like had she remained as that impossible figure of the anthropologist's dream, the intact-because-uncontacted native subject. And perhaps the winds of the final dream will grant him some kind of imaginative escape velocity that will lift him beyond the defensive battlements of his agriculturalist assumptions to a height from which he can at last survey with clear eyes the alternative life, the Other's life, that the barbarians represent.

As to the central image of the Girl offering up to him a loaf of bread, I must take issue with those otherwise perceptive critics who wish to see it as a "peace offering" (Gallagher, "Torture" 284), or a "sacramental gesture of conciliation" (Attwell 83), or a "vision of basic human endurance . . . in the face of difficult odds" (Head 91). Given our deep cultural associations with the giving and breaking of bread, these readings are understandable, almost reflexively persuasive, but that is because they emerge from an agriculturalist worldview that the novel asks us—and nudges the Magistrate—to reconsider. Instead, I wish to read it as the unconsoling image that, could our narrator only see it for what it is, might resolve his final puzzlement over that which "stare[s him] in the face," but that he cannot yet grasp. The bread, I would argue, is yet another of Coetzee's robust allegories that can express several things at once: the one deep link with Joll that he hasn't quite discovered and thus hasn't yet repudiated, the root cause of Empire's violence that he hasn't yet analyzed, and the conceptual millstone that prevents him, perhaps even in his final dream, from soaring free of the walls and the flooded, ruined fields they once commanded. I realize how second nature it is to look at one figure offering bread to another and to see in such an act of peace, a ceremony of reconcilement—but, as the Magistrate himself would have the Girl believe, this is not what you think it is.

BECAUSE COETZEE's larger, anthropological frame has not been adequately perceived, many sensitive and sympathetic critics of the author have decried what they describe as *Life & Times of Michael K*'s political quietism. What they are reacting against is the fact that Michael not only refuses aid to the enemies of the (future, warring) apartheid state that hectors, imprisons, and exploits him but that he also fails to figure forth, in either deed or thought, any successor regime that might be more racially inclusive, more economically egalitarian, or even simply more pacific. The locus classicus of such objections is Nadine Gordimer's 1988 review of the novel, in which she claims that although Coetzee is "fiercely moved" by the plight of nonwhite South Africans, he "does not believe in the possibility of blacks establishing a new regime that will do much better," and thus she detects "a revulsion against all political and revolutionary solutions" running through the narrative. According to Gordimer, this antipathy prevents the author from "recogniz[ing] what the victims [of apartheid], seeing themselves as victims no longer, have done, are doing, and believe they must do for themselves" (6). These sentiments are echoed and amplified by Derek Wright, who sees the novel implying "that the land is to be returned not to the blacks but to itself," and that while "these two things could, conceivably, be the same, . . . there is no indication in the book that they will be"—a conclusion that leads Wright to dismiss Michael as "a hero of the white ecological Eighties" (440). Anthony Vital is equally disappointed to find *Life & Times* suggesting "that however good it would be to remove the apartheid regime, the nation, at a profound level, is not worth fighting over"—a mistaken resignation, in his opinion, since "it is the nation state that provides the arena in which people are fated to seek improvement in their lives" (99–100). Even Hardt and Negri, coauthors of the venerable *Empire*, warn that, by itself, an absolute refusal "of work and authority" like that manifested by Michael (and by Melville's Bartleby) is "empty," since although such characters may constitute "beautiful souls, . . . their being in its absolute purity hangs on the edge of an abyss," because "their lines of flight from authority are completely solitary." Instead, Hardt and Negri require an "exodus" that "create[s] a real alternative," where "as part of [our] refusal, we ... construct a new mode of life and above all a new community" (204). A consensus of political disappointment thus appears to enshroud the novel.

But while all of these critics are correct in perceiving that the book offers little hope to those attempting to overthrow repressive regimes by means of armed struggle at the level of the nation-state, they have no real explanation for *why* the novel seems to downplay this mode of action, given its author's consistent public positions on apartheid. The answer, I believe, is to be found precisely in Coetzee's engagement with contemporary anthropology, and especially with the notion of the agricultural trap, an engagement that, despite the apparent local pacifism that puzzles and disappoints some readers, enlists Michael in a longer-term struggle whose stakes remain, in their own way, deeply political. We can begin by noting that in *White Writing: On the Culture of Letters in South Africa*, published in 1988, Coetzee is sympathetically responsive to many assertions of professional anthropology's new, emergent paradigm. Take, for instance, the notion that the turn from hunting and gathering to agriculture, far from giving birth to the very concept of leisure, was in fact "the first step in a long increase in drudgery" (Scott 95) that largely extinguished leisure for everyone except elites, and that in turn spawned pervasive cultural slanders that depicted foragers as lazy beings unable to defer gratification or plan for (i.e., worry about) the future. Coetzee scrutinizes European explorer/settler descriptions of the Cape's indigenous "Hottentots" (properly, the KhoiKhoi), taking particular note of how these indigenous people are chronically figured as indolent and providing an exhaustive catalog of such characterizations. While doing so, he notes that the KhoiKhoi were represented as retrograde examples of humanity on both rational and religious grounds, since, on the one hand, to "the [Enlightenment] science of Man, the spectacle of wholesale idleness is inherently scandalous" (11), while at the same time "early Discourse of the Cape effectively excludes the Hottentot from Eden by deciding that, though he is human, he is not in the line of descent that leads from Adam via a life of toil to civilized men" (25).

Coetzee, apparently intrigued that so historically recent an encounter between invading agriculturalists (i.e., the European settler-colonialists) and pastoralist hunter-gatherers (the KhoiKhoi) has produced a literature so close to home, singles out the English explorer William John Burchell, who, diverging from his fellow colonialists, declares the Hottentots "the happiest of mortals" (32–33) and reminds his readers that Rousseau believed mankind's golden age to have occurred in "the phase of leisure intermediate between savage indolence and the ... invention of metallurgy and agriculture" (24).[1] Viewing the invaders' discursive field as a whole, however, Coetzee detects a telling imaginative lacuna in the settler mindset, which he quite lyrically describes:

> Nowhere in the great echo chamber of the Discourse of the Cape is a voice raised to ask whether the life of the Hottentot may not be a version of life before the Fall (as Bartolomé de las Casas suggested in respect of the Indians of the New World), a life in which man is not yet condemned to eat his bread in the sweat of his brow, but instead may spend his days dozing in the sun, or in the shade when the sun grows too hot, half-aware of the singing of the birds and the breeze on his skin, bestirring himself to eat when hunger overtakes him, enjoying a pipe of tobacco when it is available, at one with his surroundings and unreflectively content.... No one bothers to put, save rhetorically, the ethical question: which is better, to live like the ant, busily storing up food for the winter, or like the grasshopper, singing in the sun all day, heedless of the morrow? (18–19)

Coetzee himself, however, is quite clearly fascinated by this question and seems at times to imply what his own answer might be: "With our wider historical perspective, we might also appreciate better what a massive cultural revolution is entailed when a people moves from a subsistence economy to an economy of providence, from pastoralism to agriculture—a move, indeed, in which the notion of *work* may be said to make its appearance in history" (34, Coetzee's italics). This answer is even implied in his epigraph to the volume, a passage from Ovid in which Pallas inaugurates agriculture when commanded to plow and then to sow the earth with dragon's teeth. Furthermore, once we understand that the agricultural trap associates humanity's transition from hunting and gathering to field tillage with the rise of the first ancient grain states, and that these political entities depended upon unprecedented levels of coercion, social stratification, physical drudgery, and psychic simplification (Scott 9–10, 170–76), then we can see the Magistrate's desire in *Waiting for the*

Barbarians to exist in the "time of the cycle of the seasons" (153) rather than inside "the history that Empire imposes on its subjects" (178) as a similar (if forlorn) fantasy of escape into a preagricultural social condition. Hence, there is much explanatory value in seeing the protagonist of Coetzee's subsequent *Life & Times of Michael K* as a figure who, fitfully but significantly, embodies and enacts that longed-for condition.

It is probably the case that Michael's role as an embodiment of preagricultural practices has been masked by his self-description as a "gardener"—by the fact that he plants and tends to crops with loving care whenever he is allowed to do so. But anthropologists are insistent that the lifeways of hunter-gatherer bands who opportunistically scatter seeds in likely ground must be strictly distinguished from the wholly different social arrangements necessitated by the fixed-field, tilling-intensive, sedentary agriculture undertaken in the early (and present-day) grain state (Barker 60–69; Rowley-Conwy 63). As Melinda Zeder asserts, "Cultigens and domestic animals were incorporated into the general round of subsistence strategies, sometimes for thousands of years, with little disruption of the traditional hunter-gatherer way of life" (99). Peoples who, when conditions were right, sporadically sowed seeds on the edges of flood plains or promising riverine patches remained, like K, "dispersed and highly mobile, and lived in small settlements. They might be shifting cultivators, pastoralists, fisher folk, hunter-gatherers, forages, or small-scale collector-traders. They might even plant some grain and eat it, but grain was unlikely to be their dominant staple as it was for state subjects" (Scott 229).

Once Michael breaks out onto the veld, we are told that "this was the beginning of his life as a 'cultivator,'" and I would suggest that Coetzee carefully chooses the word to differentiate his protagonist from the (few) farmers and (many) farm laborers whom he encounters throughout the novel, social roles that are tied to privately owned, fixed-field, stoop-worked, grain-state agriculture. We can hear the author's desire to parse this difference in the Medical Officer's overtly sarcastic tone as, having joined K's interrogation, he suggests that Michael confess the truth about his "recent agricultural enterprise" (140). In the Officer's opinion, it doesn't qualify as one—the novel, I believe, concurs, but sees what Michael does not as sub-, but rather as ante- (and perhaps anti-)agricultural. Indeed, at the novel's end, Michael chastises himself for planting his pumpkins too much in the style of a farmer and too unlike the manner in which a hunter-gatherer would disperse them: "Then my mistake was to plant all my seeds together in one patch. I should have planted them one at a time spread out over miles of veld in patches of soil no larger than my hand, and drawn a map and kept it with me at all times so that every night I could make a tour of the sites to water them. Because if there was one thing I discovered out in the country, it was that there is time enough for everything" (183). Clearly, one can cultivate plants without, literally or even figuratively, domesticating oneself.

Dominic Head affirms that "K's life as a cultivator is only possible when he escapes the camps" (103), and thus it is illuminating that, in redescribing the rise of the ancient grain states, James Scott provocatively labels early agricultural cities such as Uruk and Akkad as "late-Neolithic multispecies resettlement camp[s]," a term that clarifies the fact that Jakkalsdrif, Kenilsworth, and their like stand in the novel as epitomes of the agricultural state, with their rations of mealie-porridge, their gangs of corvée labor, and elaborate bureaucracies of control (Scott 140–44), for, as Head would have it, such camps function as "anti-nomadic device[s]" (103). Head goes on to view the camps through a Foucauldian lens, but one of the most revisionist assertions of those who posit an agricultural trap is that the primary function of the iconic walls of ancient grain states—and even of the Great Wall of China (Scott 29, 137–38, 233–34)—was to keep an unfree labor force in place rather than to keep "barbarians" out (Manning 34). As the guard at Jakkalsdrif warns Michael, "You climb the fence and I'll shoot you dead, mister" (85), while later the Medical Officer wonders whether the camps might "not close down" even "when the war is over," since "camps with high walls always hav[e] their uses" (147). Coetzee's implication is that so long as agriculture and the grain state endure, the walls that coerce hunter-gatherers into becoming full-time and unfree tillers of the soil will also persist.

When Michael is arrested for vagrancy in Prince Albert, his charge sheet lists him as "CM"—that is, colored male—and "NFA," indicating that he has no fixed abode. Many critics, understandably interested in Michael's resistance or lack thereof to the apartheid regime, have focused on the first abbreviation. But one can admit that the novel is very much about the ways in which successive Cape states from the colonial era through the apogee of apartheid attempted to control the mobility of specific racial groups by means of everything from sidewalk bans, to pass laws, to the establishment of Bantusans—and still admit that, given our concerns *here*, it is the second abbreviation that is more resonant. To belong to no permanent settlement is, in the eyes of the grain state, to be a "nomad," a "barbarian," and to thus betray a nature that is less than fully human. This distinction has been at the center of agrarian ideology from the time the agricultural trap first snapped shut right up until the present day: "From Thomas Hobbes to John Locke to Giambattista Vico to Lewis Henry Morgan to Friedrich Engels to Herbert Spencer to Oswald Spengler to social Darwinist accounts of social evolution in general, the sequence of progress from hunting and gathering to nomadism to agriculture (and from band to village to town to city) was settled doctrine. Such views nearly mimicked Julius Caesar's evolutionary scheme from households to kindreds to tribes to peoples to the state (a people living under laws), wherein Rome was the apex, with the Celts and then the Germans ranged behind" (Scott 9). Furthermore, although the police report goes on to list Michael as "Unemployed," the fact is that there is simply "a radically different tempo to the lives of hunting and fishing peoples . . . a rhythm that farmers often read as indolence" (Scott 53). In the eyes of agriculturalists, hunter-gatherers are "uncaptured at the very least and, at worst, represent a nuisance and threat that must be exterminated." K's serial arrests are therefore as much about habits of locomotion as they are about his coloration, since "weeds, varmints, vermin, and barbarians—the 'undomesticated'—threaten civilization in the grain state. They must either be mastered and domesticated, or failing that, exterminated or rigorously excluded from the domus" (Scott 221). Under agriculturalist ideology to be errant in the sense of chronically mobile is also to be errant in the sense of sinning.

Unsurprisingly, those inculcated in established agrarian mythology look with condescension and pity on the "unfortunate" hunter-gatherer, and thus Robert, the veteran prisoner of Jakkalsdrif, declares K a "baby" who has "been asleep all [his] life" (88), while the Medical Officer's early assessment is that he is "a poor helpless soul" (141). For his part, Michael is quite aware that he is being seen through the lens of an agriculturalist ideology, as in his perception of young Visagie's assessment of him: "He thinks I am an idiot who sleeps on the floor like an animal and lives on birds and lizards and does not know there is such a thing as money" (62). Of course Michael *does* live partly on birds and lizards, but here he is cognizant that grain-eaters disparage such fare, just as he understands that his burrow-shelter would be scoffed at by those who live behind walls and fences, that they would "shake their heads and say to each other: What shiftless creatures, how little pride they took in their work!" (101). Thus it follows that, throughout the novel, Michael's extreme leanness is taken as a marker for his degraded condition, for his perverse rejection of the (supposed) cardinal benefit of sedentary agrarianism. It is only after a prolonged and inquisitive exposure to K that the Medical Officer begins to recognize that there might be a way to view him outside the grain state's assumptions, inadvertently stating a truth when he muses that "maybe he eats only the bread of freedom." One can, at this point, hear him cease thinking of Michael's way of life as degraded and begin to consider it as radically alternative: "Maybe he is just a very thin man" (146).

This issue of what Michael eats and how often is of central importance. Whereas the traditional narrative of the agricultural revolution envisions a cultural win-win, in which humanity traded a precarious and brutal existence of hunting and gathering for a more "civilized" existence made possible by a forward leap in food security, the rival account highlights the new "diseases of sedentism and crowding" (chiefly due to chronic contact with domesticated animals) that were exacerbated by "an increasingly agricultural diet [that was] deficient in many essential nutrients." Thus, within and without the walls of the early city-states, "a diet that weakened the vulnerable" was combined with "new infectious diseases which carried them off" (Scott 107). Nor was this inferior nutrition reliably available, the frequency of accounts of famines in the ancient historical record "suggest[ing] the opposite" of the received mythology, so much so that "famine was the mark of a maturing agricultural society, the very badge of civilization" (Manning 69). Within the camps and on corvée labor details, Michael is often fed penurious portions of grain-based foods such as "mealie-porridge" (70) and "soft white bread" that he vomits up (123). Other products of sedentism, such as the wine, milk, and bread he consumes after returning to the seaside, make him feel "that what he had previous thought of in himself as tough and rope-like was becoming soggy and fibrous" (177). As he eventually tells the Medical Officer: "I can't eat the food here, that's all. I can't eat camp food" (146). Encompassing the related ills of the late-Neolithic multispecies resettlement camp, K laments an "earth stamped so tight" by the crowded prisoners that "nothing would ever grow there again" (104), while the Medical Officer admits that "dysentery and hepatitis are rife, and of course worms" (160). In sum, the deterioration of Michael's physical health after being forced inside the fences of Jakkalsdrif and Kenilsworth roughly parallels the overall declension that many anthropologists now conclude was imposed upon the bodies of former hunter-gatherers herded within the walls of ancient cities, wherein a relatively healthy and robust existence was traded for one likely to be nasty, brutish, and short.

Of course Michael also eats meagerly when he is outside the camps, living as a hunter-gatherer. But here Coetzee makes his point through a remarkable strategy, for when K is a free man tramping across the karoo in the guise of a Paleolithic forager, his hunger, though present, does not seem to matter, almost as if it were a neutral condition that can be recognized without being deplored. It would seem, for instance, that K's caloric intake reaches its minimum during his stint in the mountains after his first flight from the Visagie farm. There, he literally becomes a cave dweller, and his diet also takes on a prehistoric cast, since "he made a fire and roasted a lizard he had killed with a stone" (65). During the ensuing days, "he felt hungry but did nothing about it. Instead of listening to the crying of his body he tried to listen to the great silence about him" (66). Leaving the carcer[e]al farms far behind and below him, he feels himself "becoming a different kind of man ... if there are two kinds of man" (67). This new (actually, old) *Homo sapien* must still eat in order to live, of course, but something fundamental about nourishment has changed: "In his first days in the mountains he went for walks, turned over stones, nibbled at roots and bulbs. Once he broke open an ant-nest and ate grubs one by one. They tasted like fish. But now he ceased to make an adventure of eating and drinking." He feels hunger, but hunger no longer, as in his earlier days, presents itself a *problem* that must be solved: "As a child K had been hungry, like all the children of [his charity school,] Huis Norenius. Hunger had turned them into animals who stole from one another's plates and climbed the kitchen enclosure to rifle the garbage cans for bones and peelings. Then he had grown older and stopped wanting. Whatever the nature of the beast that had howled inside him, it was starved into stillness" (68). Michael's ability to practically live on air—and to live happily, at that—seems to embody Sahlins's original conception of hunter-gatherers as "the first affluent society" (1–2). It is only when K returns to the fruited plain below, entering Prince Albert, where "the smell of peach-blossom envelope[s] him" (69), that hunger can again force him to perform actions against his inclinations and can trouble his clarity of purpose. It is only when he smells the agricultural food at the infirmary there that he experiences "the first hunger he had known for a long time," and is "not sure that he wanted to become a servant to hunger again" (71). Given that falling into the agricultural trap involves the promulgation within grain states of a vertical hierarchy of casts and classes that contrasts sharply with the egalitarianism of hunter-gatherer bands (Brody 185–86; Manning 18), a "servant to hunger" seems a synoptic description of the typical denizen of an early farming state.

If Michael's sojourn in the vicinity of the cave lets us glimpse his fullest embodiment of the hunter-gatherer's way of life, his pair of residences at the Visagie farmstead is where he comes in closest contact with agricultural life while still a free man. For the most part, this proximity does him no harm. For instance, on his first visit Michael discovers a herd of goats, but because he possesses none of the required pastoralist skills, he finds he must *hunt* them as if they were game in the wild. "Armed with nothing but his penknife," he attempts to use main force and then surprise, finally drowning one of the animals in a pond, whereupon he is mentally shaken by its death throes. When he finds he cannot consume all the goat's flesh before it begins to spoil, though, he does not resolve to abandon hunting, but merely to hunt prey more appropriate to his nomadic predilection: "The lesson ... seemed to be not to kill such large animals" (57), whereupon he returns to stalking birds and lizards.

It is also at the farm that he plants his beloved pumpkins and melons, which, to reiterate, is an activity completely consistent with his identity as a hunter-gatherer. But there are moments during his stays there when he wishes for and flirts with the accoutrements of settled life (recall his self-criticism), and Coetzee is not blind to the genuine attractions of sedentism, though he always depicts them as carrying an attendant price in the coin of worry. During his second visit to the farm, for instance, "the ripening of the pumpkins brought a new anxiety" (114), including questions of storage and spoilage. But what he fears most is exactly what the tillers of early agricultural states had best reason to fear: confiscation of his crop by the powerful (Scott 132–34, 140–41). Simultaneous with—and in part because of—this fretting, Michael begins longing for the products and practices made available by the walled grain city, imagining "how much easier it would all be ... if there were a fence around the dam, a fence of stout wire mesh" (117). And, when he at last harvests what pumpkins he can, he longs to enhance their flavor with the wares of agriculturalists: "And what perfection it would be with a pinch of salt—with a pinch of salt, and a dab of butter, and a sprinkling of sugar, and a little cinnamon scattered over the top! Eating the third slice, and the fourth and fifth, till half the pumpkin was gone and his belly was full, K wallowed in the recollection of the flavours of salt, butter, sugar, cinnamon, one by one" (114). Coetzee tough-mindedly perceives the agricultural trap to be baited with authentic delights.

Less enticing to the hunter-gatherer is the chronic toil required in order to till the fields of the grain state, given that "typically ... hunter-gatherers spend only three or four hours per day working at what we could call economic activities" (Gowdy xxi), keeping Sahlins's "banker's hours" (34). Indeed, for Scott, "once Homo sapiens took that fateful step into agriculture, our species entered an austere monastery whose taskmaster consists mostly of the demanding genetic clockwork of a few plants" (91), shifting the "leisure-drudgery ratio between foragers and farmers" so heavily against the latter that it is difficult to imagine the former taking up farming "unless forced to by . . . some form of coercion" (255, 20; see also Rowley-Conwy 64). Or, as Richard Manning tartly puts it, the self-serving foundation-myths of agricultural societies "had to have sprung from the imagination of someone who never hoed a row of corn or rose with the sun for a lifetime of milking cows" (23). We have already seen Coetzee musing about an era in human history before the concept of work had inculcated itself into our psyches, and, when he allows Michael to act most like a hunter-gatherer, his protagonist seems to fitfully inhabit just such a time before toil. Ensconced in the highlands, "he spent a day in idleness," during which "he felt hungry but did nothing about it," feeling no anxiety because "there seemed nothing to do but live" (66), a renunciation of exertion so profound that "he wondered if he were living in what was known as bliss" (68). As we have seen, "bliss" is in fact the very word Heathcliff uses to describe his own state of mind as he wanders the moors while refusing his daily bread.

It is back at his burrow adjoining the pumpkin patch, however, that this particular aspect of his foragers' consciousness is perfected:

> But most of all, as summer slanted to an end, he was learning to love idleness, idleness no longer as stretches of freedom reclaimed by stealth here and there from involuntary labour, surreptitious thefts to be enjoyed sitting on his heels before a flowerbed with the fork dangling from his fingers, but as a yielding up of himself to time, to a time flowing slowly like oil from horizon to horizon over the face of the world, washing over his body, circulating in his armpits and his groin, stirring his eyelids. He was neither pleased nor displeased when there was work to do; it was all the same. . . . All that was moving was time, bearing him onward in its flow. . . . [for] he was living beyond the reach of calendar and clock. (116–17)

Surely Michael has here arrived at that Great Good Place that the Magistrate of Coetzee's previous novel so longs to inhabit, the "Time of Seasons" where one could "live in time like fish in water, like birds in air, like children" (153). But, of course, in that text, it is only the "barbarians" who can exist in such a manner—"barbarian" being the epithet agriculturalists always bestow upon hunter-gatherers (Brody 6; Scott 219–21)—while the Magistrate oversees a fortified town surrounded by tilled fields. For his part, Michael at times even appears to hibernate within his burrow, sleeping "through whole cycles of the heavens" and only then "emerg[ing] into wakefulness unsure whether he had slept a day or a week or a month" (118–19). It is difficult to imagine anything farther removed from the agro-industrial imperative to "improve the time," but for the hunter-gatherer, time as experienced is already unimprovable, just as the land is perpetually Edenic (Brody 116).

Not only is the labor required by the grain state onerous, it is also often coercive and uncompensated, as we have heard in Mumford's admission that "the scepter" displayed by its king was in reality a euphemism for "the truncheon and the whip" (51–52) wielded by the brutal overseers of his fields. Given this, it is worth noting the chronic blurring that occurs in the novel between the notion of a labor camp and a prison camp:

> "This isn't jail," said the policemen, "this is a camp, you work for your food like everyone else in the camp."
>
> "How can I work when I'm locked up? Where is the work I must do?"
>
> "Fuck off," said the policeman. "Ask your friends. Who do you think you are that I should give you a free living?" (77)

Soon after this, Robert informs Michael in an ironic tone that "this isn't a prison" and asks, "Don't you know what a camp is?" He then goes on to sarcastically paraphrase the mythology of agricultural superiority: "Why should people with nowhere to go run away from the nice life we've got here? From soft beds like this and free wood and a man at the gate with a gun to stop the thieves from coming in the night to steal your money?" He continues by explaining that one of the camps' primary purposes, like the declared or implicit agendas of the early walled grain states, is to stamp out nomadism by first capturing and then enslaving the nomads: "'You climb the fence,' the man said, 'and you have left your place of abode. Jakkalsdrif is your place of abode now. Welcome. You leave your place of abode, they pick you up, you are a vagrant. No place of abode'" (78).

And who profits from the camps? According to Robert, it is "the farmers" (i.e., farm owners, not farm workers), and soon enough Michael is assigned to do field work, where a "foreman" menaces him with a "rattan stick" (82), followed a few days later by field-scything under the aggressive shouts of supervisors. Even when the camp officials themselves discuss what kind of place they are running, they cannot help revealing Jakkalsdrif and Kenilsworth as the forced-labor enterprises they in fact are. As an officer angrily asks a guard, "What do you think you are doing here—running a holiday camp? It's a work camp, man! It's a camp to teach lazy people to work! *Work!*" (91, Coetzee's italics). The Medical Officer confirms this when he becomes impatient with K's passive resistance: "This is a camp, not a holiday resort, not a convalescent home: it is a camp where we rehabilitate people like you and make you work!" (138). All this makes it clear that while the crime Michael is officially suspected of may be caching food for the rebels, his actual crime is his living as a hunter-gatherer, having no fixed abode, and avoiding the stoop labor that the agricultural state demands. *Life & Times* strongly suggests that it was the plow that turned the Magistrate's longed-for time of seasons into the time of Empire he deplores.

If, after hunter-gatherers are rounded up, slavery is a mode of grain-state violence perpetrated against an internal victim, its frequent comrade is aggressive war waged against perceived external enemies. Scott maintains that "the ancient states replenished their population by wars of capture and by buying slaves on a large scale from barbarians who specialized in the trade" (36). Brody agrees, noting the "striking links between agriculture and warfare: farmers compete with one another as well as with hunter-gatherers, and their skills were brought to bear on the development of weapons as well as farm implements. From the very beginning, they must have learned how to beat their plowshares into swords" (148). Thus, Coetzee's imagined South Africa is at war with enemies that seem to include both the domestic and the foreign. The society he depicts is thoroughly militarized, and most of the characters we meet either wear a uniform or are in the custody of those who do. The Medical Officer, recalling the participation of "labour battalions" in the "big military parades," provides an image of the denizens of the camps let out on furloughs in order to "march with spades on their shoulders" (134). Finally, in an episode whose irony is palpable, when the armed forces of the agricultural state discover Michael's clandestine arbor, they tear out his potentially nutritious pumpkins and sow the ground with land mines.

But if a mythology promulgating the "natural" superiority of agriculture over foraging is to be reproduced down the ages, more than brute violence is necessary—ideological indoctrination is required. We have already touched upon the long-standing slanders that the grain state hurls against supposedly shiftless "barbarians" enjoying no fixed abode, but at one point during his incarceration K seems to wonder if some more systematic method of persuasion is being aimed at him: "Is this my education? He wondered. Am I at last learning about life here in a camp? It seemed to him that scene after scene of life was playing itself out before him and that the scenes all cohered. He had a presentiment of a single meaning upon which they were converging or threatening to converge, though he did not know yet what that might be" (89). This passage leaves unanswered the question of whether Michael will submit or resist the big lie of the agrostate, but there are indications that attempts to inculcate him in agrarian habits of mind began early in his life, for at one point he recalls struggling with a story-problem at Huis Norenius: "Numb with terror he stared at the problem before him while the teacher stalked the rows counting off the minutes till it should be time for them to lay down their pencils and be divided, the sheep from the goats. Twelve men eat six bags of potatoes. Each bag holds six kilograms of potatoes. What is the quotient? He saw himself write down 12, he saw himself write down 6. He did not know what to do with the numbers" (110). Furthermore, the agro-culture's penetration of the everyday language of those in authority is deep and unconscious, and so, at the height of his exasperation with K, the Medical Officer shouts a word that seamlessly melds his official power to every farmer's chief anxiety: "And no one is going to remember you but me, unless you yield and at last open your mouth. I appeal to you, Michaels: *yield!*" (152, Coetzee's italics). In like manner, one of the rare surnames we hear in the novel compactly connects state authority to sedentism, for the underlings at Jakkalsdrif "later learned what had brought down Oosthuizen's wrath upon them" (93). Thus it is Captain "East-houses" who has denounced holidays and lauded stoop work, his name suggesting someone who has embraced his post-Edenic fixed abode eastward of the Garden, in the precincts of Cain.

Throughout the novel, one of K's defining traits is his verbal reticence, a trait that drives even the curious and sympathetic Medical Officer to fits of frustration. Many commentators on *Life & Times* have understood Michael's refusal to converse at any length with his various captors—to answer the Medical Officer's questions in a way the latter would find satisfactory—as Coetzee's way of representing the inaccessibility of the racial Other's experience or essential language (Gallagher, *South Africa* 164–65). All I would add to such readings is an insistence that K's silence also "speaks" when overlaid with the ideas I have been describing here. Referring to farmers' perceptions of foraging bands, Brody contends that, "in this 'wilderness,' the voices of the hunting peoples were likened to the calls of the wolf or the hooting owls: resonant, beautiful, haunting, susceptible to much sentimental and nostalgic interpretation, but not quite human. If the wild hunter-gatherers could be made to speak a *real* language, they, like their lands, could be turned into something of use and value to the settlers" (182–83). Doesn't the Medical Officer, who disbelieves the official suspicions against Michael, urge him to speak on precisely *these* grounds—that only speech that makes sense to him and his fellow officers will furnish K's own life with a meaning and a purpose? "Give yourself some substance, man, otherwise you are going to slide through life absolutely unnoticed. You will be a digit in the units column at the end of the war when they do the big subtraction sum to calculate the difference, nothing more. You don't want to be simply one of the perished, do you? You want to live, don't you? Well, then, *talk*, make your voice heard, tell your story" (140). Without a biography in the language of sedentism, he implies, K will resemble the beasts that perish—foragers always appearing as human beasts in the eyes of the grain state.

By this point the structural function of the Medical Officer should be clear, for if it is he who hectors Michael with the questions, accusations, and assumptions of a tiller's mindset, it is also he who slowly, fitfully moves toward empathy and admiration, reluctantly admitting that Michael has outpaced him in a journey toward a place that appears Edenic. Even his chronic misnaming of Michael as "Michaels," which substitutes a surname for a given one, alludes to the distance separating the personal and intimate sociality of the hunter-gatherer band from the looser, larger, cooler alliances of agricultural societies. In the end, and despite his best efforts, the Medical Officer can only become Michael's traveling companion in imagination, for he, like our culture generally, has awakened too late to the genuine attractions of the foraging life. He remains, like most of us, a settled citizen of the agro-culture, who must squint and strain to decipher the message of contentment spelled out by the wanderer's footprints.

But what, then, is one to make of the band Michael encounters when, toward the novel's end, he returns to Sea Point? On the one hand, there seems to be an untrustworthy edge to their aggressive friendliness, and while they appear in some sense to adopt K they also attempt to rob him of his seeds, as well as causing him to spill his "seed" by means of a sexual act (Derek Wright 441). They share their food with him, but the wine and bread they offer causes Michael to vomit and to void himself. The sexual services he receives are unasked for, but they also don't seem to count in his mind as much of a violation. In the end, given that the band constitutes some sort of extended family, and that they move on from place to place in search of what they can find (their baby swaddled for easier tramping), one can assume that Michael has at last found a tribe of fellow hunter-gatherers. However, they seem an unhappier version of himself, eating the cast-off food of sedentary production and moving through an urban rather than a natural environment. They appear satisfied with their lot and inclined to celebrate frequently, though their mood does not reach to the precincts of "bliss" that Michael enjoyed in the mountains. If he experienced genuine happiness in the purest stage of his foraging, they, picking through the detritus of a failed grain state, only get as far as happy-go-lucky.

Hence, the novel ends with Michael's imagined escape back into a landscape that can genuinely sustain the authentic hunter-gatherer. However, this willingness to leave the band only underscores his one crucial difference from most foragers known to anthropologists. Actual hunter-gatherers, both Paleolithic and extant, live within tight-knit communities that share material recourses equally, make decisions cooperatively, and enjoy high levels of emotional intimacy, while Michael belongs to no community at all and seeks none. His status as someone who, while representing an anthropological category, emerges from no identifiable historical culture, may save his author from the charge of creating an atavistic protagonist, in that Michael cannot be said to behaviorally recapitulate some prior version of "his people's" cultural practices. What people, after all, are "his?" Rather, Michael's Rousseauean atomism figures the life that he pursues as unique and nonreproducible, the result of an inexplicable rupture in the fabric of time through which he has somehow stepped. Orphaned and friendless, he offers no reliable road map "back," no clear method of future emulation—his solitary contentedness becoming the very marker of a way of living that we once blindly abandoned and have since irrevocably lost.

And yet there is a sense in which we, like the Medical Officer, are nevertheless compelled to follow this nearly silent messiah. This is so because, given the ecological degradations apparent in the novel's near-future present, his miniscule ecological footprint paints him as pursuing lifeways that we urgently *need* to emulate. Recall that "he thought of himself not as something heavy that left tracks behind it," but, rather, as one whose passage over the earth is like "the scratching of ant-feet, the rasp of butterfly teeth, the tumbling of dust" (97). And, apparently, once he resumes his solitary veld-walking, his requirements will continue to be minimal: "He would bend the handle of the teaspoon in a loop and tie the string to it, he would lower it down the shaft deep into the earth, and when he brought it up there would be water in the bowl of the spoon; and in that way, he would say, one can live" (184). But it seems he prefers to—or perhaps must—do such living alone; like Rousseau himself, he is a solitary walker, and, as such, difficult to accompany. Counterbalancing such radical isolation, however, are his multiple affiliations at the level of figurative implication, for he is at one and the same time a hunter-gatherer possessing most of the anthropological bona fides, a philosophe's confection, and a victim of an all-to-real apartheid regime. If he is plausibly the avatar both of Kafka's hunger artist and Sargon's unfree subject, he is also a CM in South Africa who must show his pass to the police. In Coetzee's hands, this becomes not mere confusion, but rather a richly suggestive plenitude.

Such is confirmed by the fact that even those critics most interested in showing *Life & Times* to be a commentary on the particularized political circumstances of 1980s South Africa, and who are therefore often the most disturbed by Michael's refusal to join the rebels, have always admitted that there is some aspect of him—frequently labeled as "allegorical"—that somehow seems to transcend these historical particulars. Susan Gallagher, for instance, asserts that the novel appears to offer a "millennial vision of a new heaven and a new earth" by "*obscurely* pointing toward ineffable realities transcending discursive definition" (*South Africa* 136, my italics) and goes on to declare that the text explores "an alternative way that human beings might live in relationship to the land and to each other" (156)—all without specifying very closely what this alternative might be. In like manner, Sarah Dove Heider leaves things overly general when she declares that "Michael K is the Other of everyone" because "he seems to have no culture which he embraces as his own, beyond the idea of gardening," and is thus "distinguishable mainly by his disengagement" (87). Finally, Derek Attridge admits that "K's relation to the earth and to cultivation implies a resistance to modernity's drive to exploit natural resources," but states that this "resistance ... never becomes an alternative moral norm" ("Allegory" 75).[2] What I hope I have provided, then, is a way of approaching *Life & Times* that will concretize such critics' recognition that Michael represents *some* kind of oppositional stance that transcends our familiar historical and political frames, for to recognize Michael K as a hunter-gatherer in flight from an eliminationist agro-culture is to give his vague "allegorical" penumbra a local habitation and a name.

This reading also provides a specific answer to the question of why Michael refuses to join the rebels, since we are now in a position to understand the key term "gardening" aright: "K knew that he would not crawl out and stand up and cross from darkness into firelight to announce himself [to the rebels]. He even knew the reason why: because enough men had gone off to war saying the time for gardening was when the war was over; whereas there must be men to stay behind and keep gardening alive, or at least the idea of gardening; because once that cord was broken, the earth would grow hard and forget her children. That was why" (109). Once one ceases to equate "gardening" with *any* form of fixed-field agriculture and sees it instead as a referring specifically to the hunter-gatherer way of living, much that was puzzling becomes clear. The "gardening" the rebels are likely to forget or cause others to forget is not the sowing of seeds writ large, but a foraging existence in which human traces upon the earth might approach the insectile lightness sought for by Michael. If this life is the Paleolithic life, then the Edenic echoes of the "gardening" K champions can be given an anthropological facticity that keeps it from being frustratingly amorphous or apolitically escapist, for Michael's *non serviam* now becomes recognizable as a thirst for a deeper, more comprehensive revolution. Yes, the guerillas battle against the apartheid regime, but if their eventual victory results merely in the founding of a kinder, gentler version of the sedentist, agricultural state, then this, from Michael's viewpoint (which is that of an anthropological *long durée*), would merely entail replacing Tweedledee with Tweedledum.

If in this respect the text's aspiration toward an imagined future can be seen as either wildly ambitious or resignedly despairing, its assessment of the present predicament is clear eyed and daunting. Scott Cutler Shershow, who has traced the relationship between recent currents in anthropology and Derrida's theory of writing's origins, takes notice of how the former have manifested themselves within popular culture as various "Paleo" diet plans: "It is argued that humanity evolved to be hunter-gatherers, that our genes remain those of the carnivore, and that our grain-based diet is responsible for a whole spectrum of nutritional ailments. Anyone who even glances at the discourse of these contemporary diets, especially 'Paleo,' will be struck not only by how much of it there is but also by how these dietary plans are explained, pursued, and celebrated with the fervor and passion of a religion" (110). Shershow's dismissive tone is obvious, and he seems to mock "the extravagant claims of various diet books, which trace the cause for almost every human illness to the consumption of grain" (124). I would like to say something important about Coetzee, however, by taking diet fads seriously for a moment, for nutritional prescriptions sometimes carry within themselves (even if they rarely articulate) a rough-and-ready historico-evolutionary picture of our species' trajectory (Morton, *Dark Ecology* 39–40). In Western popular culture, most diets of the postwar period focused on the number of calories consumed in a day (assumed to be high) and the number of calories expended through physical exercise (assumed to be low). The implication of this was that, nutritionally speaking, the dire inflection point for "first-world" humanity occurred within the last 250 years, when, commencing with the industrial revolution, we began to enjoy chronic nutritional abundance, to transport ourselves in motorized vehicles, and to eat processed foods. If one possesses even a moderately long-term historical vision, a 250-year-old mistake in our species' enterprise is one that seems potentially correctible. However, anyone accepting the premises underlying the supposed superiority of Paleo diets must admit that our species took a dire turn not a quarter-millennium ago but at least five to ten millennia before the present day (Scott 25–27). This is a blunder of such long standing, and whose effects have been compounding for such an extended period of time, that recovery from it appears almost impossible to imagine.

Under such a conception, the agricultural trap becomes a secular version of the Christian fall from a fruited Eden into a world of thorns and nettles that must be worked forevermore by the sweat of one's brow. And while Coetzee's representation of the forager's "cultivation" practiced by Michael, as well as the author's later commitments to animal rights, tells us that he is not one to take any culture's foodways lightly, the problem as he depicts it goes far beyond the remedies suggested by nutritional gurus, for he sees it as a political, ethical, and psychological tragedy that permeates all aspects of contemporary consciousness. *Life & Times of Michael K* suggests that an entire secular order (secular in the old sense of "persisting from age to age") must be overturned if we are to make progress toward that human possibility that exists "out of all the camps" (182)—out of, specifically, the Neolithic multispecies resettlement camps that have since metastasized into the agroindustrial complex. The Medical Officer is thus not deceived when he claims he is "not sure that he [Michael] is wholly of our world" (130), and he seems to intuit the vastness and nearly un-begin-able nature of the recuperative project K represents: "Let me tell you the meaning of the sacred and alluring garden that blooms in the heart of the desert and produces the food of life. The garden for which you are presently heading is nowhere and everywhere except in the camps. It is another name for the only place where you belong, Michaels, where you do not feel homeless. It is off every map, no road leads to it that is merely a road, and only you know the way" (166). As the Medical Officer tries in vain to convince his colleagues, Michael K was never inclined to follow the guerillas into the mountains. According to Coetzee, if the political order such rebels seek to establish is to represent a genuine and lasting revolution in the human condition, it is they who—somehow—must follow him out of the agricultural trap.

5

The Necessity of Cannibalism

THE LABELING of indigenous, nonwhite cultures as "infantile" has long been a favored rhetorical weapon in the armory of Western racism and imperialism. Therefore, any attempt to employ a Lacanian metaphor to illuminate anthropological reports and surmises about the lives of people within hunter-gatherer societies—be those societies extant or archaic—must begin by underscoring the fact that Lacan's conception of the infantile bears no whiff of opprobrium or condescension. Indeed, in Lacanian terms (and in some aspects of Freud's thought as well) our earliest days are a kind of secular Eden in which, prior to our inevitable expulsion from it, we enjoy both positive pleasures and liberating exemptions so powerful and benign that our subsequent lives are little more than a poignantly doomed quest to recapture them, and so different from the repressions and social isolations required by modernity that, could they only be realized again, they would transform our lives, communally and individually, in utopian directions. To liken the lives of forager bands to Lacan's notion of infantile life within the imaginary order is, then, contra the familiar discourses of empire, to invest them with an efficacy, a wisdom, and a happiness from which we have exiled ourselves; it is to swap our usual superciliousness toward them for chagrin at our own fallen condition.

True, making such a comparison immediately opens one up to the charge of Romantic primitivism, but even if this family resemblance must be acknowledged, it is a primitivism that is based on much less conjecture and much more anthropological practice than, say, Rousseau's. And let me be clear about the limits of what I am claiming Lacan can do in furthering our understanding of hunter-gatherers. In pointing to broad points of resemblance between a psychoanalytical theory and an anthropological conception, I am not putting forward some literalist claim that a cultural phylogeny must actually resemble a psychological ontogeny (or vice versa), but only suggesting that keeping a Lacanian schema in mind can help us to imagine more intensely and to articulate more robustly the differences in the texture of everyday life before and after the springing of the agricultural trap. I am not making a rigorous assertion about either anthropology or human psychology; rather, I am pointing out a suggestive analogy between two established fields that will prove, I hope, good to think with—especially, perhaps, when we try to think about hunter-gatherers within the imaginative realm of literature.

Take, for instance, what is perhaps the signal delight of—to employ Freud's parallel terminology for a moment—this early "oceanic state" of the nursing infant: the absence of boundaries between self and other, experienced as a merging of the child's existence with that of its primary nurturer. This, says Lacan, is unconsciously recalled as our sole, short-lived reprieve from our subsequent "isolation in the prison-house of self," a solitary confinement that stands as "the cost of modern autonomy" (Kilgoure 246). When, therefore, observers of hunter-gatherer bands remark upon the communal cohesion, consensual decision-making, and physical intimacy that characterizes such human groups (Lorna Marshall; Brody 113–14), the similarities between the Lacanian child and the foraging band become resonant. By contrast, the lives of "advanced" and "civilized" people appear to be impoverished by a kind of social and spiritual atomism, evoked by Daniel Defoe with surprising power in the *Serious Reflections of Robinson Crusoe* (1720), a text whose fictional hero earlier lived in fear of, and expressed a loathing for, the hunter-gatherers he encountered:

> What are the sorrows of other men to us, and what their joy? Sometimes we may be touched indeed by the power of sympathy, and a secret run of the affections; but all the solid reflection is directed to ourselves. Our meditations are all solitude in perfection; our passions are all exercised in retirement; we love, we hate, we covet, we enjoy, all in privacy and solitude. All that we communicate of those things to any other is but for their assistance in the pursuit of our desires; the end is at home; the enjoyment, the contemplation, is all solitude and retirement; it is for ourselves we enjoy, and for ourselves we suffer. (2–3)

This passage has been read as expressing the existential alienation endemic to life under capitalism, as indeed it does, but it may be that an understanding of capitalism can be furthered by recognizing it as a particular mode of agriculturalism, or, rather, as farming's most fateful precipitant, and that the crucial climacteric of our cultural trajectory occurred not when people began trading commercial shares but when they began harnessing themselves to plowshares.

There are other salient parallels between the psychoanalytic view of childhood and certain anthropological readings of prehistory. For instance, if, as is often claimed, a robust conception of the notion of "scarcity" is responsible for the birth of modern economics, then it is worth noting that the absence of a need to compete with others for resources is a hallmark both of Lacanian infancy and of the forager band's basic social assumptions. If the primordial environment provides sufficient abundance, or if abundance is simply defined as a satisfaction with what the environment reliably provides, then the material world—the land, in the largest sense—need not be parceled out into tracts of mine and thine. So it is significant for us that Lacan conceives of the imaginary order as a place where we appear to enjoy a pleasurable interpenetration of our body's material substance with the matter that constitutes the larger world, matter that only later we will come to see both as alien to ourselves and as pervasively divided up, owned, and guarded. It also matters that when we moderns "learn to be social" we do so by "learning to say no, to sacrifice or give up ... the initial contact one has with the natural world" as surely as we give up physical contact with our "first human objects" (Rivkin and Ryan 572). This is not merely a matter of territory, but also of the experience of time, for the pervasive feeling among foragers of abundance and stable sufficiency, which negates the need for material competition, also entails, by modern standards, a radical lessening of anxiety concerning the future, indeed a conception of time itself as unpressured, nonlinear, nonentropic, and nonteleological, just as Lacan's infant gives no thought to a morrow of which it cannot conceive, a positive absence that, says the psychoanalyst, one later aches to somehow recapture and reexperience. And, finally, if anthropologists such as Marshall Sahlins are insistent upon both the lightness and brevity of the diurnal work needed to sustain a community of hunter-gatherers (34–35), especially when compared with the chronic stoop labor required of most nonelites in agricultural societies, then in this respect, too, the forager is akin to what some of us once were in the midst of our imaginary bliss, summoning the sustaining nipple with only a brief spasm of our breath.

Let us now push this metaphorical connection a single step farther. What is it, according to Freud and Lacan, that keeps us from returning to our blissful infant state? The physical circumstances of our bodies have altered, of course, but this is not the only or even the most effective bar against any attempted return to the mother's breast. Rather, it is the incest taboo that signals our internalization of the decree that "the mother's body is barred," and that that bar "can never be crossed," despite the fact that "all our desires throughout life will consist of attempts to come to terms with this separation" (Rivkin and Ryan 572). My contention is that, in the disparate literary works we will soon take up, representations of hunter-gatherers trigger something akin to the incest taboo—or provoke a panicked reaction over the prospect of violating it—and that this frantic response manifests itself as the cry of "Cannibal!" In these texts, before curiosity and wonder toward foragers can be expressed, before sympathy for or envy of their condition can properly manifest themselves, our narratives (or characters within them) self-terrify by discovering and then anxiously promulgating the horrible news that hunter-gatherers consume human flesh, thus violently repressing any desire to return to the Edenic state of egalitarian sociality, environmental symbiosis, and happy leisure that such peoples might enjoy. To put this in ecocritical terms, the sight of robust and contented foragers induces a fit of solastalgic panic (since agrognostic faith cannot tolerate doubt), which can only be quelled by the temptation-canceling assertion of man-eating.

It is interesting that Freud himself referred to the oceanic stage as anthropophagous because it involves the oral ingestion by the infant of the mother's physical substance, rendering "the Golden Age of the infant ... a cannibalistic experience of fluid boundaries between self and world, who are joined in a symbiotic oneness" (Kilgour 244).[1] My point, however, is that, in varying degrees and through various strategies, Prospero, Robinson Crusoe, Charley Marlow, and Coetzee's Cruso all "discover" anthropophagy in the hunter-gatherers they encounter in order to inoculate themselves against, as Marlow himself puts it, the temptation of "go[ing] ashore for a howl and a dance" (36). Patrick Brantlinger, in specific reference to Conrad, asserts that, since the advent of Lévi-Strauss, "for modern Europeans ... as for Romantics, the association of primitive life with paradise has once more become possible. For the Victorians, however, that association was taboo, so repressed that the African landscapes they explored and exploited were painted again and again with the same tar-brush image of pandemonium[, such that] when they penetrated the heart of darkness, [they] discover[ed] lust and depravity, cannibalism and devil worship" (*Darkness* 194–95). As I hope to show, this taboo manifests itself not just during the imperial apex of the late nineteenth century, but well before that era as well.

Let us be clear: the accusation of anthropophagy has been one of the most potent rhetorical weapons in the long project of racial Othering undertaken by a host of interrelated racist and imperialist discourses, a "Western racial projection" (Hulme "Scene" 3) that has stood as the justification for the derogation, subjugation, and massacre of indigenous people at the hands of colonialists, settlers, and pseudoscientists. As Maggie Kilgour puts it, "Cannibalism is the tool of empire, be it the British empire or the empire of [Victorian] anthropology" (240). Indeed, according to that radical skeptic concerning man-eating, Walter Arens, "the operational definition of cannibalism in the sixteenth century was resistance to foreign invasion followed by being sold into slavery" (51). Such is undeniable, and, thus, when I speak about the cannibal libel as a defense mechanism against the thoughtful and envious consideration of the lives of foragers, this claim seeks neither the replacement nor even the subsumption of that same libel's central position in the annals of racism and imperialism. Just as, in the previous chapter, the country that Joseph K traverses is specifically apartheid South Africa while being at the same time a figure for the grain state writ large, so, too, here the historical specifics of interracial encounters from the early modern period to today need not become blurred amid my own investigation involving a longer *durée*. After all, it is no coincidence that Caliban, the natives Crusoe encounters, Marlow's indigenous passengers on the steamship, and Coetzee's Friday are all nonwhite. All I am suggesting is that, amid all the illuminating scholarship on the racial and imperial implications of cannibalism, there is another aspect of the Other yet to be fully considered.

I should also note that my argument does not entail perfect agreement with Arens's thoroughgoing wariness about the prevalence of actual acts of cannibalism throughout history. (There is a lively back-and-forth from 1979 wherein Arens takes Marshall Sahlins to task for a review in which the latter, while debunking assertions of gustatory cannibalism, allows claims for ritualistic cannibalism to stand.) All my argument requires is what I, as an interested layman in this debate, am in fact persuaded of: that, across the historical record, charges of cannibalism have far outnumbered actual instances of it. It may be the case that some of those who study the cannibal libel in the context of imperialism are "hard skeptics" à la Arens, and that is fine, though the logic of their arguments would not be diminished if all shared my own view that while starvation cannibalism has been frequently documented, and while isolated instances of ritual man-eating are at least plausible (though the motives of its reporters must always be closely scrutinized), gustatory anthropophagy is nothing more than a racist myth (see Brantlinger *Cannibals* 28–35; Malchow 41–45). The only thing that occurs with undeniable frequency is the hurling of the "cannibal" charge, the targets of which include several of the fictional foragers represented in works of English literature.

Assertions about a culture's supposedly cannibalistic practices, when not directly meant as an incitement to genocide, are sometimes part of a discussion about their foodways, couched in cooler and more general terms. Recall the words of that eminent Victorian anthropologist John Lubbock, who asks that our abhorrence of Stone-Age atrocity be tempered with a dollop of sympathy for primitive starvelings simply outmatched by the challenges of their environment: "The true savage is neither free nor noble; he is a slave to his own wants, his own passions; imperfectly protected from the weather, he suffers from cold by night and the heat of the sun by day; ignorant of agriculture, living by the chase, and improvident in success, hunger always stares him in the face, and often drives him to the dreadful alternative of cannibalism or death" (586). As mentioned in chapter 1, Lubbock's observation is not at all unusual—during, before, or after his own time—since it has always been a working assumption of the agriculturalist mindset that hunter-gatherers could not possibly forage enough food to provide themselves with a sufficient or satisfying diet, hence the inevitability of their casting ravenous looks upon each other at the end of each day's frustrating meander (Lestringant 123). As Caliban, whose name is generally agreed to be an anagram for "cannibal" (Goldberg 4, Go 467–68) declares, "I must get my dinner" (1.2.332–32)—though this utterance constitutes "a blank non-sequitur" to the "bitter imprecations" directed at him from Prospero that immediately precede it (Warner 104). Indeed, it is unclear whether Caliban speaks thusly in anger, in resignation, out of self-loathing, or in some other register altogether. There might even be some smugness in his tone, when one considers how the jolly pioneers of the Virginia Company (chronicles of whose travails were a source for *The Tempest*) found themselves quickly becoming dependent upon the Native Americans (who both hoe-farmed and foraged) for *their* dinners (Hulme *Colonial* 128; Gilles "New World" 198). In turning first to Shakespeare's late romance, I would like to focus upon just how various characters do, or sometimes don't, go about securing their meals, as well as how they imagine others might do so. By approaching the play in this manner, I hope to illuminate some of the tensions between agriculture and foraging that suggest Shakespeare's awareness of, and interest in, his own culture's anxieties about the existence of seemingly happy societies who eschew the plow.

In Prospero, we see a man who apparently wishes his table to be furnished by the products of fixed-field agriculture, for he seems hell-bent upon completing the first required task of the settler-farmer: clear-cutting the existing forest. The Magus, we learn, directs Caliban to continually cut down trees (as he will later order Ferdinand to haul around their felled trunks), but, as Vin Nardizzi points out, from "his very first words in the play, Caliban seems aware that his efforts are in excess of Prospero's need: 'There's wood enough within' (1.2.317) he responds from offstage to Prospero's summoning" (*Wooden Os* 114). This stripping has apparently proceeded so relentlessly that, despite the play's heavy borrowings from Ovid, "the eco-hallmark of Ovid's Golden Age—the virgin forest—is absent" (130), leaving only "the line-grove which weather-fends [Prospero's] cell" (5.1.10) as a poignant remnant. Nardizzi points to Prospero's requirement of firewood for heat and cooking and links such needs to the Jacobean-era difficulties of supplying London's cookfires ("Wood" 376–78), but, as Gabriel Egan's catalog of maniacal lumberjacking within the play suggests, indoor heating can't be the only driver of such felling:

> Prospero's main activity since his arrival on the island has been its deforestation. The play is insistent about this activity and its rapidity: "Fetch in our wood" (1.2.314); "There's wood enough within" (1.2.316); "Fetch us in fuel. And be quick" (1.2.368); "*Enter Caliban . . . with a burden of wood*" (2.2.0); "torment me / For bringing wood in slowly" (2.2.15–16); "I'll bring my wood home faster" (2.2.71–2); "I'll . . . get thee wood enough" (2.2.160); "I'll bear him no more sticks" (2.2.162); "Nor fetch in firing / At requiring" (2.2.180–1); "*Enter Ferdinand, bearing a log*" (3.1.0); "no more endure / This wooden slavery" (3.1.61–2); "Am I this patient log-man" (3.1.67). Suffering this relentless arboreal labour, it is hardly surprising that Caliban's fantasy of revenge includes the poetic justice of killing Prospero with a stake through the stomach (3.2.91). (155)

Nor, Egan points out, is the shipwrecked and supposedly homesick Prospero building a vessel on which to escape the island, for there is no mention of one being under construction, nor does Prospero order the axing stopped when he captures a passing craft. In the end, Egan concludes that

Prospero "continues clearing wood as though he meant to stay and colonize the island" (157), becoming a "settler-master" (169) who dreams, like his old friend Gonzalo, of founding a "plantation" (2.1.140)—that is, an agricultural complex worked largely by unfree labor (though, as we shall see, Gonzalo elides this aspect in his fantasy).

Yet Prospero states that he wishes to leave the island, manipulates the other characters to ensure his departure, and gives every indication that he is about to board ship for home as the play concludes. What can reconcile this seeming contradiction? Perhaps we must see Prospero as "a colonialist *malgré lui*" (Halpern 267)—that is, as someone so thoroughly imbued with an agriculturalist mindset that when he sees virgin land he automatically begins preparing it for the plow. According to the ideology of farming, that is just what any civilized person *does* with "waste" land like the island's onetime virgin forest: he clears it, "improves" it, so that it may be gathered within the physical and psychological pale of civilized life. Under such a reading Prospero, despite—or, better, because of—his extensive book learning, is a prime example of an unconscious subject in Althusserian terms, someone unable to think outside the hegemonic assumption that land is always and everywhere *for* plowing, with the result that he continually orders his slave to perform labors which do nothing to speed his own return to Milan.

But what about that social dreamer Gonzalo? Is he better able to think outside the rectilinear fields of the farming mindset? Perhaps, momentarily, and yet his imaginative flights remain vulnerable both to external corrections and internal contradictions. Spinning out his golden-age idyll for the shipwrecked conspirators and echoing Ovid, he imagines his Great Good Place as specifically nonagricultural:

> I'th'commonwealth I would by contraries
> Execute all things. For no kind of traffic
> Would I admit; no name of magistrate;
> Letters should not be known; riches, poverty,
> Bourn, bound of land, tilth, vineyard, none;
> No use of metal, corn, or wine, or oil;
> No occupation, all men idle, all;
> And women too, but innocent and pure;
> No sovereignty—(2.1.143–52)

This speech, a close paraphrase of John Florio's translation of Montaigne's essay "On Cannibals," can't help but impress readers familiar with today's view of hunter-gatherers, given the way it equates a nonfarming society with one that is also nonhierarchical and possessed of abundant leisure. If this wasn't enough, after a few lines of interruption Gonzalo redescribes his postagricultural utopia, this time linking the leisure afforded by the refusal to plow with a lack of intragroup violence that also pricks up the ears those interested in the idea of the agricultural trap:

> All things in common nature should produce
> Without sweat or endeavor. Treason, felony,
> Sword, pike, knife, gun, or need of any engine
> Would I not have; but nature should bring forth
> Of its own kind, all foison, all abundance
> To feed my innocent people. (2.1.156–61)

Within this evocation of a future abundant society so strongly resembling Sahlins's first abundant society, the ordering of ideas—leisure, then the absence of weapons, then again a nature that provides without the need to be wrung out by toil—seems to figure its "engine" as a plow and to equate it with those other, more obvious implements of violence. In other words, it reads remarkably like modern anthropology rendered into poetry.

But, of course, the interruption that separates these passages is famously deflating, for, to Gonzalo's assertion that he would allow "no sovereignty," Sebastian replies, "Yet he would be king on't," prompting Antonio to add that "the latter end of his commonwealth forgets the beginning" (2.1.153–54). Jonathan Bate explains that "Gonzalo gets into a tangle in his speech, and can be mocked by Sebastian and Antonio, precisely because of the incompatibility between the Golden Age ideal of no law, no property, no need to till the land, and his own Iron Age mentality which thinks in terms of the right to plant, of sovereignty and rule" (52). But in one sense the conspirators' snarky interjection is superfluous, for Gonzalo fatally undercuts his presentation of a new, plowless Eden by beginning his remark with the fatal conditional "Had I plantation of this isle" (see Kasdan 94). It seems as though Prospero is not the only European in the play who can't erase the necessity of sowing from his deep assumptions about how the world must work. At the level of the play's rich fabric of classical allusion, such undermining may have begun dozens of lines earlier, back when Gonzalo began his tutorial about contemporary Tunis being the remnant of ancient Carthage, an idea that also draws Sebastian and Antonio's derision:

GONZALO: This Tunis, sir, was Carthage.
ADRIAN: Carthage?
GONZALO: I assure you, Carthage.
ANTONIO: His word is more than the miraculous harp.
SEBASTIAN: He hath raised the wall, and houses too. (2.1.79–84)

The "miraculous harp" mentioned here is that of Amphion, who conjured up the battlements of Thebes by means of it. In Shakespeare's day, the "seven-gated" Thebes of Greek tragedy would have stood as the very pattern of a walled grain city; thus, even if Gonzalo succeeds, as the conspirators suggest, in "bring[ing] forth more islands" by "sowing the kernels of it in the sea" (2.1.87–88), *The Tempest,* by associating Gonzalo with a wall-builder, casts doubt that such a harvest will actually come to fruition without *somebody's* stoop labor. Or, since "raised"/"razed" is an aural contronym, perhaps we should see it as the play's premonitory fear of ruination in the cereal-free fantasy Gonzalo is soon to articulate.

But if Gonzalo's ante/anti-agricultural discourse is framed as a dubious utopian fantasy, there is another character in the play who actually "get[s] his dinner" without tilling a field. A fact sparingly mentioned by critics is that Caliban is a "hunter-gatherer" (Gilles "Masque" 698–99, "New World" 198), a "forager, hunter, and fisherman" (Orgel 65).[2] This relative lack of interest is all the more surprising given how straightforward the play is about Caliban's foodways. For instance, when recalling the days just after Prospero's arrival on the island, Caliban makes it clear that he showed the newcomer not the best places to *plant,* but the best places to *forage*: "And then I loved thee / And showed thee all the qualities o'th'isle, / The fresh springs, brine-pits, barren place and fertile" (1.2.337–39). Later, when he offers to show his new master, Stephano, how to thrive on the island, what he offers to instill is precisely the knowledge of the hunter-gatherer:

> I prithee let me bring thee where crabs grow;
> And I with my long nails will dig thee pig-nuts,
> Show thee a jay's nest, and instruct thee how
> To snare the nimble marmoset. I'll bring thee
> To clust'ring filberts, and sometimes I'll get thee
> Young scamels from the rock. Wilt thou go with me? (2.2.144–49)

In addition, two ambiguities—or, if you like, two cases of overdetermination—make it at least plausible that Shakespeare might have been intrigued by the hunter-gatherer as a discrete category of humanity, and thus by the challenges that such a figure could present to traditional equations of farming with "civilized" societies. These are, first, the varied historical and literary sources for Caliban himself, and, second, the geographical ambiguity of Prospero's island. The scholarship on the former is vast, but emerges in the end more at a place of cumulative abundance rather than of irreconcilable division. It seems beyond doubt, for instance, that in creating Caliban Shakespeare drew on reports of Native Americans emanating from both propagandists for, and critics of, the Virginia Company (Gillies, "Masque" 675–83). However, Caliban's lack of some stereotypical accoutrements of "stage Indians" (Vaughan and Vaughan 275; Skura 65) suggests that the author had also absorbed a much wider variety of travel narratives emanating both from Europeans encountering the New World (Mowat 34–35) and from those plying the militarily contested Mediterranean, all of which renders his character a "composite formation" with antecedents in far-flung parts of the globe (Hulme, *Colonial* 108, "Prospero and Caliban" 128; Lupton 6–7). Closer to home, Caliban also possess traits drawn from the venerable folkloric figure of the European wild man (Vaughan and Vaughan 60–71; Sturgess 120), as well as from derogatory accounts of the Irish (Egan 157), while simultaneously functioning as "a more general representation of anarchy [and] social uprising" in England itself (Marshall 386–87). It seems possible, then, that Caliban has been conceived as belonging to a category of human being that *includes* American Indians but is not exhausted by or coterminous with them (Vaughan, "Indian" 152), and hence that a coherent conception of Caliban as a hunter-gatherer is not embarrassed by, say, his lack of face paint or the fact that the Powhatans hoed small patches of maize. What I am trying to suggest is that the human and literary models for Caliban are sufficiently diverse that, when one tries to find an element that might bind them all together, the fact that most of them either didn't participate in fixed-field agriculture or were accused of lacking that specific cultural attainment emerges as a plausible common thread.

This same suggestive generality, of course, applies to where in the world Prospero's place of exile might be meant to reside, since the Mediterranean, the Western Atlantic, and the Caribbean are all candidates. This generic quality seems to unburden the island from the need to feature or favor any specific historical, literary, or climatological characteristics, opening it up as a theater of the possible, where either radically new beginnings or bold revivals of some golden age (such as Gonzalo's) can be mounted, tested, and, if found too unsettling, debunked. Additionally, such ambiguity can allow an encounter with "the dark backward and abysm of time" (1.2.50) that might be, as I suggested at the outset, both psychological—as Prospero intends—and anthropological simultaneously.

If it is clear from all this where Caliban the hunter-gatherer "get[s] his dinner" of pine-nuts, filberts, and marmoset meat, it is not quite so clear where Prospero gets *his* dinner, or what exactly it consists of. Many readers simply assume that Caliban is coerced into being "the provider of Prospero's food" (Orgel 65; see also Lamming 152; Hulme *Colonial* 247), and no one could be faulted for thinking so. After all, the clear-cutting of fields is still ongoing, and there is not a word in the play of any crops that have already been planted, so, logically, Caliban must be providing Prospero's meals through his foraging. Caliban's own words on the subject, however, are a bit oblique. When he lists the tasks he believes he will no longer have to perform for his new master, Stephano, we get the following:

> CALIBAN: [*Singing*] No more dams I'll make for fish,
> Nor fetch in firing
> At requiring,
> Nor scrape trencher, nor wash dish,
> Ban, ban, Ca-caliban
> Has a new master—get a new man. (2.2.156–61)

It is his building fishweirs that seems to clench the matter—freed from Prospero's domination, he will do so no more, or at least less frequently (since fish-trapping is a common strategy of hunter-gatherers). It is interesting, then, that when Prospero explains to Miranda that they must suffer Caliban's noxious presence because of the services he renders them, he refuses to name the provision of food, or at least resorts to a euphemized generalization at the crucial moment:

> But as 'tis
> We cannot miss him. He does make our fire,
> Fetch in our wood, and serves in offices
> That profit us. (2.1.311–14)

Gillies explains that European settlers in Virginia were very impressed with the local Powhatans' mastery of fish-trapping, a technique the latter closely guarded and that the settlers, dependent on Indian food, never learned, thus making Caliban's threat to stop building them a serious matter. Worse, "the notion that Caliban possess a technology unmastered by Prospero must have deconstructed the hierarchy of skill, power, value, and right that is presupposed in Prospero's subjection of Caliban," and, thus, says Gillies, the subject is "elided," "buried," and "suppresse[d]" by the play ("New World" 198). But if Caliban's possession of a technique that Prospero lacks does in fact seem a convincing explanation of the latter's embarrassment, our perspective can still offer a relevant addition. Most hunter-gatherers don't (and didn't) "work for more than a few hours on any one day" because, "for them, the key to a full stomach [is] knowledge, not labour: where the game [will] be, when the fruit [will] ripen, how to hunt wild boar and catch shoals of fish" (Mithen 165). So here may be a further source of Prospero's discomfort, as well as a partial explanation for all the *useless* work he orders Caliban to do *unless* that work is anticipatory to agricultural production. If Prospero enjoys a groaning board, and yet no one has worked very hard to produce it—Caliban's complaints being mainly about his enslaved condition—then the whole notion that hunger can only be conquered by taking up the labor-intensive plow, as well as its binary complement that foragers are chronic starvelings, goes all to smash. There is, after all, not a whisper of evidence that Caliban suffered from hunger prior to Prospero's arrival on the island. Gillies explains why Caliban's threat to cut off food is buried amid milder material, but here is a way to understand Prospero's denial of his dinners' obvious origins as well.

That the Magus is represented as anxious about food and the agriculture that—to his mind—is the only fit way of producing it can be seen in the two magical illusions that he (through the intermediary of Ariel) produces. The first one, meant to torment the conspirators, involves luring them toward a banquet that is suddenly snatched away from them as they reach for it.[3] The episode seems to weigh down rather than advance the plot—unless, that is, we posit that Prospero is motivated to show himself in complete control of the island's food supply. Later in the play he still seems to have edibles on his mind, since, when explaining to the conspirators that they remain mentally foggy as a result of his spells, he tells them: "You do yet taste / Some subtleties o'th'isle" (5.1.123–24), a reference to elaborate pastries served between courses and decorated with allegorical figures.

The proof in the pudding, however, arrives in the form of the wedding masque he mounts to celebrate the union of Miranda and Ferdinand.

This production features Iris, herald of the rainbow; Ceres, goddess of the harvest; and Juno, goddess of the skies, in a contest of mutual congratulation and a spectacle of fruitful cooperation. Between its opening, which features Iris addressing Ceres as "most bounteous lady," and praising her "rich leas / Of wheat, rye, barley, vetches, oats, and peas" (4.1.60–61), and its conclusion amid a dance of naiads and "sun-burned sicklemen" (4.1.134) just done with their reaping, Ceres delivers a song of agricultural triumphalism:

> CERES: [*Singing*] Earth's increase, and foison plenty,
> Barns and garners [i.e., granaries] never empty,
> Vines, with clust'ring bunches growing,
> Plants, with goodly burden bowing;
> Spring come to you at the farthest,
> In the very end of harvest.
> Scarcity and want shall shun you,
> Ceres' blessing so is on you. (4.1.110–17)

This looked-for moment, when spring will begin the very moment autumn's harvest is concluded, is, interestingly, the stated goal of the contemporary supermarket industry, whose corporate term of art for the winter offerings in their produce sections is "permanent global summertime" (Blythman). And, while the echoes of Ovid's golden age in the masque have been long understood and well elaborated (Gillies "Masque" 690–97), what seems to have been overlooked is that it is also an echo of the Old Testament book of Amos.[4] That prophet, after repeated and increasingly fevered denunciations of his fellow Israelites (and especially of the way they distribute farmland), concludes his jeremiad with a promise that, if repentance and repair will be at last undertaken, the result will be the cancellation of winter (and, as bonus, the conversion of hills to bottomland): "Behold, the days come, saith the Lord, that the plowman shall overtake the reaper, and the treader of grapes him that soweth seed; and the mountains shall drop sweet wine, and all the hills shall melt" (9:13). Recalling this alternative source of Ceres's song renders it less an act of cultural nostalgia and more a millenarian prophesy. After all, how far toward Ovid's paradise lost can plowing ever get you, given that, as Bate reminds us, for Ovid "agriculture is . . . a Silver Age phenomenon" (53)? Scriptural prophesy, however, "moves from paradise lost to paradise regained, from Eden through the wilderness to Cannan, the land flowing with milk and honey, and hence from retrospection to prophecy" (Levin 5).

When swords are beaten into plowshares, *then* will arrive the kingdom of permanent global summertime.

And yet, for all the confident prophesy of agricultural bounty, it is Caliban—or, at least, the shadow that forager casts within Prospero's mind—who brings the masque to a hasty and discordant end:

> *Prospero starts suddenly and speaks*
> PROSPERO: [*Aside*] I had forgot that foul conspiracy
> Of the beast Caliban and his confederates
> Against my life. The minute of their plot
> Is almost come. [*To the spirits*] Well done! Avoid! No more.
>
> *To a strange, hollow and confused noise* [*the spirits*] *heavily vanish* (4.1.139–42)

If, says Gillies, the entire performance has been "an inverted echo of the unreclaimed 'fens' that inspire Caliban with [the] images of disease" he hurls at Prospero, then he elsewhere admits that the reasons for the breakup of the masque still seem inadequate ("Masque" 690, "New World" 200). For, indeed, in the famous speech that follows, something fundamental to Prospero's worldview seems all at once to have been fatally undermined, as he explains to a "dismayed" Ferdinand about the "baseless fabric" of his now "insubstantial pageant," while composing a dirge that seemingly untunes Amphion's wall-building music: "The cloud-capped towers, the gorgeous palaces, / [And] The solemn temples" of the world "fad[e]" and disappear even as he speaks (4.1.147–56). Prospero may vanquish Caliban by the play's end, but it is a victory that seems the result of continual psychic repression: "This thing of darkness, I / Acknowledge mine" (5.1.274–75). And if, finally, one of the unanswerable questions about *The Tempest* is whether Prospero means to take Caliban home with him to Milan or to leave him behind on the island, my reading must admit to a preferred answer. The image of Caliban back in possession and contentedly getting his copious and varied dinners by means of unlaborious hunting and gathering—would this not darken those two-thirds of Prospero's thoughts not already dedicated to his own approaching death, aggressive promoter of all things agricultural that we know him to be?

This issue of Caliban's *happiness* in his once and future foraging is all to the point and leads us into at least a pair of other debates about the play. First, is Caliban's remarkable and redemptive speech about the aural and visual beauties of the isle—prompted by Stephano and Trinculo's alarm over Ariel's hidden piping—a recollection of the location's *natural* effects, or are we to understand that his memories are all the result Prospero's *special* effects? That is, did the landscape sing to Caliban before the Magus arrived, or only after he washed up and began casting spells?

> Be not afeard; the isle is full of noises,
> Sounds, and sweet airs, that give delight and hurt not.
> Sometimes a thousand twangling instruments
> Will hum about mine ears; and sometime voices,
> That if then I had waked after long sleep,
> Will make me sleep again; and then in dreaming,
> The clouds methought would open, and show riches
> Ready to drop upon me, that when I waked
> I cried to dream again. (3.2.127–35)

If one is open to the idea that *The Tempest* is at least sympathetically curious about the lives of hunter-gatherers, then one is likely to lean toward the view that Caliban is here remembering a time when he used to forage his food without interference or quotas from Prospero. (Besides, why would Prospero grant his "slave" such a gratuitous boon of a dream?) It is as if that which most viscerally motivated the Virginia Company—the prospect of gold—were to become, to those attuned to the island's floral and faunal riches, Wordsworth's "simple produce of the common day," allowing Caliban to delight in the presence of that which is precious to an earlier kind of abundant society. His vision is thus "a metaphor of balanced biodiversity borne on musical harmony, with the 'thousand twangling instruments' as interconnected species exchanging resources through mutualistic relations" (Heidi Scott 644)— or, if one prefers, the enjoyment of golden-age nature. This conclusion in turn affects one's answer to the uncertainty over whether Gonzalo, in confecting his utopian fantasy, is merely playing the obsequious courtier by trying to cheer up the grieving sovereign Alonso, or whether he perceives something powerful in what he terms the "lush and lusty" (2.1.51) environment that inspires him. I would urge that, despite Prospero's ongoing attempt to redeem the island from its Paleolithic condition, Gonzalo seems to have caught phrases of the same primordial music that solaces Caliban.

Which brings us back to the question of his anagrammatic name. Why should *The Tempest* christen him in a way that suggests cannibalism while at the same time making it clear he doesn't practice it and never has? The word came into being through Christopher Columbus's initially careless misrendering of the name of an Amerindian culture and his subsequent ascription of anthropophagy to those misnamed people when he found it expedient to do so (Arens 44–48). This was a process of coinage (or, better, of counterfeiting) that "did not rely on empirical evidence" (Goldberg 4) at any point. Although there is no indication that Shakespeare himself knew the details of the word's provenance, the anagram makes it seem as if he knew very well the *process* by which such a cultural libel arrived on the scene, since the *result* is the garbled articulation of a visceral fear that casts aspersions upon a cultural Other. Who, after all, named Caliban? We are not told whether it was Sycorax, Caliban himself, or Prospero. But, given what we know of the Magus, it seems like something he *could* plausibly have come up with; its anagrammatic nature communicates both a carelessly superior attitude toward the "empirical facts" of Caliban's actual foodways, and an almost instinctive cultural slander directed at foragers as a class. Prospero, it seems, shares more with Columbus than an extended sea journey. And so Meredith Anne Skura makes an excellent point about the potential ethical effect of the anagram: "Caliban is no cannibal—he barely touches meat, confining himself more delicately to roots, berries, and an occasional fish; indeed, his symbiotic harmony with the island's natural food resources is one of his most attractive traits. His name seems more like a mockery of stereotypes than a mark of monstrosity, and in our haste to confirm the link between 'cannibal' and 'Indian' outside the text, we lose track of the way in which Caliban severs the link *within* the text" (67). *A mockery of stereotypes.* It is as though the play understands what kind of slander the sight of a genuine hunter-gatherer will instantly, instinctively provoke in us and manages to get there first, mocking us atop the dubious height from which we had unconsciously hoped to look down upon foragers. *The Tempest,* through the knowing smile of Caliban's allusive name, suggests that we might be people tying ourselves in knots so as not to violate a taboo. Now that we know how our reaction-formation—our solastalgic panic—has been anticipated and wittily put before our eyes, we can perhaps bestow a diagnostic (and appropriately anagrammatic) label on this propensity to cry "cannibal" whenever we see a forager: I would nominate "Calibanism."

I suggested at the outset that keeping the incest taboo in mind would be helpful in understanding the way in which various texts try *not* to think about the attractions of hunting-and-gathering lifeways, and it so happens that links between Oedipal crimes and anthropophagy were already common in Shakespeare's time. *Mundas Novus*, the widely popular (sixty editions in six languages by the end of the 1520s) digest of reports from Columbus, Da Gama, Vespucci, and others, repeatedly insisted that New World cannibals also casually committed acts of incest (Lestringant 28–30). It may be that the two practices are linked by more than the slanders of conquistadors, for Lévi-Strauss has remarked that cannibalism "is an alimentary form of incest" (141), while René Girard muses that "we are perhaps more distracted by incest than by cannibalism . . . only because cannibalism has not yet found its Freud" (277). At any rate, as Arens points out, when it comes to besmirching cultural Others, the charge of cannibalism and the charge of incest usually come packaged as a kit: "There are two reasons for this equation. First, like eating human flesh, incest is a striking indication of a lack of culture. As a result, cannibals were also accused of having no incest taboo. Subsequent investigations by professional anthropologists, with their interest in kinship and marriage systems, have laid this myth to rest. Second, in many cultures, including ours, there is a symbolic equation between sex and eating" (146).

So it is not surprising that in the forager Caliban's backstory there hangs a faint haze of incest mingled with the suggestion that, in the sole company of his mother Sycorax, he enjoyed an idyll of sustained imaginary-order pleasures. After all, one of Prospero's assertions about the "damned witch" involves a sexual crime apparently so disturbing that it must only be spoken of in the most general terms: "For one thing she did / They would not take her life" (1.2.263–67). According to the Magus, once she had arrived on the island and given birth to Caliban, her crimes only continued when she confined Ariel to a tree for not complying with her "earthy and abhorred commands" (1.2.273). However, this clearing of a space in which she and her son can share the island wholly between themselves inaugurated an era which Caliban apparently found quite satisfactory, at least in contrast to the time after Prospero's arrival. For his part, Prospero attempts to demean Sycorax further by insisting that in old age her body had "grown into a hoop" (1.2.259), but this imagery merely renders her frame into a womb entire for the prolongation of Caliban's incestuous, anthropophagical, imaginary delights. As most readers feel, there is something manic about Prospero's denunciations of Sycorax, and while this may in part be because she resembles him too closely in being yet another ruthless, usurping colonizer of the island, it also might be because, as mother of the living forager he holds in uncomfortable proximity to himself, she is too closely associated with ways of getting one's nourishment whose attractions he doesn't dare admit. The time was Caliban got his dinner from the forest in peace and plenty, but Prospero seems not only interested in describing that time as dystopian but also in "by the spurs pluck[ing] up / The pine and cedar" (5.1.47–48) that—intolerably embarrassing to the agriculturalist mind—still supply *his own* dinners.

This peace and plenty that the play seems willing to imagine as the natural state of foragers takes on added resonance in light of the fact that Shakespeare was prosecuted for grain hoarding and price-gouging at Stratford during a food shortage in 1598. Could it be that his involvement in, or even his complicity with, the feast-and-famine cycle of grain cultivation and commodification led him to imagine sympathetically those cultures that he knew once—or yet still in distant lands—obtained their sustenance *without* "bourne, bound of land, tilth, [or] vineyard" (2.1.149)? Certainly there are moments in *Coriolanus* and *King Lear* in which grain supplies fail and thereby untune many a civil chord, and though Prospero seems eager to begin farming his plantation, part of the enchantment of the isle as we come to experience it surely flows from the fact that, despite all the feverous wood-chopping, plowing has not yet begun. Perhaps there were moments, especially after 1598, when Shakespeare wistfully fantasized about a world in which it never had.

ALTHOUGH *ROBINSON CRUSOE* (1719) was written before many of the conjectural historians touched upon in chapter 2 were active, surely the heart of Defoe's novel and the mainspring of its perennial appeal has always been its hero's progress, with the help of only a few salvaged modern tools, through something very like the stages of cultural development later put forward by those speculative anthropologists (Barbaret 112; Novak, "Survey" 194). His first years on the island, for instance, are spent as a hunter-gatherer, and he thinks himself "well . . . furnish'd for [his] Subsistence" as he scours the landscape for game provided with a gun, yet mentally prepared to continue his stalking when "his Ammunition should be spent" (47). Foraging grapes and melons between considered pulls of the trigger, a typical day during this period sees him consuming "a Bunch of Raisins for [his] Breakfast, a Piece of the Goat's Flesh, or of the Turtle for [his] Dinner broil'd . . . and two or three of the Turtle's Eggs for [his] Supper" (76). All in all, he finds this primal stage of sustenance-getting rather satisfactory, at least from a material perspective: "But I had no Need to be venturous; for I had no Want of Food, and of that which was very good too; especially these three Sorts, *viz.* Goats, Pidgeons, and Turtle or Tortoise; which, added to my Grapes, *Leaden-hall* Market could not have furnish'd a Table better than I, in Proportion to the Company; and tho' my Case was deplorable enough, yet I had great Cause for Thankfulness, that I was not driven to any Extremities for Food; but rather Plenty, even to Dainties" (80).

Though hunger does not prod him, he nevertheless wastes no time in trying to attain the subsequent stage of cultural development by becoming a pastoralist. His earliest attempts to tame a kid and some pigeons fail, but after he builds a set of necessary enclosures the parrot Poll "began now to be a mere Domestic" and a second kid pent up within a fence "became so loving, so gentle, and so fond, that it became from that Time one of my Domesticks also" (82). As his phrasing suggests, Crusoe is well on the way to establishing a proper *domus*, and he knows how to value the pleasures of settled ranching over the (supposed, since earlier denied) rigors of peripatetic foraging, just as agriculturalist ideology decrees he should: "This little wandering Journey, without settled Place of Abode, had been so unpleasant to me, that my own House, as I call'd it to my self, was a perfect Settlement to me, compar'd to that; and it rendred every Thing about me so comfortable, that I resolv'd I would never go a great Way from it again" (81–82).

Crusoe's arrival at the next, and fateful, stadial mode must intrigue anyone familiar with the concept of the agricultural trap, for one day he is startled to *find himself already* a farmer without the exact intention of becoming one and certainly without his usual calculation of an action's future implications. Investigating an unexpected patch of green where he had long ago emptied out a dusty sack rescued from the ship, he is "surpriz'd and perfectly astonish'd, when, after a little longer Time, [he] saw about ten or twelve Ears come out, which were perfect green Barley of the same Kind as our *European*, nay, as our *English* Barley" (58). Progress toward a steady and sufficient harvest is slow, however, and indeed it is "not until the 4th Year that [he] could allow [him] self the least grain of this Corn to eat, and even then but sparingly." This is in part because Crusoe finds himself a man in need of a farmer's almanac (no Georgic poem for him) that will lay out the proper times for planting and harvesting particular species of crops—he "lost all that [he] sow'd the first Season, by not observing the proper Time; for [he] sow'd just before the dry Season" (59). Ever self-sufficient, though, he tries various "Experiment[s]," varying month and ground until he eventually becomes the "Master of

[his] Business, [who] knew exactly when the proper Season was to sow; [such that he] might expect two Seed Times, and two harvests every Year" (77). This allows Crusoe to pen the almanac he himself once lacked, and the reader is invited to peruse his chart detailing the seasonal rainfall, position of the sun, and direction of the wind, compiled in the service of nurturing bumper crops (78). Though it is beyond the scope of this chapter to pursue further, *Robinson Crusoe* recapitulates the process whereby writing itself came into being as a response to the agriculture's historically unprecedented requirement for complex bookkeeping.

There are three further aspects of his early farming career that find echoes in modern-day anthropological accounts of the rise of agriculture. First of all, he is quite straightforward about the sheer difficulty, compared with foraging, that attends the processes of sowing, reaping, and milling cereals. "It might be truly said, that now I work'd for my Bread; 'tis a little wonderful, and what I believe few People have thought much upon, (*viz.*) the strange multitude of little Things necessary in the Providing, Producing, Curing, Dressing, Making and Finishing this one Article of Bread" (86). Each in turn, the challenges of plowing, harrowing, harvesting, grinding, cleaning, mealing, and baking are complained of, as "all this ... made everything tedious to [Crusoe]" (86–87), sometimes even requiring him to be "much abroad in the Fields ... even before it was thorow Daylight" (131), though eventually each of these impediments to a square meal of porridge is overcome. Throughout these pages the shipwrecked city-boy is the *inverted* image of Mithen's hunter-gatherer, likened above to Caliban, since Crusoe's "key to a full stomach" is precisely labor rather than knowledge. Second, his turn to agriculture seems to bring about a change in his religion, for once he "saw Barley grow there, in a Climate which [he] kn[e]w was not proper for Corn, and especially that [he] knew not how it came there, it startl'd [him] strangely, and [he] began to suggest [to himself], that God had miraculously caus'd this Grain to grow without any Help of Seed sown" (58). The castaway backslides occasionally amid the many setbacks of his farming (66), but over time the "Anguish of [his] Soul" that he once felt "as [he had] walked about ... on [his] Hunting" abates (82–83), and as his crop matures and prospers he eventually comes to see his status as a sower as providential. Fixing upon a scriptural verse (Ps. 78:19) whose metaphor is appropriately nutritional, he "admir[es] the Hand of God's Providence, which had thus spread [his] Table in the Wilderness" (95), later exclaiming, "What a Table was here spread for me in a Wilderness, where I saw nothing at first but to perish for Hunger" (107). His turn to the sky gods of agriculturalism is complete. Finally, there is the irony, unperceived by Crusoe but, as Conrad's Marlow might say, ominous in the light of later information, that he harvests his first crop not with a scythe but with "one of the Broad Swords or Cutlasses" (86) salvaged from the ship.

In general, though, Crusoe's career as a planter produces yields that trace the cheery upward curve touted as the norm by apologists for agro-culture, where gains in efficiency produce increases in bounty that mutually reinforce each other. The first indication of this is his need for successively larger containers in which to store and transport his grain, which evolve from "Wicker-ware ... Baskets" (79) to "Earthen Vessels, which indeed [he] wanted sorely" (87). But just as baskets must give way to pottery, after three years such primitive amphorae are also rendered inadequate to his burgeoning harvests.

> And now indeed my Stock of Corn increasing, I really wanted to build my Barns bigger. I wanted a Place to lay it up in; for the Increase of the Corn now yielded me so much that I had of the Barley about twenty Bushels, and of the Rice as much, or more....
>
> Upon the whole, I found that the Forty Bushes of Barley and Rice, was much more than I could consume in a Year. (90)

But if his personal requirements are fully met, he eventually finds reasons to justify opening ever greater amounts of acreage to cultivation. The mere sighting of the footprint, for instance, provokes in Crusoe a generalized anxiety about the future, prompting him to "reproac[h him]self with [his] easiness, that would not sow any more Corn one Year than would just serve [him] till the next Season as if no Accident could intervene to prevent [him] enjoying the Crop that was upon the Ground." As a result, the castaway "resolv[es] for the future to have two or three Years Corn beforehand, so that whatever might come, [he] might not perish for want of Bread" (113). As Lucinda Cole notes, "In Defoe's fiction from *Robinson Crusoe* on, the accumulation of food against future contingencies seems, at once, prudent, nearly compulsive, and almost totemic, a strategic warding off of psychological distress and [a] channeling [of] deep-seated fears into seemingly productive activities" (151). Beset by what might be termed the "anxiety of agriculture," there is no such thing as too much.

Never mentioning any threat to his store posed by vermin (Cole 145–46), Crusoe frets instead that the Caribs will "find" (116) his expanding grain fields and make a feast of them, though he never imagines they will learn from his plantings and attempt to grow their own. The footprint also prompts a behavioral reversion that counts as a stadial advance, for though he "needed not hunt any more about the Woods" (121), he begins routinely carrying firearms again, the reason being that he has now become primarily a hunter of men. When someone actually arrives in the person of Friday, this technically exponential increase in population (a result that agroideology also spins as a natural and always desirable result of planting) pushes Crusoe in a by now familiar direction: "I begun now to consider, that having two Mouths to feed, instead of one, I must provide more Ground for my Harvest, and plant a larger Quantity of Corn, than I us'd to do; so I mark'd out a larger Piece of Land" (154). By the time the Spaniards arrive toward the end of the novel, Crusoe compacts with them to "dig and cultivate some more Land, as much as [he] could spare Seed to sow," since, as one of the new colonists reminds the now-Governor, "the Children of *Israel* ... yet rebelled even against God himself that deliver'd them, when they came to want Bread in the Wilderness" (177–78). Almost the last thing we hear is that he has "shar'd the Island into Parts with 'em," but "reserv'd to [him]self the Property of the whole" while "engag[ing] them not to leave the Place" (220), a set of arrangements that seems to render Crusoe both the gentrified landlord of tenant farmers and the feudal master of unfree serfs.

So, if Crusoe briefly finds himself a preagriculturalist who can nevertheless reliably get his dinner and yet works tirelessly and successfully to transcend that initial stage and regain the supposed physical and psychic safety of fixed-field agriculture, the question remains: Are there other preagriculturalists depicted in Defoe's novel? The answer is both yes and no. If, as Peter Hulme tells us, "Crusoe's island is situated by the text in the estuary of the Orinoco, within sight of Trinidad," and if "the Amerindians that feature in the book, including Friday, are all referred to as Caribs" (*Encounters* 176), then Defoe is borrowing for his fiction a people who both foraged and practiced slash-and-burn agriculture. However, the novel depicts *its* Amerindians as 1) *entirely* preagricultural, and 2) almost *exclusively* cannibalistic. As Hulme points out, "By 'cannibal' [Crusoe] seems to understand that Friday will eat nothing but human flesh," and he is undoubtedly right that this paints the Caribs as "so depraved and stupid ... that it has never occurred to them to taste the flesh of the animals living on [the] islands" (*Encounters* 210; see Boucher 126). But what interests me is the dark fantasy of the agricultural unconscious that this blatant absurdity also betrays—for, as we shall see, Defoe's Caribs seem to be cannibals *because* they don't plow. That is, every time *Robinson Crusoe* depicts someone who doesn't practice farming in the European manner, another label—that of "cannibal"—instantly intrudes itself, enacting a panicked recoil from methods of gathering sustenance that must not be allowed to speak their actual names. Thus, whenever the text attempts to represent a person who does not consume cereal grains, it has difficulty imagining any possible alternative food for him beyond the substance of his fellow men.

It is striking, for instance, how saturated is Crusoe's brain with the figure of the cannibal, how quickly that figure interposes itself into any consideration of his own condition, and how thoroughly it precludes his consideration of the novel's Caribs as performers of any action other than anthropophagy: Defoe floods the zone with man-eating. Even before Crusoe has set eyes on the island, he and Xury assume that, were they to go ashore in West Africa, they must take precautions that the "wild Mans . . . shall Eat neither of us" (20). Later, once he is shipwrecked, Crusoe's reckoning of his general geographic position takes the form of several different place-names joined nevertheless by one salient characteristic—that is, he first estimates that he has washed up on "the *Savage* Coast between the *Spanish* Country and the *Brasils*," which is populated by "the worst of *Savages*; for they are Cannibals, or Men-eaters, and fail not to murther and devour all the humane Bodies that fall into their Hands" (80). Subsequently he shifts his nomenclature, but not his anxiety, stating that he knows "by the Latitude that [he] could not be far" from what he now terms "the *Carribean* Coast," and that this shore is inhabited by "Canibals, or Man-eaters" (91). Finally, he claims that, like himself, the Spaniards have been wrecked upon "the *Cannibal* Coast, where they expected to have been devour'd every Moment" (176).

It would seem that he imagines anthropophagy not only when he looks outward at the geography but also during moments of introspection, for after his first years on the island but before he sees the footprint, he admits to loneliness and hardship but marks his supreme luck in encountering "no Savages to murther and devour [him]" (97). Later, after discovering the sign in the sand but before any direct danger has yet emerged, Crusoe confesses that "the Dread and Terror of falling into the Hands of Savages and Canibals" tortures him, and that the "expectation every Night of being murther'd and devour'd before Morning" has maimed his newfound spiritual life, putting him into a frame of mind in which he "seldom found [him] self in a due Temper for application to [his] Maker, at least not with the sedate Calmness and Resignation of Soul which [he] was want to do" (119). If this were not enough, John Richetti notices that Crusoe's terrors also interfere with his agricultural pursuits, changing him "from a planter-colonist into a fearful observer as much of his own shifting desires and fantasies as of the coastline for cannibal enemies" (53). Wretched before a threat of a physical danger that is also clearly a form of "cultural castration" (Haggerty 83), his brain overwhelmed by scenarios of exterminating all the anthropophagous brutes, he admits to being "so full of it [i.e., the cannibal threat], that [he] often dreamed of it" (122), even though he understands that "the Expectation of Evil is more bitter than the Suffering, especially, if there is not room to shake off that Expectation, or those Apprehensions" (133). But that is precisely the point: there is no psychic *room* left within Defoe's protagonist to see nonfarmers as anything but full-time cannibals. And this crowding-in of cannibal thoughts, to the exclusion of all other cultural possibilities, is physically reinforced by the fact that although the Caribs (if Friday is any indication) eat *only* human flesh, they consume that food *only* after rowing out to Crusoe's island. This inconsistency (i.e., they do it all the time, and they take special pains to only do it in my face) seamlessly stiches up the feverous anthropophagic nightmare that encloses the castaway. Crusoe thus undergoes "the same experience as Columbus two centuries earlier: he thinks so much about the Cannibals that in the end he encounters them" (Lestringant 141–43, 137).

Luckily for civilization, agricultural bounty can soothe the savage breast (and appetite). Distressed to find that the otherwise tractable Friday "ma[kes] nothing" of the cannibal feast's gristly remnants and indeed suggests that he and his new master "dig [the dead Caribs] up again and eat them" because he "had still a hankering Stomach after some of the Flesh" (149–50), Crusoe decides to engineer a conversion, one perhaps as serious in its way as the hero's own conversion from worldliness to Christian piety. In order to "bring Friday off from his horrid way of feeding, and from the Relish of a Cannibal's Stomach," he introduces him to the viands of more advanced stages. First he gives him meat from a slaughtered kid, which Friday "seem'd very glad of[,] . . . and lik'd it very well," a success he follows up with that ur-staple of the fixed field, bread. So persuasive are these loaves that, although Crusoe has complained often enough about how difficult it is to till a crop, Friday agrees to work "very hard" at stoop labor and to do so "cheerfully" once he is told "what it was for; that it was for Corn to make more Bread, because he was now with me, and that I might have enough for him, and my self too" (154). When the castaway later asks Friday whether he would revert to man-eating were he to return home, the latter is anxious for his master to understand that he has been transformed from sinner into evangelist: "He lookt full of Concern, and shaking his Head said, *No no,* Friday *tell them to live Good,* tell them *to pray God,* tell them *to eat Corn bread, Cattle flesh, Milk, no eat Man again"* (162). It is worth noting that this conversion to agriculture occurs with greater swiftness and confidence than Friday's parallel conversion to Christianity. Apparently the Carib, like many a nonagriculturalist, has been worshipping a forest god, "*Benamuckee,* who liv'd but a little way off" (156). His redirection toward the transcendent sky god correlated with farming occurs, but it is slower to be accomplished, with Friday depicted as putting various religious difficulties to Crusoe that resist the white man's ability to unknot. Christ, Satan, a sense of sin, the hope of grace and redemption—these all are borne home to Friday in time, but it is cornbread that knocks him down on his way to Damascus.

Which leaves us, it would seem, only with the man-eating wolves of the Pyrenees. As Cole sees it, "What Crusoe describes in the Pyrenees is a weather-sensitive system populated by opportunistic carnivores sometimes driven by uncontrollable appetites," while "the violence of encounters between hot-blooded creatures (human or otherwise) is precisely what his colony, with its nascent infrastructure of agriculture and storage, is intended to prevent" (161). Judith Still agrees with this linkage, asserting that "a parallel is implicitly established between the cannibal horde in the Americas and [the] European wolfpack" (186). But if this strangest of novelistic addendums is best seen as a repetition-compulsion consequent upon Defoe's harrowing imaginative encounter with foraging-figured-as-anthropophagy across the earlier sections of his novel, there are yet a few ancillary points to mention. The first is that, for preagriculturalists, wolves are not a species singled out for special opprobrium—that only occurs in the practices and the poetic imagery of pastoralists and farmers, for whom the wolf is the very symbol of the unreclaimed wilderness, just as the dog (a domesticated wolf) acts as guardian of the domus (see Still 214). As we understood back on Crusoe's island, Defoe's hero conquers such a wilderness by advancing through the progressive stages of civilization in a way that telescopes anthropological development, and so it is worth mentioning that something seems stadially out of joint about the Pyrenees episode. There, on what the protagonist called "The Field of

Battle," it is not a matter of a pastoralist or farmer/rancher defending his flock from canid predators, but rather of two human armies maneuvering for tactical advantage:

> And presently after we saw about a hundred coming on directly towards us, all in a Body, and most of them in a Line, as regularly as an Army drawn up by experienc'd Officers....
>
> I verily believe there were three hundred of them. It happn'd very much to our Advantage, that at the Entrance into the Wood, but a little Way from it, there lay some large Timber Trees, which had been cut down the Summer before, and I suppose lay there for Carriage; I drew my little Troop in among those Trees, and placing our selves in a Line, behind one long Tree, I advis'd them all to light, and keeping that tree before us, for a Breast Work, to stand in a Triangle, or three Fronts, enclosing our Horses in the Center. (215, 216)

This could be a participant's description of Blenheim, and the bizarre gratuitousness of the entire episode seems to suggest a panicked doubt about whether the true enemies of herders and sowers are animal pests or an animalistic kind of human. As Carol Houlihan Flynn argues, both on the island and in Europe, "Crusoe must separate himself from the savage-animal world that can eat him up. If there is to be an eating chain, he must be the one ordering it. For not to order it is to become consumed" (154). In line with this, the very last report Crusoe gives us concerning his island speaks of a ceaseless war-to-the-death between farmer and cannibal, in which we are told that "300 *Caribbees* came and invaded them, and ruin'd their Plantations," and that the tillers "fought with that whole Number twice, and were at first defeated, and three of them kill'd," but that they battled on until at last they "renew'd and recover'd the Possession of their Plantation" (220). When it comes to dealing with human beings who refuse the plow, apparently man is a wolf to man.

IF ROBINSON Crusoe is distressed about cannibals even before he sets eyes on one, Conrad's Charlie Marlow appears quite blasé about the man-eaters with whom he rubs elbows over the taffrail. One explanation for such nonchalance might be to say that Marlow adopts the world-weary imperviousness to atrocity modeled in the narratives of such macho Victorian unflappables as Burton and Stanley. And if, as seems clear, Conrad drew on contemporary press reports of supposed cannibalism in the Free

State (Eastly) in order to, well, flesh out his own experience on the Congo, he deliberately eschewed their tone of outraged sensationalism. There is, of course, a "sensationalism" in just bringing up the subject of cannibalism, but this is a separate issue from Marlow's performative deadpanning: "Fine fellows—cannibals—in their place. They were men one could work with, and I am grateful to them" (35). Brantlinger perfectly captures the unconvincing nature of these fine fellows' own anthropophagous confession when he notes that "the headman of Marlow's cannibal crew gets in a few phrases of pidgin-minstrelese" (*Darkness* 271): "'Catch 'im,' he snapped with a bloodshot widening of his eyes and a flash of sharp teeth. 'Catch 'im. Give 'im to us.' 'To you, eh?' I asked. 'What would you do with them?' 'Eat 'im!' he said curtly and, leaning his elbow on the rail, looked out into the fog in a dignified and profoundly pensive attitude" (40). A feeble scene, to be sure, but it does confirm that, in Conrad's fictional Belgian Congo, cannibalism is meant to be taken as a "fact" operative in the novel's (to Western eyes) exotic but formally realistic setting. It is "real," and apparently just another of those obscenities walking about under the blaze of noon whose presence accounts for the "air of horrific verisimilitude" (Eastly 116) Conrad is at pains to construct.

But, interestingly, several aspects of the novel suggest that cannibalism is just a word—possessed, like the Little Russian, of a certain outré "glamour"—but really no more than a charge one would expect to find on the lips of those mounting a "fantastic invasion" (57) of a place they fear and don't understand. Take, for instance, the conspicuous absence from the text of that "primal scene of 'cannibalism' as 'witnessed' by Westerners" in "whatever genre" they are writing in—a scene central to *Robinson Crusoe*—in which a European "stumbles across the remains of a cannibal feast" (Hulme "Cannibal Scene" 2–3). If I am briefly arguing from an absence here, I have good company within the text, for if Marlow is placid about meeting "cannibals" he gets quite exercised by the fact that no acts of cannibalism actually occur: "Restraint! What possible restraint? Was it superstition, disgust, patience, fear—or some kind of primitive honour? No fear can stand up to hunger, no patience can wear it out, disgust simply does not exist where hunger is.... Restraint! I would just as soon have expected restraint from a hyena prowling amongst the corpses of a battlefield. But there was the fact facing me—the fact dazzling, to be seen, like the foam on the depths of the sea, like a ripple on an unfathomable enigma" (41–42). In fact, the supposed man-eaters on board have at least two nonhuman foods to eat: the "rotten hippo meat" and the "half-cooked dough of a dirty lavender colour they kept wrapped in leaves" (41). Furthermore, Kurtz, who has apparently adopted the most shocking of native practices, is discovered in a severely emaciated state, "the cage of his ribs all astir" on the stretcher because at his station there hasn't been "a mouthful of invalid food for months" (58–59). Even the great man's marquee atrocities argue against rather than for cannibalism, since the heads he has had placed on stakes are fully fleshed. And, finally, as Peter Firchow convincingly argues, since man-eating is, as we have just seen, readily speakable in the text (Marlow even makes a few jokes about it), Kurtz's "unspeakable rites" can't involve cannibalism, but instead must allude to his being approached as a deity in ceremonies that might or might not involve human sacrifice, a practice quite distinct from cannibalism (110–23). So, there is an irony in Marlow's scorn at receiving information that the victims whose heads Kurtz displays were "rebels": "I shocked him excessively by laughing. Rebels! What would be the next definition I was to hear? There had been enemies, criminals, workers—and these were—rebels" (58). The next outrageous definition, of course, is "cannibal," and it has emerged from Marlow's own lips.

But why should the text affirm and deny anthropophagy at the same time? Perhaps this paradox is a marker of the same solastalgic anxiety at the sight of hunter-gatherers that we have seen operating in our previous works. Here is Marlow's most sustained meditation in the novel on what appear, implicitly, to be foragers:

> It was unearthly, and the men were—No, they were not inhuman. Well, you know, that was the worst of it—this suspicion of their not being inhuman. It would come slowly to one. They howled and leaped and spun and made horrid faces; but what thrilled you was just the thought of their humanity—like yours—the thought of your remote kinship with this wild and passionate uproar. Ugly. Yes, it was ugly enough; but if you were man enough you would admit to yourself that there was in you just the faintest trace of a response to the terrible frankness of that noise, a dim suspicion of there being a meaning in it which you—you so remote from the night of first ages—could comprehend. And why not? The mind of man is capable of anything—because everything is in it, all the past as well as all the future. (36)

Here, amid a complicated interplay of attraction and repulsion, is one of the hard kernels of Conrad's racism: his eminently reliable narrator looks out on another culture and reads it as all license all the time. There is no acknowledgment that Marlow might be glimpsing a society in which rules of custom and law instill some version of the "holy terror of scandal and gallows and lunatic asylums" (49) as they do in the metropoles of empire. In other words, it is a perfect example of imperialist pseudoanthropology.

But if it appears doubtful from the deck of the steamboat that the howling dancers respect civilized checks upon behavior such as the incest taboo, and if this is partly what makes the spectacle "ugly enough," this passage, because it is almost the only one in the novel where Africans are not seen laboring under coercion, also hints at an exemption from daily toil that is harder to render unattractive. After all, if the Africans are exclusively depicted as either suffering de facto slavery or engaging, as here, in ritual behavior, then the Africans are by default depicted as strangers to work in their "natural" state (recall that Marlow found "worker" a laughable definition when applied to them). Meanwhile, it has long been understood that *Heart of Darkness*—a "workplace fiction," despite its nightmarish content (Sayeau 344)—expresses ambivalence toward the Victorian Gospel of Work (Watts 55). On the one hand, Conrad asserts that "a man is a worker. If he is not that, he is nothing" (*Life and Letters* 190), and Marlow confesses that what prevents him from "going ashore for a howl and a dance" is a devotion to work—his commitment "to put bandages on those leaky steam-pipes" and "get the tin-pot along by hook or by crook" (36), such that his very dreams center upon rivets. This is no mere personal quirk, either, for, employing the imperial plural in the novel's opening pages, Marlow insists that what saves "us" from abandoning ourselves to uncivilized license is "efficiency—the devotion to efficiency" (6). And so, in his struggle to withstand the "flabby, pretending, weak-eyed devil of a rapacious and pitiless folly" (16), it is quite true to say that Marlow "finds no better weapon than that of his own industry" (Gaston 203).

Yet he also admits, "I don't like work. I would rather laze about and think of all the fine things that can be done. I don't like work—no man does." This confession prompts him to append the anxious self-correction that he *nevertheless* values "what is in the work—the chance to find yourself" (29). But this precarious antithesis is in turn undercut by his later admission that the devotion to toil provides only a "surface truth" sufficient for regulating the unimaginative minds of "mere fool[s]" who, possessed of "sheer fright and fine sentiments, [are] always safe" (36). Such dullards are perhaps represented by the "not . . . very enthralling" Tower or Towson or Towser whose technical manual exhibits "an honest concern for the right way of going to work" (38), but that proves a feckless scripture against the moral hazards unleased by Kurtz and Company. It is thus worth remembering that, despite Marlow's crediting of toil with both the promotion of individual self-knowledge and the reinforcing of racial ideals, he describes most of his labor in the register of complaint. The text's cannibalism may therefore be present—as Freud would insist the incest taboo is present—only to stave off a genuine node of attraction, in this case the golden-age (and perennial) dream of sufficiency without labor: "An appeal to me in this fiendish row—is there? Very well. I hear, I admit" (36). So Marlow's odd lack of concern about the presence of cannibalism and his odder excitement about its absence registers the novel's lack of belief in its own deployment of anthropophagy, alerting us to the merely diversionary nature of the abhorred practice in Marlow's narrative. The "fine fellows" are cannibals in name only, while their exemption from toil is mouthwateringly attractive.

TURNING AT last to Coetzee's *Foe* (1986) we find another novel in which there is much talk about cannibals but vanishingly little evidence of the genuine article. *Foe* is a text in which, on one level, the suspect cry of "anthropophagy" can be explained as the author's critique of colonialist discourses that slanderously misconstrue the racial and cultural Other in order to lubricate the wheels of conquest. So, if—as we might expect from our previous analyses of *Waiting for the Barbarians* and *Life & Times of Michael K*—there is also in *Foe* an engagement with the agroideological disparagement of foragers, it is to be expected that this thread will intertwine tightly with the novel's anticolonialist critique.

One motif that clearly furthers *both* purposes is Coetzee's depiction of Cruso's island as a stage upon which a fractured revival of *The Tempest* takes place, with Cruso, Susan, and Friday playing Prospero, Miranda, and Caliban/Ariel, respectively (Gallagher 180–81; Murphy 193; Attridge, *Ethics* 66). Cruso, for instance, is, like Prospero, directing the preparation of the island for agriculture through the construction of his "terraces" (a full discussion of which must wait until the following chapter) and disdaining to build a boat, while Susan, Miranda-like, "had never known such a storm, and pitied the poor mariners at sea" (28). Friday, for his part, resembles Caliban not only in his racial distinctness from the European castaways but also in the fact that he "smell[s] of fish" (6) and does "his chewing between his front teeth, like a fish" (24). Susan, meanwhile, spies him "bearing on his shoulder a log or beam nearly as long as himself" and "making an offering to the god of the waves to cause the fish to run plentifully, or performing some other such superstitious observance" (31). Later, when both are in England, she wonders "how he differ[s] from one of the wild Indians whom explorers bring back with them" (150), accusing herself of an abduction akin to the one Stephano contemplates toward Caliban. Furthermore, Friday seems to enact Ariel's famous song, "scatter[ing]," in Susan's surmise, "the petals over the place where your ship went down, and scatter[ing] them in memory of some person who perished in the wreck" (87), a victim who has, as Foe now in turn imagines, suffered a sea-change: "Picture the hundreds of his fellow-slaves—or their skeletons—still chained in the wreck, the gay little fish (that you spoke of) flitting through their eye-sockets and the hollow cases that had held their hearts" (141). Friday likewise reprises Caliban's ambiguous song of liberation and renewed bondage: "He does not know what freedom is. Freedom is a word, less than a word, a noise, one of the multitude of noises I make when I open my mouth. His master is dead, now he has a mistress. That is all he knows" (100–101). Finally, toward the end of the novel, Susan acknowledges a thing of darkness as her own: "I do not love him," she says of Friday, "but he is mine" (111). As has been frequently and forcefully pointed out (Spivak 13–16; Gallagher 183–92; Head 119–28; Rickel 164–66; Attridge, *Ethics* 81), it matters greatly that what Friday "must" have suffered or "should" be feeling can only be filled in with the speculative words of white Europeans. I would only suggest that if Coetzee can figure Michael K, his "coloured" victim of apartheid, simultaneously as a hunter-gatherer, then he can do the same with Friday, his revenant of both Defoe *and* Shakespeare's imagined native, bestowing upon him attributes of the forager that supplement and enlarge the part he so evocatively plays in a tragedy of colonialism.

For all that Friday cannot communicate the truths of his own life in a way that whites might understand, the novel is crowded with reasons why the European nightmare of man-eaters is mostly a delusion. First of all, the racist-imperialist function of the anthropophage is clearly on view, since while Susan states that she "met no cannibals" in Brazil, Cruso insists that the country is "full of cannibals" (13) and that in Africa as well the "forests teem" (24) with them, the better to justify European conquest of such locales. As Susan is well aware, those with power command the levers of language, making Others into first enemies, then slaves, as convenience dictates: "I say he is a cannibal and he becomes a cannibal; I say he is a laundryman and he becomes a laundryman" (120). The cannibal is also cast as a kind of primal psychological terror, an infantile boogeyman that comes to the fore, for instance, when Cruso is "in the grip of the fever" (12) or when children wish to taunt a stranger (55). The man-eater also gains traction from his utility as a metaphor for various states of spiritual anxiety, since Susan believes that Cruso imagined cannibals partly "to spur himself to vigilance" against the "abiding sleep" of sloth (82) and muses that "surely eating human flesh is like falling into sin: having fallen once you discover in yourself a taste for it, and fall all the more readily thereafter" (94).

Then, too, there are the economics of Grub Street, for Susan accuses Foe of being a man "who knows above all how many words can be sucked from a cannibal feast, how few from a woman cowering from the wind" (94), calling him a hack who wishes to fill in the longueurs of Cruso's actual story "by inventing cannibals and pirates" (121). In a telling figure of speech, Foe complains that the true story of the island "is like a loaf of bread. It will keep us alive, certainly, if we are starved of reading; but who will prefer it when there are tastier confections and pastries to be had?" (117). Even Susan herself, who, unlike Foe, receives no pay for her narratives, wishes they nevertheless contained that spice which the writer-for-money doesn't scruple to inject: "If we were nearer the heavens there, why was it that so little of the island could be called extraordinary? Why were there no strange fruits, no serpents, no lions? Why did the cannibals never come? What will we tell folk in England when thy ask us to divert them?" (43). Indeed, she finds the island so dull that she admits "it mattered not who came, Spaniard or Muscovite or cannibal, so long as [she] escaped" (35).

An overdetermined libel, then—but could part of what it obfuscates be Friday's identity as an erstwhile hunter-gatherer, *despite* the novel's politically valent insistence on the opacity of his biographical particulars? There are hints, gestures. Perhaps the most sustained of these is simply Friday's passive resistance to the maniacal agriculturalism practiced by Cruso, since one thing at least that can be said about the white man's terrace-building here is that Friday is no eager participant in it. Seeing Friday mope about in England, Susan calls it "a terrible fall . . . from the freedom of the island where he could roam all day, and hunt birds' eggs, and spear fish, when the terraces did not call" (56)—"call" being a euphemism for Cruso's demands that this laborious preparation of the land for crops be unceasing. Later, as a castaway in Britain, Friday is given no choice but to consume the fruits of the plow, resulting in a pair of predictable results, addiction and declining health: "He is become a great lover of oatmeal, gobbling down as much porridge in a day as would feed a dozen Scotsmen. From eating too much and lying abed he is growing stupid. Seeing him with his belly tight as a drum and his thin shanks and his listless air, you would not believe he was the same man who brief months ago stood poised on the rocks, the seaspray dancing about him, the sunlight glancing on his limbs, his spear raised, ready in an instant to strike a fish" (57).

Despite his deteriorating physical condition, and his missing (or willfully unused) tongue, Friday is able to express himself on at least two occasions. The first involves his playing of an offered recorder, which he "so far mastered . . . as to play the tune of six notes [Susan] will forever associate with the island and Cruso's first sickness." This melody, however, "he played over and over all morning," a repetition she disparages: "How like a savage to master a strange instrument . . . and then be content forever to play one tune upon it! It is a form of incuriosity, is it not, a form of sloth" (95). Her first step in teaching him a more Western music is to imitate his own (to her mind) monotonous ditty, but "the music we made was not pleasing: there was a subtle discord all the time, though we seemed to be playing the same notes" (96). Soon her attempts to get him to vary his melody also end in failure, leading her to exasperatedly claim that "we cannot forever play the same tune and be content. Or so at least it is with civilized people" (97). All of this insistence on savage versus civilized music sounds like a metaphor depicting—to use the terminology of Coetzee's earlier novels—a barbarian being urged by an enwalled townsman to give up the cyclical time of the seasons and conform himself to the progressive, cumulative, purposive time of empire. Susan at last concludes that when Friday pipes "his soul [is] more in Africa than in Newington" (98).

Such a mental geography may apply as well to his only other artistic production, the writing of hieroglyphics on pieces of Foe's foolscap. At first glance, Susan thinks he is drawing "leaves and flowers," but soon discovers that "the leaves were eyes, open eyes, each set upon a human foot: row upon row of eyes upon feet: walking eyes" (147)—or, according to traditional iconography, a walking wisdom, a wisdom gained and preserved only through mobility. If we extend this (in a positive sense) pedestrian gloss to his second act of writing, the two can be related, for now his penning of "rows and rows of the letter *o* tightly packed together" (152) suggests a map of the foragers' cyclical journeyings, inscribing at the same moment the ancient symbol of perfection. And if what Friday writes seems to echo the scribblings of Stevie in Conrad's *The Secret Agent*, these are not the utterances of an idiot savant (though even Susan suspects him at times of idiocy), but an "excellent dumb discourse" representing a lost design for living. So, when Susan awakens from the rapture induced by her joining in Friday's endlessly whirling dance, she retains "an intimation that I had been far away, that I had seen wondrous sights . . . for what I had seen in my trance, whatever it had been—I could summon back nothing distinct, yet felt a glow of after-memory, if you can understand that—had been a message (but from whom?) to tell me there were other lives open to me than this one" (103–4).

If there is indeed a higher wisdom in a life of walking—provided it is the proper kind of walking—Susan has already discovered that attempting to forage in the modern world will bring down hard names and threats of violence. When she and Friday seek respite at an inn from their footsore trek between London and Bristol, they are told that "this is a clean house, we do not serve strollers or gipsies" (102). (It is on this trip, by the way, that a hungering Susan has recourse to "acorns," though this is as close as she herself will get to escaping Iron Age cuisine.) Soon after their rough expulsion from the tavern, they are accosted on the steps of a church by an old man: "'Are you gipsies then?' said he—'Are you gipsies, you and he?' For a moment I was lost for words. 'He has been a slave, now he is returning to Africa,' I repeated. 'Aye,' he said, 'but we call them gipsies when they roam about with their dirty faces, men and woman all higgledy-piggledy together, looking for mischief.' And he got to his feet and faced me, propped on his stick as though daring me to gainsay him" (108). Before long Susan is preemptively assuring people that "we were not gipsies" (109) and eventually admits that tramping has caused her to resemble "a filthy old gipsy-woman" (125). "But we *call* them gipsies"—the wandering cannibals of a colder clime.

It all makes one suspect that Coetzee was familiar with the last accusation of cannibalism laid against a European cultural group, an incident from Vienna in 1782 when a band of Roma were accused of "having cooked and eaten a few dozen Hungarian peasants," a crime to which some of them confessed under torture, after which forty-one of their number were hanged—though a subsequent investigation happily discovered that all the supposed victims were very much alive (Avramescu 9, 265n20). What *Foe* seems to know, then, is what *The Tempest* appears to suspect, and what our remaining texts unconsciously confess: that to acknowledge the existence of peoples who happily subsist without agriculture is either to confront—or, more often, to impulsively avoid confronting—a deep-seated anxiety. To the mind steeped in agriculturalist assumptions, the happy, healthy, leisured, egalitarian hunter-gatherer is always already a rebuke, a self-incrimination, an intolerable questioning of a bargain struck so deep in the past and seated so deep in the psyche that it feels like the texture and terms of unmediated existence itself. As our works in this chapter illustrate, it is often easier *not* to look, to mask the disturbing person reaching for berries with, paradoxically, a more comforting person who is sharpening her teeth. There is an intentional and witty reversal of this idea in *Foe*, wherein Susan, trying to come to terms with the fact that she "cannot look at Friday's lips without calling to mind what meat must once have passed them," decides that she must overlook his mouth altogether, for "we must cultivate, all of us, a certain ignorance, a certain blindness, or society will not be tolerable" (106). But for Crusoe, Marlow, and Cruso, the best way not to see a *forager* is precisely to manufacture a cannibal instead, for that creature who is so ideologically convenient to the colonialist hungry for conquest is no less convenient for the farmer trying to justify earning bread by the continuous sweat of his brow. Like the incest taboo, the anthropophage gives us a reason for specifically *not looking back*, for not daring to reacquire what the world says is lost—what the world says is *well* lost. The man-eater is that consoling mirage that allows us, exiles from Paradise that we are, to say, along with Milton's Adam, that "idleness had been worse," and, almost, to believe it.

6

What Walls Want

GIVEN AGRICULTURE'S immediate and unceasing requirements for defensive architecture, we can profitably think of walls and cereal grains as what biologists call "obligate symbionts"—that is, as two organisms that can thrive only in each other's presence. This mutual interdependence stretches back to the earliest beginnings of fixed-field tillage and is bound up with the properties of cereals that first baited the agricultural trap. The fact is that while some fraction of the foodstuffs that foragers gather can be preserved through drying or smoking, most of it must be eaten within a short time after it is picked. A supposedly prime benefit of harvested grain, by contrast, is that it can be hoarded and processed into food at a later date, though this obliges the farmer to find storage vessels that will keep it at least partially protected from the incursions of moisture and rodents. When thinking of such primordial means of containment, earthenware may naturally come to mind, and yet "the earliest settlement at Jericho precedes the development of clay pottery, considered a milestone because, without fired vessels, storing grain on any large scale is impossible. The first wall of Jericho would thus have created its own granary, a vessel for whatever surplus its inhabitants had been able to gather from the fields around it. This status as a repository of grain—and thus of life itself—was both the city's power and its chief vulnerability" (Oles 23–24). A vulnerability because grain's ability to be stored (and measured and taxed) also means that the accumulated labor-products of agriculturalists, unlike the diurnally perishing finds of hunter-gatherers, provide a tempting target for raiders. Thus, like the later, larger "construction described in the Old Testament, the earliest wall of Jericho almost certainly defended the settlement against human foes" (Oles 23). Indeed, when it comes to Neolithic city ramparts, it is largely pointless to attempt a discrimination between those designed for storage and those reared for defense, since the ability to perform the first task already implies a need to undertake the second (Leick 80–81). Anxiety about the harvest always outlasts its harvesting.

If the walls of the grain city at one and the same time signify a cultural fall into endemic violence and a supposed protection against that very menace, then they bear an intriguing relationship to the mark of Cain, which is simultaneously a sign of divine anger and a signet of heavenly protection. The Yahwist of Genesis thus appears to promulgate a deep anthropological truth by insisting that the inventor of agriculture was the world's first murderer as well as its first urban architect. (Even Cain's famous question—"Am I my brother's keeper?"—seems one that, from what we know of forager bands, would only occur to an urbanite.) Certainly this biblical conflation of physical infrastructure and ethical topography gestures toward a historical reality, as Thomas Oles explains: "The spiritual aspects of walls are inextricable from practical ones; indeed, it would not have been possible for a premodern person to draw such a distinction. From Skara Brae to Uruk to Babylon, walls were part of people's spiritual apparatus, not because there was some point at which, after discovering their many uses, people chose to invest them with this power, but rather because they were integral to the material and psychic culture of the societies that built them" (43–45).

This intertwining of mortar and mentality will be the focus of this chapter, for in each of our texts "civilized" tillers will battle "savage" hunter-gatherers, and between these antagonists will fall the shadow of crenellated ramparts. Furthermore, in each of them the perceived need to wall out the forager will result in a psychological walling-in of the farmer, the construction of a straitened Grange of the mind circumscribing empathy and possibility. Agriculture's battlements, supposedly reared in order to secure, maintain, and memorialize the happiness of those within them, offer their physical shelter only at the cost of spiritual incarceration.[1] And if they are charged with the vital offices of reminding the plow-driver that he has definitively escaped the moral darkness of the forest, and of crowning his sedentary life of stoop labor with a monument of compensatory triumph, it should not be surprising that any perceived breach in their solid, protective surface must be instantly, sometimes frantically, mended.

But for a moment before we turn to the showy obsessions of Crusoe and Cruso, or the sensational horrors witnessed by Victor and Marlow, we should remind ourselves that ideology manifests itself in quieter, more contemplative moments as well, and that literature is also capable of registering such persuasive whispering. As most readers recall, the butt of Robert Frost's "Mending Wall" seems to be the speaker's unimaginative or incurious acquaintance who "will not go behind his father's saying" that "good fences make good neighbors" (ll. 43–45). The speaker himself, by contrast, appears keen to investigate the deep assumptions behind our desire to build and maintain such barriers:

> Before I built a wall I'd ask to know
> What I was walling in or walling out,
> And to whom I was like to give offence.
> Something there is that doesn't love a wall,
> That wants it down. (ll. 32–36)

Yet, as has been frequently pointed out, it is not the speaker's adjacent fellow farmer who has instigated the wall-mending, but himself. It is *he* who notices the gaps, *he* who is apparently unsettled by them, and *he* who sets their repair in motion: "I let my neighbor know beyond the hill; / And on a day we meet to walk the line / And set the wall between us once again" (ll. 12–14). Thus, even while admitting that "there where it is we do not need the wall" (l. 23), he finds himself lifting rocks alongside his acquaintance, whom he suggestively depicts as an "old stone savage" (l. 40) because of the fellow's unthinking adherence to farmers' bromides. "Mending Wall," whose deceptively light ironies barely begin to register before its forty-odd lines are done, reminds us that the ideology of agriculture, like most ideologies, nudges us rather than tackles us, accomplishing its ends not by means of Amphion's rampart-raising crescendo, but through our daily placement of a stone upon a stone.

IN *ROBINSON CRUSOE* we are so frequently and copiously informed about each new wall the castaway constructs that his erections threaten to become formidable barriers to readerly pleasure, if to little else. As we witnessed in the previous chapter, Crusoe is anxious to race through several millennia of stadial development during his single generation of island solitude, and we soon discover that, at least in his mind, the linear feet of fortification he raises is just as—or even more—important a marker of his progress through these stages than any accumulating number of barley sheaves. Like the primordial agriculturalists of Jericho, he begins erecting walls from a fear of "voracious Creatures as [well as] cruel Savages" (65), though years later he admits encountering "no ravenous Beast, no furious Wolves or Tygers to threaten [his] Life" and "no Savages to murther and devour [him]" (97), and that thus "as it appear'd afterward, there was no need of all this Caution" (45). But, then again, as wall after wall is painstakingly constructed, one begins to suspect that their purpose is in fact more spiritual than practical, that they are most important not as means of physical security but as "securities" in the sense of visible markers of his civilized condition: "All this Time I work'd very hard, the Rains hindering me many Days, nay sometimes Weeks together; but I thought I should never be perfectly secure 'till this Wall was finish'd; and it is scarce credible what inexpressible Labour every Thing was done with, especially the bringing Piles out of the Woods, and driving them into the Ground, for I made them much bigger than I need to have done" (56).

As he works his way from foraging though pastoralism toward agriculture, his walls proliferate much faster than his flocks or his cereals, until the ramparts themselves come to seem the primary crop that he is raising. Barriers first sprout at his cave residence, which he "resolv'd to strengthen with a Work, Wall, or Fortification made of double Piles, lin'd within with Cables, and without with Turf" (53). Later, his separate "Country-House" is "surrounded ... at a Distance with a strong Fence, being a double Hedge, as high as [he] could reach, well stak'd, and fill'd between with *Brushwood*" where he "lay very secure" (75). Varmints nibble his early crops, a problem for which he sees "no Remedy for, but by making an Enclosure, about it with a Hedge," which he accomplishes "with a great deal of Toil" until it is "totally well fenc'd" (85). Later he discovers new planting-grounds, which requires "fenc[ing] them in with a good Hedge" (87). Next, he longs for a herd, which likewise entails "some enclosed Piece of Ground, well fenc'd either with Hedge or Pale[,] ... [a] great Undertaking for one Pair of Hands" (106). For this last endeavor, he at first grandly imagines that his "Hedge or Pale must have been at least two Mile about" until he realizes that his stock would simply remain undomesticated amid such an extent of park, though even after settling for a much smaller circuit-wall he immediately "enclose[s] five several Pieces of Ground to feed them in" (107). The climax of this wall-building craze is described in language that borders on the maniacal:

> Adjoining to this I had my Enclosures for my Cattle, that is to say, my Goats: And as I had taken an inconceivable deal of Pains to fence and enclose this Ground, so I was so uneasy to see it kept entire, lest the

Goats should break thro', that I never left off till with infinite Labour I had struck the Out-side of the Hedge so full of small Stakes, and so near to one another, that it was rather a Pale than a Hedge, and there was scarce Room to put a Hand thro' between them, which afterwards when those Stakes grew, as they all did in the next rainy Season, made the Enclosure strong like a Wall, indeed stronger than any Wall. (111)

All this, mind, occurs *before* he spies the footprint in the sand; afterward, his efforts, as well as the resulting girth of his ramparts, are redoubled:

So that I had now a double Wall, and my outer Wall was thickned with Pieces of Timer, old Cables, and every Thing I could think of, to make it strong; having in it seven little Holes, about as big as I might put my Arm out at: In the In-side of this, I thickned my Wall to above ten Foot thick, with continual bringing Earth out of my Cave, and laying it at the Foot of the Wall, and walking upon it; and through the seven Holes, I contriv'd to plant the Musquets, of which I took Notice, that I got seven on Shore out of the Ship; these I say, I planted like my Cannon, and fitted them into Frames that held them like a Carriage, that so I could fire all the seven Guns in two Minutes Time: This Wall I was many a weary Month a finishing, and yet never thought myself safe till it was done. (117)

All that has been quoted above represents but a sample of Crusoe's regularly recurring descriptions of his walls, but it should be enough to explain why, when his rescuers at last arrive, "all [he] shew'd them, all [he] said to them, was perfectly amazing [to them]; but above all, the Captain admir'd [his] Fortification" (186).

It should be noted that in *Robinson Crusoe* the notion of walls and cereals existing as obligate symbionts strains to become more than merely a helpful metaphor, for to a surprising extent his bulwarks are composed of living flora. Returning to his country "Bower," for instance, the castaway finds that the "Stakes, which [he] had cut out of some Trees that grew thereabouts, were all shot out and grown with long Branches," providing his original palisade with a kind of natural camouflage, a process he decides to encourage at his original cave-house: "This made me resolve to cut some more Stakes, and make me a hedge like this in a Semicircle round my Wall; I mean that of my first Dwelling, eight Yards distance from my first Fence, they grew presently, and were at first a fine Cover to my Habitation, and afterward serv'd for a Defence also, as I shall observe in its Order" (77). Toward the end of his exile, when this "castle" (his term) reaches its peak of invulnerable invisibility, it is in part because the byproduct of one of his crops—"the Rice Straw, which was strong like Reeds" (151)—is woven into its protective structure. When the waste of the field literally becomes the matrix of one's granary walls, who with confidence will divide the wheat from the chaff?

If, from within the serrated circuit of the agricultural trap, walls are meant to overawe, to exclude, and to discredit wanderers, this brings us directly to the footprint, and to the question of why Crusoe's discovery of it should be, to employ Christopher Miller's succinct phrase, such "a concussive event" (64). Derrida, pursuing his fascination with a text that he declares "can and must . . . be read as a short treatise of anthropology or ethnology" (103), draws our attention to a passage in which Crusoe, after much thought, perfects his "Grindstone" by "contriv[ing] a Wheel with a String, to turn it with [his] Foot, that [he] might have both [his] Hands at Liberty" (61). Derrida then muses:

> There would be much to say . . . about the invention of a technical apparatus, a machine indeed, that . . . liberates one's hands. The liberation of the hand, a certain freeing of the hand, is considered to be the access to what is proper to man, and an essential moment in the hominization of the living creature. . . . [Consider] what Heidegger says about the hand . . . when he claims precisely that the animal has no hand, but merely prehensile paws, or claws, etc. whereas only *Dasein* supposedly has what can properly be called hands with which it salutes, gives, thinks, and acts (*handelt*). And thought itself, he says, is a *Handeln*. And there is no animal *Handeln*. (82–83)

Let us add to Derrida's discussion Stephen Bertman's demonstration that Defoe was familiar with a story concerning the classical philosopher Allistipus, a story told by the Roman architect Vitruvius and anthologized by Erasmus and other aggregators of ancient wisdom (130–35). In this anecdote, Allistipus is shipwrecked by a storm on a desert coastline, but, seeing some mathematical equations scribbled in the sand, tells his fellow castaways, "Take heart, my friends, for I see the footprints of man!"—"man" here being meant in the sense of civilized people as opposed to ignorant barbarians. According to Bertman's persuasive surmise, "Processed through Defoe's mind . . . the symbolism of the Classical tale became inverted: footprints, actual rather than metaphorical, came to foreshadow not the presence of civilized men but of a savage, while joy was replaced by fear" (134). According to Crusoe's math, the footprint's five digits add up to the sum of all fears.

I would align the two passages above to refine what *kind* of "savage" it must (in imagination) be whose footprint concusses Crusoe. If all of his mighty labors to escape the condition of the forager and to accelerate himself through the anthropological stages—an accomplishment he both forwards and announces by constructing prodigious lengths of bulwarks—can be seen literally, spiritually, and metaphorically as the work of his *hands*, then the *footprint* becomes the synoptic reminder of the wandering, foraging condition he has so tirelessly labored to leave behind. For while part of his terror over the print is undoubtedly a terror of the *Other*, the castaway also expresses a second thought, "that this Foot might be the Print of [his] own Foot, when [he] came on Shore from [his] Boat" (115). Derrida pounces on this doubt of Crusoe's in a passage that we may fruitfully read through the lens of our own anthropological interests:

> He then wonders even more anxiously if this bare footprint is not that of his own foot. His own foot on a path he had already taken. Just as Poll the parrot returns to him only the echo of his voice, so the bare footprint is the *unheimlich*, uncanny, for being quite possibly his own, on a path already trodden, that he has always described without knowing it, described in the sense that to describe a movement is also to execute it. Fundamentally, he cannot decide if this track is his own or not, a track left on a path that he does not know if he has already trodden, broken or walked—or not.... Am I a revenant of myself that I cross on my path like the trace of the other, on a path that is already a return path or a path of revenance, etc?.... When I discover this path and this track, have I not already been this way, already, without knowing or wanting to, decided to go this way?.... The other man, the step of the other man—is it not me again, me alone who, returning like a revenant on the circular path of the island, become an apparition for myself, a specular phantom? (48–49)

I want to emphasize that, in taking this suggestion of Derrida's as a description of Crusoe's fear of the-savage-*as*-hunter-gatherer, we are relying not merely on some implicit hint of Defoe's concerning Crusoe's interest—or on Crusoe's general capability of being interested—in theories of biblical history or other protoanthropological debates, but on the protagonist's direct account of his own not-so-distant experience. As we saw in the previous chapter, at several points during the novel's first quarter

Crusoe confesses to being a rather happy and satisfied forager, even as he simultaneously betrays a growing anxiety to become a prospectively happier and even more physically satisfied agriculturalist. He clearly informs us of the way he once employed his feet to find his sustenance—prior, of course, to abandoning such primitive tramping in order to busy his hands in the civilized and civilizing construction of the myriad ramparts required by pastoralism and agriculture. As Simon Verey points out, although "Crusoe may have used primitive methods[,] ... in his determination of boundaries he is modern, civilized man" (153–55), which is to say he is agricultural man, *Homo murorum*, man the wall-builder. Crusoe's career reminds us that in anthropological terms the boundary marker between our species' lengthy "before" and our brief "after" is nothing other than the boundary marker itself.

Finally, Crusoe is also handy at building walls within his own psyche, which perhaps explains why he is able to pursue farming with such alacrity even while complaining at length about the "Pains" it costs him not only to build walls but also to clear land, plant seeds, scare pests, reap grain, grind kernel, and bake bread. But if he suffers in body the fate of all the nonelites who stoop-work the fixed fields of the grain state, he also has recourse to a persistent fantasy: that he is the king of such, and thereby, at least in fancy, the regal recipient of all the fruits of agricultural toil who performs of none of it. "I descended a little on the Side of that delicious Vale, surveying it with a secret Kind of Pleasure, (tho' mixt with my other afflicting Thoughts) to think that this was all my own, that I was King and Lord of all this Country indefeasibly, and had a Right of Possession; and if I could convey it, I might have it in Inheritance, as completely as any Lord of a Mannor in England" (73). A bit later he reflects that "if I pleas'd, I might call my self King, or Emperor over the whole Country which I had Possession of" (94), and indeed before long (and after sufficient fortification) his cave-house becomes his "Castle, for so I think I call'd it ever after this" (112). For a while, of course, the threatened invasion of Carib "cannibals" seems to dampen his daydreams of sovereignty, though he still manages to instruct his tamed "cannibal" Friday that his title and his name are both to be "Master" (149). And then again, when Englishmen finally arrive on the island, he insists that they address him as its "Governor," while during the ensuing hostilities against the mutineers he additionally proclaims himself "Generalissimo" (192).

Since Crusoe is thus self-crowned, it is clarifying to be reminded of a fact that time and habituation have blinded us to: that crowns, the objects we have come to see as the very symbol of kingship, had their origin in the ancient Near East as representations of the crenellated defensive walls of the grain city, compacted to encircle the head of its absolute ruler and to thereby iconically remind all who beheld them of the physical "foundation" of kingly authority (Van De Mieroop 51–52). One wonders, then, whether it is just Defoe's endowing of his protagonist with a knack for math and engineering that dictates that so many of Crusoe's fortifications—the many concentric ones at his cave-castle, the several at his "Summer House"—are circular or semicircular. Perhaps their shape not only physically streamlines but also psychologically compensates for the many irksome "Pains" he took to build them. Regardless, what we are witnessing in Crusoe's compulsive rampart-building is his unrestful tracing of a repeated orbital trajectory around the hyperobject that is agriculture, a massive black hole whose diameter he cannot adequately discern and whose gravity he can never escape.

The first words we hear from Victor Frankenstein are to the same purpose as the first from Crusoe—namely, to inform us of the city of his origin. "I am by birth a Genevese," Victor tells us, "and my family is one of the most distinguished of that republic," adding that his forebearers, including his father, have "been for many years counsellors and syndics" (19)—the syndic being the chief magistrate of Geneva. (Little William later blurts out this fact of his ancestry with instantly fatal results.) The proud, annunciatory tone of this initial paragraph already alerts us that Frankenstein's natal city will mean more to his subsequent narrative than Crusoe's will to his, and indeed nearly every page of Shelley's novel engages with intellectual doctrines and historical developments closely associated with Geneva. Since the author of *A Discourse on the Origins of Inequality* was born there, and since in 1794 the metropolis was the site of a bloody Jacobin uprising, "Rousseau and Revolution" could stand as a concise but sufficient answer to a question of why the novel is set largely in that city's environs (Randel 469–76), though it is of course also relevant that the tale was conceived and begun by Shelley within five miles of its walls. And there *were* walls encircling Geneva in 1816—rather extraordinary walls—and it is on their symbolic relevance to our concerns in *Frankenstein* that I now wish to focus.

After returning grief-stricken to "the environs of Geneva" only to find that "the gates of the town were already shut," Victor wanders about lamenting the death of his brother William, but soon enacts a scene with a long precedent in the struggle between agriculturalist and forager. He sees a man emerging from the forest, a man fundamentally different than himself—racially different, to be sure (Malchow 16–18), but also alien in that this other's method of obtaining his sustenance is grounded in constant movement rather than in settled, civilized dwelling. True to form, Victor's reaction to this stepping forth from the wilderness is rage:

> As I said these words, I perceived in the gloom a figure which stole from behind a clump of trees near me: I stood fixed, gazing intently: I could not be mistaken. A flash of lightning illuminated the object, and discovered its shape plainly to me; its gigantic stature, and the deformity of its aspect, more hideous than belongs to humanity, instantly informed me that it was the wretch, the filthy daemon to whom I had given life. What did he there? Could he be (I shuddered at the conception) the murderer of my brother? No sooner did that idea cross my imagination, than I became convinced of its truth; my teeth chattered, and I was forced to lean against a tree for support. The figure passed me quickly, and I lost it in the gloom. Nothing in human shape could have destroyed that fair child. He was the murderer! I could not doubt it. The mere presence of the idea was an irresistible proof of the fact. I thought of pursuing the devil; but it would have been in vain, for another flash discovered him to me hanging among the rocks of the nearly perpendicular ascent of Mount Salêve, a hill that bound Plainpalais to the south. He soon reached the summit, and then disappeared. (55)

The walls of Geneva, whose curfewed gates in this scene exclude and expose one of the city's most privileged sons, were crucial to the polity's self-conception. Each December 12 the citizens commemorated "The Escalade," an unsuccessful attempt in 1602 by troops of the Duke of Savoy to scale the already impressive defensive walls of the city. The resulting repulse of the invaders has remained "a much-commemorated defining episode in the history of the republic" (Randel 486) down to the present day. Furthermore, the folk song that sprang up to celebrate this victory, "Cé què l'ainô," or "The One Above," speaks of citizens atop these battlements who "mock and laugh" at the "scoundrels" below, and soon became the de facto anthem of the city. Nor did the progress of Enlightenment (and the evolving sciences of warfare) physically diminish these walls, as was frequently the case elsewhere. An account of 1732 notes that the Genevese could yet boast "fine, strong and large Bastions, a double Row of Ditches, very wide and deep and almost every where dry (which are the safest)," as well as a "Tower called *Caesar's*, on the side of the *Rhone*, and another large round one towards *Savoy* called *Maitre*" while "on the side of the Lake they have forifyed the Port or Harbour with a double Row of strong Stakes drove down into the Water." Indeed, the author admits that "it would be too tedious to mention all the Parts of their Fortifications, Contermines, Ravelins, and a hundred such Names, which Necessity & Industry hath invented against Power & Violence" (Le Mercier 62–63). And this was *before* the city received a massive and comprehensive set of Vauban-style (i.e., star-shaped) fortifications in the mid-eighteenth century, reinforcements that were both militarily redundant and visually hypertrophic, covering nearly as much area as the city they supposedly protected. Not that such a build-out far beyond the needs of martial security was anything new; it simply represented a modern instance of "the tendency, widespread in Mesopotamia, to build city walls so massive and imposing that they exceeded any military need," since, like Geneva's, "the wall of Uruk was as much a public expression of power and wealth as a defense against enemies" (Oles 32). Unlike many such erections, however, these Genevan walls were not demolished until the middle of the nineteenth century and were thus visible at their maximum extent during Mary Shelley's sojourn in the area. If they are mentioned only in passing in her novel, their looming facticity remains relevant, for whereas a motto of the wall-swaddled Genevan Republic was "*Immota manet*, that is to say, It remains unmoveable" (Le Mercier 59–60), among those attributes that render the Creature intolerable to Victor is his terrifyingly prodigious *mobility*.

When Victor isn't harping on the Creature's evil nature or ugly countenance, he seems mostly to notice the velocity with which he covers ground (Mayer 238). Calling him an "animal" who is bound to "elude all pursuit" (56), Victor affirms that the Monster bounds across glaciers "with superhuman speed" (74) and "descend[s] the mountain with greater speed than the flight of an eagle" (117). Later, as the scientist mourns over the graves of his family, the Creature is able to soundlessly sneak up within whispering distance of him, only to then "fle[e] with more than mortal speed" (164), eventually leading Frankenstein on a cross-continental trek that he finds "a toilsome march" (165) but that his quarry accomplishes with relative ease. But surely the most impressive overland (and overwater) feat that the Creature undertakes is the one in which he follows Victor from the peaks of the Alps to "one of the remotest of the Orkneys" (130) in order to monitor the latter's fulfillment of his promise to build a female. Marshall Brown, amid a helpful attempt to parse out what is merely superlative (i.e., "quantitatively impressive") about the Creature from what might be downright supernatural (and thus "qualitatively alien"), finds this epic act of bloodhounding difficult to categorize:

> Other aspects of the plot, however, are harder to explain, even if less flamboyant. How does the monster so infallibly track Frankenstein? Though rarely seen, it appears always to be close at hand and never at a loss for means of locomotion and transport. A single glimpse of it at a great distance leaves Walton awestruck; how, then, is it able to remain unnoticed as it follows Frankenstein to "one of the remotest" of the Orkney Islands—"a place" that is "hardly more than a rock"—and then watches over him for an extended period [130]? Similarly, at the end, the monster has passed out of sight before Frankenstein is rescued by Walton's boat: how does it know when it is being amateurishly tracked and where Frankenstein has left off? Nothing in the novel is presumed to violate the laws of nature, but there is much like this in the plotting that remains unaccountable. Food is always to be found, weather is not a problem; though early in its existence the monster sometimes suffers from the cold, later it promises to live easily in the wilds of South America, saying that its "food is not that of man" [115], and according to Frankenstein it can "exist in the ice caves of the glaciers" and possesses "faculties it would be vain to cope with" [116]. (149–50)

I would suggest that, once we open ourselves to the possibility that one (among many) of the Creature's functions is to stand as Shelley's speculative figure for a primordial hunter-gatherer, his tracking of Victor across a thousand miles of terrain emerges not as supernatural teleportation but as the employment of an ancient human skill. This talent, she implies, is moribund in modern people like Frankenstein, but is simply a "natural" ability of Victor's unnatural stage-one creation. Certainly the Creature's relentlessly focused hunt vividly contrasts with Victor's intolerable dawdling along the same route, as the latter plays tourist on the Rhine, visits superfluous "philosophers" in London and Oxford, and otherwise endangers by frivolous delay his supposedly beloved fianceé, whose life hangs in the balance. Later, the retrospective image conjured by Victor drinking in the sight of picturesque "ruined castles" between Strasbourg and Rotterdam (123) while the Creature keeps steady pace with him along the nearest ridgeline is genuinely haunting. Victor, though (once it occurs to him), apparently finds this same idea enraging, for his most signal act of cruelty toward his creation occurs at the exact moment *when*—and,

I would argue, in part *because*—he becomes cognizant of the Creature's unbounded ability to walk at will across the landscape.

> I trembled, and my heart failed within me, when, on looking up, I saw, by the light of the moon, the daemon at the casement. A ghastly grin wrinkled his lips as he gazed on me, where I sat fulfilling the task which he had allotted to me. Yes, he had followed me in my travels; he had loitered in forests, hid himself in caves, or taken refuge in wide and desert heaths; and he now came to mark my progress, and claim the fulfilment of my promise.
>
> As I looked on him, his countenance expressed the utmost extent of malice and treachery. I thought with a sensation of madness on my promise of creating another like to him, and trembling with passion, tore to pieces the thing on which I was engaged. The wretch saw me destroy the creature on whose future existence he depended for happiness, and, with a howl of devilish despair and revenge, withdrew. (133)

Frankenstein's report here about the Creature's face revealing "malice and treachery" just at the moment when his fondest dreams are about to be realized is the scientist's most obvious act of psychological projection, inviting us to entertain alternative explanations of his (i.e., Victor's) reaction.

If, as I have been suggesting, the Creature's superlative ability to roam contributes to Victor's perception of him as the unsettled and unsettling hunter-gatherer—and whose potentially propagative mate must therefore be destroyed—this is not the only place in the novel where the Monster has played such a role. Huddled in a lean-to outside the DeLacey cabin, separated from those immiserated agricultural workers by a wall, and picking up from them a fragmentary but apparently sufficient knowledge of life in "the time of Empire"—or in that of the "*Ruins of Empires*" (91)—there, too, he embodies the uncontained barbarian. But Victor (whose surname means "stones of the Franks") feels a city-dweller's distaste for such a cultural outsider, for a being who is "ostentatiously rural rather than urban" (Malchow 19) even before he hears the Creature's narrative, peremptorily telling him on the glacier that "there can be no community between you and me; we are enemies" (75). If, then, the book's final chapters depict the culmination of a barbarian's revenge against an urbanite, this is not only because the usual binaries of city-dwelling master and foraging slave have been reversed but also because the Creature succeeds in transforming Victor into a wanderer like himself, leading him across "the wilds of Tartary and Russia" (164) to their posthumous reunion in the arctic. It only remains for Walton, in the novel's final paragraph, to report that the (again supremely mobile) Creature becomes "lost in darkness and distance" (181), an obscurity that, while it may reiterate his final exile from the symbolic order (Comitini 194), also evokes the anthropological chasm that separates him from the modern world. At an earlier point in this revengers' journey, Frankenstein, pursuing his foe, spies "the print of his huge step on the white plain" (164). Clearly this moment is for Victor a confirmative rather than, as it was for Crusoe, a concussive event, but it is equally clear that the scientist and the castaway share a conviction that such a horrid sign can only have originated someplace beyond the civilized pale, that it can only exist as a synoptic hieroglyph of nomadism, and that therefore the only fitting response to it is hatred and fear.

IF, AT a crucial moment, Victor finds himself outside city walls that, given his status as a civilized man, should rightly enfold him, a similar eviction befalls the collective representatives of Western civilization in *Heart of Darkness*. Thanks to a long critical history, we are by now familiar with thinking our way into Conrad's text by picking up on inversions of expected hierarchies (Chetham 304). Marlow's first pronouncement, which is about the British heartland, is that "this also ... has been one of the dark places of the earth" (5), and going forward from there we now easily accept whiteness becoming a kind of implacable darkness, rationality assuming the lineaments of madness, forward motion tracing out a retrograde journey, etcetera, etcetera. One such inversion, however, has not received due attention. If, as we have seen, agriculture is the very marker of civilized life (at least according to the ideologies of farmers), and if walls are the obligate symbionts of cereal grains, then there is no ambiguity concerning on which side of the wall civilization dwells: obviously and everywhere, on the *in*-side (notwithstanding the tilled fields' literal position outside of, but spiritually beneath and under the eye of, the battlements). A corollary of this long-digested theorem is that if a city wall is being besieged—if enemies are probing it, undermining it, bombarding it, attempting to circumvent it—these would-be invaders can only be the houseless barbarians who know not the plow and a settled existence, but who instead wander restlessly across the face of the earth. In Conrad's novel, however, the question of who one finds inside the ramparts and who outside is just as disconcerting as the other shattered binaries cited above.

That the tropical vegetation of the Congo is conceived by Marlow as the wall of some mysterious but beckoning city is suggested even before he arrives on the river, when he gazes from his French transport at "the edge of a colossal jungle" that "r[uns] straight like a ruled line," making it appear "as if Nature herself ha[s] tried to ward off intruders" (13–14). Once amid the camps of the company, he discovers that "the wall of matted vegetation stand[s] higher than the wall of a temple," leading him to ask puzzledly, "What was in there?" (27). Nor does his assuming command of his steamboat prevent him from craning his neck back in awe at the frozen tsunami that looms over him and his fragile craft: "The great wall of vegetation, an exuberant and entangled mass of trunks, branches, leaves, boughs, festoons, motionless in the moon light, was like a rioting invasion of soundless life, a rolling wave of plants piled up, crested, ready to topple over the creek, to sweep every little man of us out of his little existence. And it moved not" (30). Thus the steamer paddles slowly upstream "between high walls," chugging along the pediments of "trees, trees, millions of trees, massive, immense, running up high," a "curtain of trees" that "made you feel very small, very lost" (35). (Indeed, the river appears at times to be a kind of moat surrounding the jungle's battlements, though a moat that, disconcertingly, never links up with itself.) Before long this rampart is again figured as more architectural than organic, with "the living trees, lashed together by the creepers" such that "the undergrowth might have been changed into stone, even to the slenderest twig, to the lightest leaf" (39). Adding to Marlow's unease before this seemingly "quite impenetrable" barrier is the feeling that "eyes were in it, eyes that had seen us," but whose "serried ranks" (43–44) of trunks render it opaque and "heavy like the closed door of a prison" (56), though he continues to perceive the milling of "the crowd . . . behind the curtain" (66). More unnerving still, he has caught the echo of this metropolis's civic alarum summoning its denizens to man the ramparts, noting "the tremor of far-off drums, sinking, swelling, a tremor vast, faint; a sound weird, appealing, suggestive and wild—and perhaps with as profound a meaning as the sound of bells in a Christian country" (20). Like the agrarian's anxious caricature of a barbarian outside the gate, Marlow puzzles and fantasizes about the wonders piled up within the portal, longing to break the seals of secret treasuries he cannot lay eyes on.

Of course these European nomads do more than merely gaze up at bulwarks they desire to pierce, but their attempts to assault this torrid Byzantium prove feckless at best: "Pop, would go one of the eight-inch guns; a small flame would dart and vanish, a little white smoke would disappear, a tiny projectile would give a feeble screech—and nothing happened. Nothing could happen. There was a touch of insanity in the proceeding, a sense of lugubrious drollery in the sight" (14). This futile bombardment is renewed when Marlow steps ashore, where he observes that "a heavy and dull detonation shook the ground, a puff of smoke came out of the cliff, and that was all. No change appeared on the face of the rock" (15). Nor, farther upriver, can weapons of smaller caliber better penetrate palisades as closely planted as any of Crusoe's, since when "the pilgrims ... ope[n] fire with their Winchesters" they succeed only in "squirting lead into that bush" (45). No wonder, then, that he perceives the "high stillness" of the green wall enduring such attacks with "its ominous patience, waiting for the passing away of a fantastic invasion" (33) or, yet more ominously, preparing "a terrible vengeance" for the same (57).

As every citizen of the grain city understands, nomadic savages often attempt to ape the sophisticated civil infrastructure of settled life, often with risible results. Thus, when Conrad's Europeans attempt to erect their own walls around their various "stations," the outcome is a "crazy fence of rushes" in which "a neglected gap was all the gate it had" (21), or a "rotten fence" that only signals what a "flabby devil [is] running that show" (21, 23). In their favor, these hapless copyists have ambitions to rebuild their fortifications with stronger materials, but this plan, too, seems unlikely to prosper: "The business entrusted to this fellow was the making of bricks—so I had been informed—but there wasn't a fragment of a brick anywhere in the station, and he had been there more than a year—waiting. It seems he could not make bricks without something, I don't know what—straw maybe. Anyways, it could not be found there, and as it was not likely to be sent from Europe, it did not appear clear to me what he was waiting for. An act of special creation perhaps" (24). Marlow himself, of course, is likewise made to wait interminably for his cherished rivets. Only later on does he discover an engineering text that might conceivably be helpful to the company's imitative efforts, a book that inquires "earnestly" into "the breaking strain of ship's chains and tackle.... and purchases," but, alas, it lies neglected and is annotated, he believes, "in cipher" (38), making it a text before which the invaders are as good as unlettered. Even, at long last, the magnificent and reclusive Kurtz is discovered to have bungled the perimeter of his compound, for "they would have been even more impressive, those heads on the stakes, if their faces had not been turned to the house" (57)—personal vanity undermining what should have been at least a potently demoralizing spectacle to besiegers; recall that Coetzee's beleaguered Magistrate also decorates his ramparts with "armed dummies" (177), also to little effect. Taken all in all, the Europeans' incompetence at rearing walls throughout *Heart of Darkness* seems to turn a common racist trope on its head: monkey see, monkey do.

It only remains to note that, even at the story's very beginning, the unnamed frame-narrator casts not just the tale itself, but also its teller and its listeners, as all alike situated outside an "uncrackable" bastion that is bound to frustrate all penetrative desires: "The yarns of seamen have a direct simplicity, the whole meaning of which lies within the shell of a cracked nut. But Marlow was not typical (if his propensity to spin yarns be excepted), and to him the meaning of an episode was not inside like a kernel but outside, enveloping the tale which brought it out only as a glow brings out a haze, in the likeness of one of these misty halos that sometimes are made visible by the spectral illumination of moonshine" (5). A common complaint against *Heart of Darkness* is that it attempts too obviously, through the deployment of ominous generalities, to inflate its own exoticism. But, if my argument is at all convincing, it is also one of its intentions to be—in the sense such a term once possessed when cities were still enshelled by walls—thoroughly *suburban*.

THIS MOTIF of Conrad's that, alongside others, figures Europeans as so many feckless barbarians is, of course, at cross-purposes with Marlow's steady valorization of his sense of vocation throughout the text. Marlow finds the Western way of work salvific, though, as mentioned in the previous chapter, he protests so much in this regard that one begins to suspect his deepest motivation is a kind of envy directed toward all the howlers and dancers on shore, who seemingly have no need to inflate the benefits of punching a clock. In *Foe*, by contrast, no such ambivalence concerning the nature of labor seems to operate, for there is a critical consensus that Coetzee, disciple of Beckett that he is, will entertain no neo-Carlylean consolations for the repetitive tedium of holding down a steady job.[2] Thus, Cruso's efforts to construct his island "terraces" are "seemingly futile" (Attwell, *South Africa* 107) and "apparently pointless" (Prentice 96) and constitute nothing more than a series of "absurd projects" that prove him "intellectually moribund" (Wade 211). As Susan Barton puts it, it is all "a stupid labor" (35). The problem is, this general agreement that Cruso's wall-building is a figure for meaningless toil has apparently precluded any substantive discussion of its specifically agro-cultural purpose. Given Coetzee's endorsement of the notion of the agricultural trap, my contention is that while his castaway's actions are far from being benign, their very allegiance to a tiller's ideology also renders them anything but meaningless.

Cruso, a farmer by deep cultural instinct, sees in imagination—as he trudges toward it in body—the promised land he knows he himself will never enter:

> "Is it your plan to clear the whole island of growth, and turn it into terraces?" I asked. "It would be the work of many men and many lifetimes to clear the whole island," he replied; by which I saw he chose to understand only the letter of my question. "And what will you be planting, when you plant?" I asked. "The Planting is not for us," said he. "We have nothing to plant—that is our misfortune." And he looked at me with such sorry dignity, I could have bit my tongue. "The planting is reserved for those who come after us and have the foresight to bring seed. I only clear the ground for them. Clearing ground and piling stones is little enough, but it is better than sitting in idleness." And then with great earnestness, he went on: "I ask you to remember, not every man who bears the mark of the castaway is a castaway at heart." (33)

Cruso's rhetoric here is indeed Carlylean, and he elsewhere asserts that "on the island there is no law except the law that we shall work for our bread, which is a commandment" (36). But our specific concerns should also prompt us to recognize that his actions are closely reminiscent of Prospero's, since that previous castaway also cleared fields for planting, even though he, too, was apparently bereft of seed. And if Susan is correct that Cruso looks forward to "at last, the coming of a golden-haired stranger with a sack of corn" (67), then this desire seems retrospectively fulfilled by the descent of Ceres in Prospero's masque. The efforts of Coetzee's castaway, whatever else they do or don't accomplish, contribute to an already lengthy list of intertextual resonances with *The Tempest*.

But I would argue that they do more, or that they add up to more, or that at least they were tending to before Cruso was abducted from his island of laborious contentment. Susan may be right when she pronounces his terrace-building "a foolish kind of agriculture" (34), but if we pause for a minute to contemplate the physical relationship between walls and plowing, we will see that such an activity is in fact a peculiarly *concentrated* kind of agriculture. Terrace farming creates fixed and level fields on both sides of a rampart, permitting planting to occur at both its foot and its apex and transforming a maximum amount of previously untillable hillside into arable acreage. Whereas plowed fields on a plain often retain strips of the locale's original vegetation to serve as boundary markers and windbreaks, the terraced hillside is a terrain exhaustively altered by the hand of humans, often leaving no clues as to what grew there before the sowers and masons arrived to transform it. Terrace farming is, in a real sense, the combination of clear-cutting with mountaintop removal. Thus, what Cruso attempts is the thoroughgoing transformation of the island's physical substance from something natural into something cultural, into something *agricultural*. And if Susan denounces such a plan as "foolish," she herself is not immune from an ideology that valorizes tillage as a primordial source of meaning and truth. When, for instance, she attempts to defend the facticity of her own biographical existence (against the possibility of her being a mere fiction flowing from the pen of Foe), she does so by arguing for Bahia's reality through a methodical iteration of that country's agricultural products. Notice here, too, the deliberate mention of both the finished foodstuff and the cereal or domesticated grass from which it is processed:

> Whereas the silence I keep regarding Bahia and other matters is chosen and purposeful: it is my own silence. Bahia, I assert, is a world in itself, and Brazil an even greater world. Bahia and Brazil do not belong within an island story, they cannot be cramped into its confines. For instance: In the streets of Bahia you will see Negro women bearing trays of confections for sale. Let me name some few of these confections. There are *pamonhas* or Indian corn-cakes; *quimados*, made of sugar, called in French *bon-bons*; *pão de milho*, sponge-cake made with corn, and *pão de arroz*, made with rice; also *rolete de cana* or sugar-cane roll. These are the names that come to me; but there are many others, both sweet and savoury, and all to be found on a single confectioner's tray on the corner of any street. (122)

In like manner, the agricultural terracing that Cruso undertakes is in part meant to confirm his identity, as if he, too, believes that only a place that will produce a harvest can truly be said to exist in the world. Anxious about questions of legacy, Susan asks him, "Is it not possible to manufacture paper and ink and set down what traces remain of these memories, so that they will outlive you?" Cruso's answer frustrates her, but is definitive: "'I will leave behind my terraces and walls,' he said. 'They will be enough'" (17–18). So Cruso is in fact doing something more than just preparing the ground to someday receive a plow; he is also building a familiar species of structure that, historically, proclaims a personal legacy while symbolizing and supposedly legitimizing the unequally distributed wealth that accumulates from agricultural production. Recall that the island is "a great rocky hill with a flat top, rising sharply from the sea on all sides except one," and that "in the centre of the flat hilltop was a cluster of rocks as high as a house," where "in the angle between two of these rocks Cruso had built himself a hut of poles and reeds" (7–9). Susan comes near to grasping what would have been the architectural endpoint of the castaway's terracing when complaining of it later to Friday:

> First, the terraces. How many stones did you and your master move? Ten thousand? A hundred thousand? On an island without seed, would you and he not have been as fruitfully occupied in watering the stones where they lay and waiting for them to sprout? If your master had truly wished to be a colonist and leave behind a colony, would he not have been better advised (dare I say this?) to plant his seed in the only womb there was? The farther I journey from his terraces, the less they seem to me like fields waiting to be planted, the more like tombs: those tombs the emperors of Egypt erected for themselves in the desert, in the building of which so many slaves lost their lives. Has that likeness ever occurred to you, Friday; or did news of the Emperors of Egypt not reach your part of Africa? (83–84)

While Susan's reading of Cruso's motivations ring true, her geography and archaeology are a bit off, for, even before the time of the pharaohs, pyramids were erected in Mesopotamia that featured not the smoothly diagonal ascensions of those found in the Valley of the Kings, but were instead constructed from of a series of stepped terraces, with a house-sized temple centered on the topmost that served as a receptacle for the local divinity and His or Her holy accoutrements. What Cruso seems intent on constructing is a ziggurat, that quintessential physical statement of the grain city's agriculturalist ideology and, indeed, its agriculturalist theology. Thus it is too facile to dismiss his labors as merely absurd, for they show him to embody the very spirit of Farming Militant, the same spirit that motivated Prospero and Defoe's Cruso to either clear cut an island or to sow it far beyond the dictates of necessity or diligence. Coeztee's Cruso is thus the inheritor of a viewpoint concerning terrain writ large, concerning the landscape tout court, that assumes it is always and everywhere *for* plowing, that if it is not farmed, it is "waste" land. Just how Coetzee evaluates this age-old malady of thought is registered by his castaway's headgear, for he sports "a tall cap rising in a cone" (8), a crude blueprint of his architectural dreams that simultaneously makes him out to be the iconic Fool (or is it the iconic Pharaoh?). Just as the conical head bandages that David Lourie wears in *Disgrace* transform him into the twinning Castor of his hated youthful neighbor, Pollux, here, too, a hat means more—and worse—than its wearer understands.

Centering our attention on the walls required by agriculture can also suggest something about the vexing question of Friday's life before he fetched up on the island. Getting there, however, will require that we follow a slightly circuitous path. After Friday and Susan have endured their tramp from London to Bristol and back again, the latter confesses in a letter to Foe about an expedient she employed to obtain money during the journey: "Arriving in Marlborough, I found a stationer's and for half a guinea sold him Pakenham's *Travels in Abyssinia*, in quarto, from your library. Though glad to be relieved of so heavy a book, I was sorry too, for I had no time to read in it and learn more of Africa, and so be of greater assistance to Friday in regaining his homeland. Friday is not from Abyssinia, I know. But on the road to Abyssinia the traveler must pass through many kingdoms: why should Friday's kingdom not be one of these?" (107). I will say more about this Pakenham momentarily; for now, though, I would suggest that, given how frustrating (for readers) and indeed how infuriating (for Susan) is Friday's inability or refusal to speak the story of his previous life, we should take her hint and look for his origins "on the road to Abyssinia." After all, no other African place is ever mentioned as a conjectural rival. Furthermore, when it comes to English letters, Abyssinia is notorious for having been conjured more often by stay-at-home poets than reported on by actual visitors, so if it emerges as largely a metaphorical destination, that robs it of no literary precedent as a place redolent of cultural origin-stories. And, finally, wouldn't the denizens of Coetzee's reconstructed eighteenth-century England have reflexively referred to Friday precisely as an "Ethiopian"?

Just such an Abyssinian expedition of the mind seems to be what Susan undergoes when she imitates and abandons herself to Friday's circular dance (Murphy 189–90). Slipping into "a kind of trance" as she whirls, she awakens to "the intimation that [she] had been far away, that [she] had seen wondrous sights," and concludes that Friday must dance in order "to remove himself, or his spirit, from Newington and England."

Afterward, her recollections are like those of a sleeper awakening from a dream: "Whatever it had been—I could summon back nothing distinct, yet felt a glow of after-memory, if you can understand that—had been a message (but from whom?) to tell me there were other lives open to me than this one in which I trudged with Friday across the English countryside, a life of which I was already heartily sick" (103–4). If this collection of images—a dreamer struggling to remember her dream, the country of Abyssinia, a whirling dancer—recalls Coleridge's "Kubla Khan," that is, as we shall soon see, all to the point.

As to Pakenham's *Travels in Abyssinia*, readers can be forgiven for assuming that it is one of Purchas's volumes or some other text with an Elizabethan or Jacobean provenance, detailing the arduous journey of an early modern explorer. In fact, it is no such thing. The only book about a journey to Ethiopia by an author so named is Thomas Pakenham's *The Mountains of Rasselas: An Ethiopian Adventure*, published in 1959. This Pakenham is the Eighth Earl of Longford, who, fresh after graduating from Oxford, traveled to Ethiopia specifically in order to locate and climb the royal alpine prisons—the *ambas*—of that country. An *amba* is a high, flat-topped mountain whose sides, for the last few hundred feet before their mesa-like summits, are perpendicular ramparts of rock, which explains their remarkable function in traditional Ethiopian statecraft. Since medieval times they have been intermittently employed as inverted, open-air dungeons in which the reigning Abyssinian king (the negus) would deposit rival male heirs to the throne along with their extended families and retinues of servants. Life amid the clouds was, relative to that led by commoners below, luxurious, but, as access to these sky-islands was controlled by a guardhouse astride the single, vertiginous path upwards, they were jails first and palaces second. Should the reigning negus die, a messenger would arrive to pluck down one of the noble prisoners, who would thereupon be installed as the new king of the nation. Since ascent was so purposefully difficult, and since there was ample acreage atop them, the ambas were invariably farmed, which, along with their residences, churches, catchments, and graveyards, made each of them into a kind of living miniature of the kingdom below.

Thomas Pakenham comes across in his first book as a serious, if quite privileged, scholar. Once Abyssinian provincial governors look him up in Debrett's, he regularly receives sufficient supplies and porters; he sighs with condescending good nature about local customs and ceremonies; he is earnestly fascinated by Ethiopia in general and by the very peculiar institution of the ambas in particular. All in all, and in part no doubt because of his era and background, young Pakenham comes across as a kind of benign, more likeable Waugh. But why would Coetzee choose this ingenuous text as the one unambiguous—if rather craftily slipped in—anachronism in his historical novel? Perhaps a brief reference by the young explorer to Coleridge provides an answer:

> During my wanderings in Ethiopia I often thought of the lines from *Kubla Khan* about the Abyssinian maid (though I have never heard of any lady who played the dulcimer in Ethiopia, nor saw one on my travels). What did she sing about Mount Abora? Did it have anything to do with the Mountain? The story of the unattainable paradise of Mount Abora sounded as though it were in the tradition of Milton and Johnson, and I idly wondered if Coleridge used them as his source. In Addis Ababa, however, I had had little chance of doing any literary research, and the matter had slipped from my mind.
>
> When I returned from my Lenten pilgrimage in Lasta I found one postcard among my mail which renewed all my thoughts on the matter and filled me with a rare excitement. It was written by a genial scholar, whom I had met in Jerusalem where he was writing a book on Herod the Great. The postscript read: "How's that Abyssinian maid? I suppose you know that Coleridge wrote 'Mount Amara' in the first draft of the manuscript. I saw it once in a Paris exhibition." This was a rare stroke of luck. With perfect propriety Coleridge as well as Johnson and Milton were to be associated with the three Mountains of the Princes. (186)

As it happens, Pakenham's "genial scholar" is correct, for the manuscript of "Kubla Khan" (held by the British Museum) clearly shows that Coleridge wrote "Mount Amara," though he apparently changed it to the "Mount Abora" we discover in all printed editions because he thought it improved the line's aural effect (at least I can discover no other reason). This is relevant because it shows that Coleridge had in mind the same amba described in *Purchase His Pilgrimage* (1613)—a book he claims he was reading when he fell asleep prior to writing "Kubla Khan"—and a source for Milton's description in *Paradise Lost* of an amba that had been mistakenly supposed to be the Garden of Eden (hence the "nor" below):

> Nor, where Abassin kings their issue guard,
> Mount Amara (though this by some supposed

> True Paradise) under the Ethiop line
> By Nilus' head, enclosed with shining rock
> A whole day's journey high. (4:280–85)

Interestingly, though, Purchas doubles the walls his Mount Amara—a place "so lovely" that some have "tak[en] this for the place of our Forefathers Paradise"—topping (at the following passage's conclusion) the ambas' nearly vertical stone neck with a second, man-made rampart rising upward from the edge of the peak's flat summit:

> It is situate in a great plaine, largely extending it selfe every way, without other hill in the same for the space of 30 Leagues, the forme thereof round and circular, the height such, that it is a daies work to ascend from the foot to the top; round about, the rocke is cut so smooth, and even, without any unequall swellings, that it seemeth to him that stands beneath, like a high wall, whereon the heaven is as it were propped: & at the top it is over-hanged with rocks, jutting forth of the sides the space of a mile, bearing out like mushrooms, so that it is impossible to ascend it, or by ramming with earth, battering with canon, scaling, or otherwise to winne it. It is above twenty leagues in circuit, compassed with a wall on the top, well wrought, that neither man nor beast in chase may fall downe.... [To describe] the plenty of grains and corne there growing ... might make me glut you ... with too much store. (6, 5:565–66)

This vision of a human-constructed wall mirroring the natural one below does not fit any Ethiopian reality, for Mount Amara (or "Geshen," as it is known today) possesses only the latter. Thus the Abyssinian amba—as disseminated by Purhase to Milton and Coleridge—is a hyperbolically walled city, encircled above *and* below in unscalable surfaces. But with or without this superfluous embellishment, the heights of Geshen/Amara starkly juxtapose the ideological claim of Uruk with the physical reality of that city and its rampart-ringed progeny: a heaven on earth that is actually a fortress, peopled by supposed princes who are in reality its prisoners.

When Milton eventually describes his *veritable* Eden, he moves it to Mesopotamia and constructs it with materials from the Bible, from Classical literature, and other sources. Interestingly, though, "with the assistance of the compendia of Purchas ... he transported thither so much of Mount Amara that Mount Paradise, in its physical aspects, is decidedly more Abyssinian than Hebraic" (Clark 144). Or, as Coetzee's Pakenham puts it,

> when Milton wrote *Paradise Lost* he drew heavily on Purchas. Though he sited his paradise in Mesopotamia, the Abyssinian paradise was awarded an honourable mention. More than this, Milton used Purchas' description of Geshen for the description of the real paradise in Mesopotamia. He took the pillars of alabaster, the single path of ascent, and the overhanging cliffs, and made them his own; but instead of Ureta's guards, the archangel Gabriel sat at the gateway. Thus the towering massif of Geshen, incongruously Abyssinian, rose out of the level plains of Mesopotamia. No ziggurat of Babylon had ever looked like this. (140)

This act of transplantation becomes even clearer in Milton's construction of Eden's walls, which, like those of Purchas, feature a natural one (though vegetated rather than rocky), surmounted by a second rampart of divine architecture (also cloaked with greenery):

> So on he fares, and to the border comes
> Of *Eden*, where delicious *Paradise*,
> Now nearer, Crowns with her enclosure green,
> As with a rural mound the champain [i.e., flat, level] head
> Of a steep wilderness, whose hairie sides
> With thicket overgrown, grotesque and wilde,
> Access deni'd; and over head up grew
> Insuperable highth of loftiest shade,
> Cedar, and Pine, and Firr, and branching Palm,
> A Silvan Scene, and as the ranks ascend
> Shade above shade, a Woodie Theatre
> Of stateliest view. Yet higher than thir tops
> The verdurous wall of paradise up sprung:
> Which to our general Sire gave prospect large
> Into his neather Empire neighbouring round. (4:131–45)

As Milton would certainly have known, the English word "paradise" traces its ancestry from two Persian roots: *para*, meaning "around," and *daeza*, designating "wall," which eventually became *paradeisos* in Greek renderings of the Old and New Testaments, such that any paradise "is by its very definition a walled place, a precinct set apart from the world"

(Oles 40). Thus, when attempting to represent the unfallen architecture of Eden, Milton seems instinctively to feel that two walls stacked atop each other are better proclaimers of divine perfection than any single battlement could be. Indeed, it is not too much to say that ramparts mark out an important horizon within our species' self-imagination, functioning as a historical obstruction that closes off our backward-looking dreams of perfection at the first Mesopotamian grain cities, for whenever we try to conjure up the paradise we once possessed, we seem to have always already reared a wall around it. Oles is anxious to remind us that "the walls of the first cities were ... not simply useful and sometimes indispensable constructions, but sites of numinous awe," and that "an encircling wall such as that of Ur or Uruk would have resembled nothing so much as the handiwork of the gods" since it marked out "the earthly manifestation of a divine realm" (43). But is this, even today, so unfamiliar a concept? In our abiding assumption that any Eden worthy of the name will *naturally* be bounded by a perimeter wall, we are all Sargon's mental subjects still. Is it only, then, as Susan suggests, "on the road *to* Abyssinia" that one can find a paradise that is not also a prison, or must one travel *away* from that oft-imagined country? As hard as it is for us today to conceive of an unwalled Eden, perhaps that is the only kind that a hunter-gatherer would be likely to aspire toward—or to always already inhabit.

Is Coetzee suggesting such a wall-less, wandering backstory for Friday? As we have already seen in *Waiting for the Barbarians* and *Life & Times of Michael K*, the author seems interested in emphasizing the deep ambivalence that always clings to the city wall: the fact that it declares a pacific garden even as it perfects a martial citadel. It is apparently to make that ambivalence felt within *Foe* that Coetzee brings Coleridge's "Kubla Khan" to bear on the mysteries surrounding Friday's origins—through the abstruse gambit of Pakenham, yes, but also by means of resonances emanating from the novel's core. Reading "Kubla Khan" with Coetzee's walls in mind—those that the Magistrate guards, those that Michael K escapes over, and now those that Cruso builds—we can begin to discern a poem that can guide our reading of *Foe* because it, too, both affirms and denies the paradisiacal associations of such erections. On the one hand, Kubla has "twice five miles of fertile ground / With walls and towers ... girdled round" and, in doing so has, like Milton's God, enclosed not a city but an Edenic greenspace, for within are

> gardens bright with sinuous rills,
> Where blossomed many an incense-bearing tree;

> And here were forests ancient as the hills,
> Enfolding sunny spots of greenery. (ll. 6–11).

Yet this is also a place "with ceaseless turmoil seething" where boulders fly like "chaffy grain beneath the thresher's flail," and amid which tumult Kubla himself hears "Ancestral voices prophesying war!" (ll. 17–30). But even if, after all this, the "sunny pleasure-dome" still retains some genuinely Arcadian essence it would be bliss to recapture, the voice who suddenly takes over the poem's last third speaks in a frustrated conditional tense, telling us of a paradise that, while it may still hover within the mind's reach, yet dangles just beyond its grasp:

> A damsel with a dulcimer
> In a vision once I saw:
> It was an Abyssinian maid
> And on her dulcimer she played,
> Singing of Mount Abora.
> Could I revive within me
> Her symphony and song,
> To such a deep delight 'twould win me,
> That with music loud and long,
> I would build that dome in air,
> That sunny dome! those caves of ice! (ll. 37–47)

This same note of frustration, of remaining chronically checked just on the brink of understanding, pervades Susan's attempts to wrest from Friday the potentially salvific information about his possibly paradisiacal homeland, taunting her as she stares into his eyes, listens to his enigmatic tunes, and scans his yet-more-enigmatic writing. It may be as Attwell suggests, that Friday's repeatedly written "O"s are his Omega, while what Foe and Susan truly desire is his Alpha—"tomorrow you must teach him *a*" (152)—that holds the key to his beginnings (*South Africa* 117), perhaps somewhere along Coleridge's river Alph.[3] Besides these serial Os, there seem few opportunities wherein to seek out legible clues to Friday's previous life, though if "Kubla Khan" is even a fragmentary map of such an undiscovered country, it suggests that we should look again at his obsessive dancing, which is itself a *kind* of O, or at least an action that describes one. This dervish-like twirling, so genuinely mesmerizing yet baffling, is nevertheless exactly what Coleridge's speaker says he *would* perform if, and only if, he could somehow grasp once again his vanished vision. Then, like Susan entranced before the whirling Friday,

> all who heard should see them there
> And all should cry, Beware! Beware!
> His flashing eyes, his floating hair!
> Weave a circle round him thrice,
> And close your eyes with holy dread
> For he on honey-dew hath fed,
> And drunk the milk of Paradise. (ll. 48–54)

As his spinning raises his robes and *possibly* reveals the "atrocious mutilation" (119) of Friday's conjectural castration to Susan, does he become in some sense an "Abyssinian maid" whose dulcimer can reveal the true Mount Abora/Amara? If so, there is all the more reason to agree with Robinson Murphy that such dancing shows how "Friday's body cannot be controlled even after undergoing geographical displacement," and that, "rather than allow England, and his overseer Barton, to determine his movement, Friday travels through his imagination to an other-space and inhabits instead the home he sees in his mind" (189). But, as myriad critics have pointed out, even Susan, who receives such hopeful intimations when she imitates his whirling, can never fully grasp what Friday may be communicating. I would only add that this might be because the Eden he is conjuring as he spins is, anthropologically speaking, too far away, too far back, too far beyond the high pales that delimit her modern conceptions, even her conceptions of Paradise.

The only remaining place where a more solid glimpse of Friday's homeland, whether walled or unwalled, must be sought is within his hieroglyph of the eyed foot. This is a rune that might, as suggested in the previous chapter, be asking those who read it to discern a wisdom that lies in mobility rather than in settling down, in daring to construct the contours of the Great Good Place from journeys rather than from bricks. It may be a tall order to peer over the wall and view the open barbarian lands beyond with a sense of daily opportunity rather than dread, but doing so might qualify, as Michael K would put it, as successfully living "out of all the camps." But if we are indeed being prodded to look back historically to a time before History, to look back on an anthropological scale, we are also being asked to look back in literary history. That is, Friday's eye superimposed upon a foot surely implores us to redirect our sight, with fresh eyes, to the perfectly formed footprint discovered by Defoe's Crusoe (Attwell, *South Africa* 114). This sign terrified that industrious castaway, but for Coetzee it may exist as something benign but likely unrecoverable. It may exist as the synoptic figure of a path toward ample sustenance that relies on the steady exertion of the feet rather than the frenzied busyness of the hands, toward a making of our way that depends for its success on an ability to know the world as it exists rather than to work it—to labor it, to toil it—into something altogether different.

If this, too, is just beyond Susan's grasping, she is nevertheless certain enough about the supposed worker's paradise that ziggurat-builders such as Cruso conjure as they stack stones (or order others to do so) and dream of planting: "Of the walls they will say, These are cannibal walls, the ruins of a cannibal city, from the golden age of cannibals" (54–55). In Coetzee's world, a moral anthropophagy seems the inevitable legacy of the ramparts required by tillers—or, rather, required by the monarchs who feed richly upon their sweat. She furthermore sums up tidily Coetzee's view of the delusive nature of the walled city as a humanly constructed imitation of realms celestial: "Is the answer that our island was not a garden of desire, like that in which our first parents went naked, and coupled as innocently as beasts? I believe your master would have had it be a garden of labour; but, lacking a worthy object for his labours, descended to carrying stones, as ants carry grains of sand to and fro for want of better occupation" (86).

As Coetzee remarks of the Western work ethic in *White Writing,* "No one bothers to put, save rhetorically, the ethical question: which is better, to live like the ant, busily storing up food for the winter, or like the grasshopper, singing in the sun all day, heedless of the morrow?" (18–19). And so young Pakenham is surely wrong when, speaking of Milton's Garden, he asserts that "no ziggurat of Babylon ever looked like this." On the contrary, Milton's flat-topped mount aptly recapitulates the form of a ziggurat, which is also the form of Abyssinian prisons, which is in turn the shape that Cruso is attempting to chisel his entire island into an imitation of. As the castaway himself tells Susan, "The world is full of islands," which draws her melancholy admission that "his words ring truer every day" (71). Yes, the walled city and its terraced temple are just like heaven—as long as you can ignore those long hours on the clock. Susan thus speaks more truly than she knows when she describes the island as "the place where Cruso spent too much time *tilling the terraces*" (121, my italics). Welcome to the time, to the labors, and to the architecture of empire.

CONCLUSION
The Timescales Fall from Our Eyes

If CULTURAL processes that are masked by ideologies operate too close to our eyes to be clearly seen, then there is an additional, paradoxical level of indistinctness involved when one tries to talk about agriculture and the ideologies that justify and valorize it, since for most people in the developed world farming is something that takes place, geographically and culturally, somewhere far removed—in some territory *profonde*, or in flyover country. And even if everyone understands that agriculture is essential for sustaining our urban society, and if many are aware of, say, farming's dire environmental effects and unethical treatment of animals, there is still a general underestimation of the ways in which, over centuries, its whispered or shouted apologetics have shaped our deepest assumptions and shut down potential avenues of doubt and challenge. Before my own encounter with anthropology's current view of farming's triumph and of how that ancient conquest transformed the way *Homo sapiens* treat the earth and each other, I can recall many instances where, so to speak, I could not see the wheatfield for the stalks. I will offer up a pair of these, both of them small and absurd, but both of which, I believe, illustrate the way that agriculturalist ideologies, even when we believe ourselves to be earnestly cogitating, manage to command the terrain and bend the furrows of our thinking.

The first occurred during my involvement with my college newspaper, back in the Paleolithic era. Between pasting up lines of type and coaxing the rickety machines that spat out our weekly twelve-page tabloid, I would sometimes thumb through the collection of graphic catalogs stored in the newsroom's cupboards. One such anthology—some encyclopedia of symbols or runic dictionary, I cannot remember exactly—contained an image that chilled and haunted me to a degree that now seems risible, or pitiable. It was one among a list of "hobo signs," a collection of chalk or charcoal marks scraped upon fence posts and tree trunks that bespoke the dangers and pleasures of riding the rails and tramping the countryside. Many of them spoke of ways to pry a morsel of charity from farmers, so that a cross signified that "religious talk gets you a meal," while a series of teardrops advised one to "tell the woman a pitiful story," or a stick-figure stooping promised "food for work." Of course many raised a warning: "Cops here bad," "Vicious dog," "Too many tramps already." The one that especially disturbed me, however, did so because it seemed entirely evacuated of the element of motivation: a raised arm wielding a stick simply declared, "You will be beaten." No "if," no "then," just the violence as a certainty, upon the mere sight of you. At the time I was inclined to take this as a marker of some existential war of each against all, of some malice collectively bred into our marrow, and it put me into a picturesque, weeks-long funk. But my meditations, in hindsight, were both historically vague and politically inert. Having subsequently encountered notions of the agricultural trap and its enduring legacies, however, I can now view the promised drubbing as something more culturally and psychologically explicable—that is, as one small example of agriculturalists' chronic and ideologically compulsive aggression against nonfarmers. Why beat a hobo on sight? Because the land is *for* tilling, and those who won't settle down and do their share of it *require* a beating, lest their uncivilized tramping tempt others to down hoe or abandon plow.

The second one dates from some years later, when I succumbed to a popular delusion. Truly, it still scourges me with chagrin to admit the first mighty rush of enthusiasm and relief I experienced at the prospect of ethanol. This biofuel, usually manufactured from corn, cane, or other commercial crops, was touted as way of powering the transportation sector while reducing net carbon emissions, and I gushed about its promise whenever given the chance; I believe I once even ruined an otherwise promising first date through my alarming enthusiasm for the topic. Of course ethanol wound up delivering none of the promised reductions in CO_2 discharges, and, indeed, seems to have increased them while aggravating the problem of farmed monocultures and arguably diverting sustenance from human mouths to the throats of gas tanks. There were skeptics from the first, but when I look back on why I was not among them, I see a younger person full of social concern, to be sure, but one firmly in the grip of an agriculturalist mindset. The notion that we might actually be able to *farm* our way out of an ecological crisis was simply irresistible in its magical abrogation of the laws of physics and its vision of a virtuous circle between what "we" already did so effortlessly and what we wanted more of. The idea that the energy with which to power something I knew to be as historically newfangled and personally unrelinquishable as the automobile by means of a practice that I also "knew" to be primal (in an experiential sense), primordial (in a historical sense), natural (in every possible sense), and in some airy way productive of good character simply swept all doubts aside. It was lucky that I was still a relatively indigent grad student at the time, and that e-trading had not yet been invented, for I surely would have bet the farm on ethanol.

If, for me, personally, the concept of the agricultural trap forced a series of intellectual reframings, I wonder if—given the recent popularity of many things "Paleo" in our culture—such mental alterations might soon proliferate, for many a public issue or newsworthy event takes on a different shading when the deep history of agriculture becomes lodged in one's mind. For instance, in Beirut on August 4, 2020, just shy of three thousand tons of ammonium nitrate, a chemical chiefly employed as a fertilizer, which had been stored for six years in giant grain silos located on the city's waterfront, caught fire and exploded. The detonation was heard in several neighboring countries, produced a looming mushroom cloud that resembled that generated by atomic weapons, and registered as one of the largest human-caused, non-nuclear explosions in history. Over two hundred people were killed outright, and over seven thousand injured; the center city of Beirut, already heavily damaged by decades of warfare and neglect, was devastated anew. Ammonium nitrate is perhaps the textbook example of a "dual-use" material: its ease of manufacture, relative inexpensiveness, and ability to be stored in bulk make it attractive to industrialized agriculture, while these same properties, when added to its propensity to explode, render it the preferred bomb material of terrorists from Oklahoma City to Bali.

It would be surprising if ammonium nitrate, whose small white crystals make it appear as if the fields to which it is applied are being sown with salt, has not already been employed in some novel or poem to inform the reader that "something has gone wrong with farming." The concept of the agricultural trap, however, suggests a slight grammatical reformulation of this warning that entails a large shift in our conventional thinking: "With farming, something has gone wrong." The difference involves a radical change in timescales, and calls forth a critical practice that Derek Woods calls "scale critique" (133–34, 137–40):

> Scale critique would be an intellectual practice attentive to the way the nature of an issue or situation alters according to the scale at which it is considered. This entails a form of deconstructive attention to concepts and assumptions: for what may seem coherent, self-contained consistent or virtuous at one scale may be very different at another....
>
> Even some activities that seem environmentally beneficial in the present, at the individual or the national scale, acquire another, destructive face at broader scales. (Clark 40–41)

And so, rather than—as we are wont to do—looking back to the industrial revolution in order to lament the perversion and pollution of a once-pristine agriculture (a perversion that some believe has led to the recent pollution of our bodies), scale critique prompts us to look back to the Neolithic and acknowledge that even when agriculture was being pursued by the world's first farmers it had already begun filling the granaries of sorrow at least as quickly and copiously as those of plenty.

This timing of our original misstep matters, for pushing it so far back in history changes its emotional valence, and hence our view of our species' cultural trajectory as a whole. To envision our farewell to health and happiness as an event that, even before we possessed the ability to write down what was happening, had already effectively occurred, makes it seem less like a strategic blunder and more like a tragic fate, less Clym Yeobright than Tess Durbeyfield. Or, to come at it from another angle, having to change our collective autobiography by replacing the narrative of the agricultural revolution with that of the agricultural trap shifts us within the traditional frame of tragedy from that early moment when hubris is displayed to the later one when anagnorisis is suffered. Consider Oedipus as our collective representative: if he is guilty of self-satisfaction early in the play, this is because the story he has told himself about his rise to the apex of the city is similar to the one that the agricultural revolution proclaimed about why we *Homo sapiens* ascended to the (supposed) apex of planetary life. We did so, we told ourselves, because we had figured things out, because, being larded with talents and energies, we had earned it. In the throes of that Old Story, we resembled Oedipus before the intervention of Tiresias, thinking back with self-satisfaction on that long summer of successes—the killing of an upstart foe at the crossroads, the outsmarting of the Sphinx, the marrying of Jocasta, the grasping of the Theban crown. What a harvest of riches for a few risks run! Surely the whole of that fortunate season of growth, wherein we transformed ourselves from orphans into kings, and that promised such a bounteous autumn, was about finding at last our latent powers, unlocking our hidden luck, inheriting our destined future. But the new narrative of the agricultural trap, of course, twins us with the Oedipus we encounter later in the play, who understands now that what once appeared to be the exercise and reward of powers wholly his own were merely baits laid by larger entities indifferent to his happiness and possessed of inscrutable purposes. It is with us as it is with Oedipus: hubris is exchanged for a radically deflated self-conception, and a story of ascent is replaced by the chronicle of a primordial Fall.[1]

If I'm not content to leave matters just there, it is not because I have a confident desire to answer the inevitable next question, "What is to be done?"—especially since attempting to do so is how many otherwise helpful literary critics have made momentary fools of themselves. Indeed, genuine anthropologists usually refrain from such gambits, while it is mostly interlopers like myself who feel emboldened to test their voices. Ah, well, then: if, concerning the cultural "package" of foraging lifeways, someone declared that "there is no going back," my head would nod in instinctive agreement, though I would momentarily, on second thought, want to make sure what was meant by "no." If one is denying the possibility of a wholesale civilizational reversion, then I would agree, for such a neo-Paleolithic is indeed fantastical, so much so that it doesn't even constitute a very interesting thought experiment. Certainly there are always voices who tell us that such denials are merely a way to mask our lack of imagination and moral courage, and I think we should be grateful to the John Zerzans of the world for keeping us honest, but surely anyone who thinks as he does must sooner or later experience the demoralization felt by Conrad's Professor over the prospects for *his* revolution:

> But after a while he became disagreeably affected by the sight of the roadway thronged with vehicles and of the pavement crowded with men and women. He was in a long, straight street, peopled by a mere fraction of an immense multitude; but all round him, on and on, even to the limits of the horizon hidden by the enormous piles of bricks, he felt the mass of mankind mighty in its numbers. They swarmed numerous like locusts, industrious like ants, thoughtless like a natural force, pushing on blind and orderly and absorbed, impervious to sentiment, to logic, to terror, too, perhaps. (*Secret Agent* 102–3)

For ten thousand years the forests and steppelands have shrunk as our own numbers have swelled, so besides the terror that surely *would* be required to persuade our industrious multitudes to abandon modernity, the math, sans some culling apocalypse, just doesn't work out (see Morton, *Dark Ecology* 66).

On the other hand, I'm sympathetic to Paul Shepherd's desire to read the all-in version of "You can't go back" as a straw man that makes an impossible cultural revanchism the enemy of a reasoned and pragmatic selection of lost techniques for living: "Societies and cultures are mosaics. They are componential. Their various elements, like genes and persons, can be disengaged from the whole. Contemporary life is in fact just such an accumulation representing elements of different ages and origins, some of which will disappear, as they entered, at different times than others. The phrase 'You cannot go back' can only mean that you cannot recreate an identical totality but it does not follow that you cannot incorporate components" (313). This metaphor he employs, of individual stones arranged into a cultural mural, possesses a certain lithic aptness, but is rather too static. The most recent work in the anthropology of hunter-gatherers is all about change and variety, emphasizing foraging cultures that acquired and then abandoned particular technologies, communities who fought with farmers while others traded with them, and peoples who continually adapted themselves to a fickle climate. As Shepherd asserts, culture, including that of the Paleolithic, is best seen as highly componential, and recent findings therefore seem to deserve a more flexible trope than he provides. A more dynamic though perhaps less optimistic metaphor might envision certain selected spiritual energies and practical strategies from a long-despised and disparaged foraging gnosis being intentionally, selectively deployed as a series of small course corrections to the megaship that is our agro-industrial-informational civilization. Such discrete tugs on the wheel might not be enough to prevent the vessel from its seemingly inevitable grounding, but it might allow us to shudder onto a flat stretch of beach rather than to fetch up upon the rocks. Salvation it's not, but it might permit salvage, and, of course, all this is hope, not prediction. But as to *any* manner of "going back" that we might someday desire and hope to accomplish, let us undertake it fully mindful of the tragic irrevocability of our stumble into agriculture's snare. We have resigned our part in the casual comedy of foraging for good, and if taking up the plow has been productive of at best a terrible sort of beauty, we should nevertheless admit our inability to relinquish our self-imposed burden and accept that we have no future but in striving to perfect and pacify the dangerous arts of cultivation.

Any chance that the practical knowledges and spiritual postures of hunter-gatherers might wind up nudging the rest of us toward more sustainable tomorrows will be the product of, historically speaking, a very recent inversion of Western attitudes toward nonfarmers. If you graphed time against foragers' perceived cultural capital, you'd get the kind of J curve produced by population growth or global warming, with a long horizontal line bending suddenly toward the vertical at the chart's far right. As the organization of this book suggests, however—and as I hope its contents demonstrate—aside from the near-total revaluation of foragers that occurred just yesterday, there is not much of a satisfying historical pattern to be mapped from a chronological arrangement of our texts. Once hunter-gatherers are reactivated in the European imagination by means of early modern exploration, conquest, and colonization, subsequent literary chronology predicts very little. Shakespeare, for instance, seems both more curious and more knowledgeable about foragers than Defoe, while both Shelley and Brontë valorize (or at least sympathize with) the "primitive" figure that Conrad can only gape at in condescending wonder decades later. Given this, I wonder if it might not be fruitful to imagine the hunter-gatherer within a framework less insistent upon rigorous historicization.

Although Freudian categories such as the id and the superego have a long history of racist appropriation in descriptions of agriculturalists' encounters with hunter-gatherers, could we not, in a more self-critical spirit, see the forager as a peculiarly reliable generator of the *uncanny*? After all, farming first required constructing the very site of the *unheimlich*, the domus, and "first required" in two senses. That is, it is unlikely that agriculture ever began to be practiced before a given community had become largely sedentary, and once farming did begin, sedentism had to continue alongside it in order for tillage to be sustained. So, literally, for millennia the hunter-gatherer has been defined by agro-culture as one who does not possess a domus, who does not desire one, and who certainly has no business within one, unless it be to plunder and kill. Yet, anthropologically speaking, it is the agriculturalist who has so recently abandoned home and community, who has exchanged an originary domus that asks to be understood for a novel one that demands to be worked. Morton underscores this notion by recalling that for Freud "uncanny feelings in the end involve the repressed intimacy of the mother's body, the uterus and the vagina out of which you came" (*Dark Ecology* 36). Indeed, Hugh Brody has argued that while "farmers appear to be settled, and hunters to be wanderers," it is actually "the agriculturalists, with their commitment to . . . farms and large numbers of children, who are forced to keep moving, resettling, colonizing new lands," such that "it is farming, not hunting, that generates 'nomadism.'" Foragers, by contrast, "with their reliance on a single area, are profoundly settled" and thus "will not go forth and multiply," believing as they do "that home is already Eden." This view renders coherent the biblical narrative of Cain, that first of farmers and first of murderers denounced by Rousseau for his bad character, who is also a perpetual wanderer: "Thus we begin to see the human being [who farms] as settled and unsettled—a person displaced from his home, roaming the harsh earth looking for land to till, for somewhere to live. He can settle in a restless way, building, inventing, shaping, and then, as need be, roam farther afield—repeating the pattern that is the farmer's destiny" (86, 74).

So, when the figure amid the wheatfield locks eyes with the figure at the edge of the forest or the steppe, which one is best described as currently dwelling "at home"? Who between the two is more firmly situated in the place where our species *belongs*, in more than one sense of that word? This, then, is the anthropological twist upon Freud's category: it is not that the hunter-gatherer is an uncanny figure herself, but that, when brought before our attention, she makes *us*, we tillers of the land, feel ourselves to be uncanny beings—at home, yet at the same time suddenly, disconcertingly, alien and adrift, even as we anxiously retreat within the walls of our domus. This inversion of the farmer's view of who wanders and who settles, forced upon us by the mere sight of who we used to be, would seem to explain the proliferation of rich and troubled ambivalences toward foragers that we have witnessed in our various texts: Gonzalo's untilled plantation, Crusoe's compulsive wall-building, Shelley's monster who is no such thing, Heathcliff's sadistic love. For beholding the forager must be akin to finding an alien footprint and suddenly wondering if it might be our own—or like meeting the enemy, and discovering they are us.

NOTES

3. Shelley's and Brontë's Solitary Walkers

1. For an argument that refuses this temptation, see Thormählen (185, 196–97).
2. But perhaps Rousseau would categorize Heathcliff not as a stage-one forager, but as a member of those "savage races" who, because they congregate into communities, albeit small ones, are nevertheless already sufficiently corrupted to have lost their natural pity: "From here [i.e., the comparisons of the self against others that occurs within any settled community] arose the first duties of civility even among Savages, and from it any intentional wrong became an affront because, together with the harm resulting from the injury, the offended party saw in it contempt for his person, often more unbearable than the harm itself. Thus everyone punishing the contempt shown him in a manner proportionate to the stock he set by himself, vengeances became terrible, and men bloodthirsty and cruel. This is precisely the stage reached by most of the Savage Peoples known to us; and it is for want of drawing adequate distinctions between ideas, and noticing how far these Peoples already were from the first state of Nature, that many hastened to conclude that man is naturally cruel and that he needs political order in order to be made gentle" (*Discourse* 166).

4. Coetzee's Carcer[e]al State

1. For further discussion of Coetzee's familiarity with Enlightenment and Romantic discourses on the relationship between idleness and philosophy, see Adelman, "Ventriloquism and Idleness."
2. This list could be extended. Laura Wright, for instance, correctly states that K is positioned "as the barbarian beyond the reach of civilization," and thus as "a victim of the forms of classification he seeks to avoid" (92), but does not touch on the fact that "barbarian," in the language of the grain state, always implies a nomadic nonfarmer. Dominic Head, meanwhile, comes to "a realization that the space in which K's experiment as a cultivator can endure does not exist, either in the expectations of the novel at this time, or in the particular terrain alluded to" (106), but does not entertain the idea that, in historical and anthropological terms, it once did. For his part, Stephen Clingman is willing to admit that Coetzee's novels

"have to do with the *longue durée* of a history of frames of consciousness," but without touching on the specifically pre-agricultural world that K appears to embody. Finally, David Attwell insists that "the Magistrate's halting steps" toward a "posthumanist, reconstructed ethics ... become elaborated more fully in *Michael K*" (97), only to figure this new morality in linguistic rather than anthropological terms.

5. The Necessity of Cannibalism

1. Kilgour also discusses cannibalism's connection with psychoanalytic views of infantile states, though she seems to suggest that cannibalism is itself an attractive regressive fantasy because it involves incorporation of and comingling with the maternal. I find it more convincing, however, to see cannibalism—or the cry of such—as the equivalent of the incest taboo that *forbids* a return to infantile incorporative pleasures.
2. Seed ("This island's mine," 202–11), says, rather confusingly, "Nor is Caliban the mythical 'hunter-gatherer' who enabled English colonization in the name of farming—even though there is an allusion to this possibility later in the play (2.ii.152–65)" (208). Perhaps she means that the ambiguously complex figure of Caliban is not *ideally* suited to the ideology of English colonizers.
3. Interestingly, the dumb-show figures who offer this meal move Gonzalo toward believing he has found rather than merely imagined a utopian community, for he seems to momentarily adopt the tone that Montaigne takes toward the Brazilian cannibals, perceiving their virtues through the fog of otherness and ranking their morality as superior to that of Europeans:

> If I should say I saw such islanders—
> For certes, these are people of the island—
> Who though they are of monstrous shape, yet note
> Their manners are more gentle, kind, than of
> Our human generation you shall find
> Many, nay almost any. (3.3.28–34)

4. I am indebted to Robert Shine for directing me toward the book of Amos in regard to this passage.

6. What Walls Want

1. As Timothy Morton asserts in *Humankind: Solidarity with Nonhuman People*, "There is an ideology of agricultural social space as such, agriculture as it was conceived in the Fertile Crescent. Agricultural space must be kept

together, precisely because of the obvious ways in which, as soon as it starts up, it causes social space to be torn apart: patriarchy, hierarchy, desertification. An underlying aspect of this rip in social space is the Severing, the walling off of human space from the symbiotic real." (22–23). By "the Severing," he means the Neolithic transition to farming.
2. The sole exception appears to be Elisabeth Kraft, who, in "The Revaluation of Literary Character: The Case of Crusoe," *South Atlantic Review* 72, No. 4 (Fall 2007): 37–58, argues that in his building program Cruso "does homage to his connection with the human race in his belief that there will be someone to follow him for whom he works and to whom he feels a vague obligation" (49).
3. In the novel's enigmatic coda, do we perhaps see Friday's Os, once flat upon the page, assume a three-dimensional, almost bodily form in the spherical bubbles he breathes out from the sunken wreck of the ship? And might such constitute an utterance at least one step closer to "the home of Friday," the "place where bodies are their own signs" (157)?

Conclusion

1. For a somewhat different discussion of Oedipus and agriculture, see Morton, *Dark Ecology*, 61–63, 136.

WORKS CITED

Adelman, Richard. "Ventriloquism and Idleness in J. M. Coetzee's *Life & Times of Michael K.*" *Textual Practice* 30, no. 4 (2016): 599–619.
Albrecht, Glenn, Gina Sartore, Linda Connor, Nick Higginbotham, Sonia Freeman, Brian Kelly, Helen Stain et al. "Solastalgia: The Distress Caused by Environmental Change." *Australasian Psychiatry: Bulletin of Royal Australian and New Zealand College of Psychiatrists* 15, suppl. 1 (2007): S95–98.
Arens, W. *The Man-Eating Myth: Anthropology and Anthropophagy*. New York: Oxford University Press, 1979.
Arens, W., and Marshall Sahlins. "Cannibalism: An Exchange." *New York Review of Books*, March 22, 1979.
Ashcroft, Bill. "Irony, Allegory, and Empire: *Waiting for the Barbarians* and *In the Heart of the Country*." In *Critical Essays on J. M. Coetzee*, edited by Sue Kossew, 100–116. New York: G. K. Hall, 1998.
Attridge, Derek. "Against Allegory: *Waiting for the Barbarians*, *Life & Times of Michael K*, and the Question of Literary Reading." In *J. M. Coetzee and the Idea of the Public Intellectual*, edited by Jane Poyner, 63–82. Athens: Ohio University Press, 2006.
———. *J. M. Coetzee and the Ethics of Reading: Literature in the Event*. Chicago: University of Chicago Press, 2004.
Attwell, David. *J. M. Coetzee: South Africa and the Politics of Writing*. Berkeley: University of Calif. Press, 1993.
Avramescu, Cătălin. *An Intellectual History of Cannibalism*. Translated by Alistair Ian Blyth. Princeton, NJ: Princeton University Press, 2009.
Barbaret, John. "Messages in Bottles: A Comparative Formal Approach to Castaway Narratives." In *Approaches to Teaching Defoe's* Robinson Crusoe, edited by Maximillian E. Novak and Carl Fisher, 111–21. New York: Modern Language Association of America, 2005.
Barker, Graeme. *The Agricultural Revolution in Prehistory: Why Did Foragers Become Farmers?* Oxford: Oxford University Press, 2009.
Bate, Jonathan. "From Myth to Drama." In *Critical Essays on Shakespeare's* The Tempest, edited by Virginia Mason Vaughan and Alden T. Vaughan, 39–59. New York: G. K. Hall, 1998.
Berry, Laura C. "Acts of Custody and Incarceration in *Wuthering Heights* and *The Tenant of Wildfell Hall*." *Novel: A Forum on Fiction* 30, no. 1 (Fall 1996): 32–55.

Bertman, Stephen. "Defoe and 'the Footprints of Man.'" *Digital Defoe: Studies in Defoe and His Contemporaries* 5, no. 1 (Fall 2013): 130–43.
Blackstone, William. *Commentaries on the Laws of England, Vol. 2*. Oxford: Clarendon, 1766–67.
Blythman, Joanna. "Permanent Global Summertime." *Ecologist*, 1 September 2004. https://theecologist.org/2004/sep/01/permanent-global-summertime.
Boucher, Philip P. *Cannibal Encounters: Europeans and Island Caribs, 1492–1763*. Baltimore, MD: Johns Hopkins University Press, 1992.
Brantlinger, Patrick. *Rule of Darkness: British Literature and Imperialism, 1830–1914*. Ithaca, NY: Cornell University Press, 1988.
———. *Taming Cannibals: Race and the Victorians*. Ithaca, NY: Cornell University Press, 2011.
Braunstein, Nestor A. "Desire and Jouissance in the Teachings of Lacan." In *The Cambridge Companion to Lacan*, edited by Jean-Michel Rabaté, 102–15. Cambridge: Cambridge University Press, 2003.
Brody, Hugh. *The Other Side of Eden: Hunters, Farmers, and the Shaping of the World*. New York: North Point Press of Farrar, Straus & Giroux, 2000.
Brontë, Emily. *Wuthering Heights*. Edited by Alexandra Lewis. New York: Norton Critical Editions, 2019.
Brooks, Peter. "What Is a Monster? (According to *Frankenstein*)." In *New Casebooks: Frankenstein*, edited by Fred Botting, 81–106. New York: St. Martin's, 1995.
Brown, Marshall. "*Frankenstein*: A Child's Tale." *Novel: A Forum on Fiction* 36, no. 2 (Spring 2003): 145–75.
Cannon, Aubrey. "Historical and Humanist Perspectives on Hunter-Gatherers." In *The Oxford Handbook of the Archaeology and Anthropology of Hunter-Gatherers*, 92–103. Oxford: Oxford University Press, 2014.
Cantillon, Richard. *Essai sur la nature du commerce en général*. Edited and translated by Henry Higgs. London: Frank Cass, 1959.
Cauvin, Jacques. *The Birth of the Gods and the Origins of Agriculture*. Translated by Trevor Watkins. Cambridge: Cambridge University Press, 2000.
Chetham, George. "The Absence of God in *Heart of Darkness*." *Studies in the Novel* 18, no. 3 (Fall 1986): 304–13.
Clark, Evert Mordecai. "Milton's Abyssinian Paradise." *University of Texas Studies in English* 29 (1950): 129–50.
Clark, Timothy. *The Value of Ecocriticism*. Cambridge: Cambridge University Press, 2019.
Clingman, Stephen. "Revolution and Reality: South African Fiction in the 1980s." In *Rendering Things Visible: Essays on South African Literary Culture*, edited by Martin Trump, 41–60. Johannesburg: Ravan, 1990.
Coetzee, J. M. *Foe*. New York: Penguin, 1987.
———. *Life & Times of Michael K*. New York: Penguin, 1985.

———. *Waiting for the Barbarians*. New York: Penguin, 2010.

———. *White Writing: On the Culture of Letters in South Africa*. New Haven, CT: Yale University Press, 1988.

Cole, Lucinda. "What Happened to the Rats? Hoarding, Hunger, and Storage on Crusoe's Island." In *Imperfect Creatures: Vermin, Literature, and the Sciences of Life, 1600–1740*, 143–71. Ann Arbor: University of Michigan Press, 2016.

Comitini, Patricia. "The Limits of Discourse and the Ideology of Form in Mary Shelley's *Frankenstein*." *Keats-Shelley Journal* 55 (2006): 179–98.

Conrad, Joseph. *Heart of Darkness. A Norton Critical Edition*. 5th ed. Edited by Paul B. Armstrong. New York: W. W. Norton, 2017.

———. *Lord Jim: A Tale*. London: Penguin, 2007.

———. *Notes on Life and Letters*. London: J. M. Dent, 1921.

———. *The Secret Agent: A Simple Tale*. New York: Penguin, 1996.

Daley, A. Stuart. "A Chronology of *Wuthering Heights*." *Wuthering Heights: The 1847 Text, Backgrounds and Criticism*. 4th ed. Edited by Richard J. Dunn, 357–61. New York: W. W. Norton, 2003.

Dalrymple, John, Sir. *An Essay towards a General History of Feudal Property in Great Britain*. London: A. Millar, 1758.

Damm, Charlotte, and Lars Forsberg. "Forager-Farmer Contacts in Northern Fennoscandia." In *The Oxford Handbook of the Archaeology and Anthropology of Hunter-Gatherers*, 838–56. Oxford: Oxford University Press, 2014.

Davies, Stevie. *Emily Brontë: Heretic*. London: Women's Press, 1994.

Defoe, Daniel. *Robinson Crusoe: A Norton Critical Edition*. 2nd ed. Edited by Michael Shinagel. New York: W. W. Norton, 1994.

———. *Serious Reflections during the Life and Surprising Adventures of Robinson Crusoe: With His Vision of the Angelick World. Written by Himself*. London: W. Taylor, 1720.

Dellamore, Richard. "Earnshaw's Neighbor/Catherine's Friend: Ethical Contingencies in *Wuthering Heights*." *ELH* 74, no. 3 (Fall 2007): 535–55.

Derrida, Jaques. *The Beast and the Sovereign*. Vol. 2. Edited by Michel Lisse, Marie-Louise Mallet, and Ginette Michaud. Translated by Geoffrey Bennington. Chicago: Chicago University Press, 2011.

Diamond, Jared. "The Worst Mistake in the History of the Human Race." *Discover* 8, no. 5 (May 1987): 64–66.

Dovey, Teresa. *The Novels of J. M. Coetzee: Lacanian Allegories*. Cape Town: Ad. Donker, 1988.

Eagleton, Terry. *Heathcliff and the Great Hunger: Studies in Irish Culture*. New York: Verso, 1995.

———. *Myths of Power: A Marxist Study of the Brontës*. London: Macmillan, 1975.

Eastley, Aaron. "Conrad, the *Times*, and Some Explorers." *Conradiana* 44, nos. 2–3 (Fall-Winter 2012): 91–125.

Eckstein, Barbara. "The Body, the Word, and the State: J. M. Coetzee's *Waiting for the Barbarians.*" *Novel: A Forum on Fiction* 22, no. 2 (Winter 1989): 175–98.

Egan, Gabriel. *Green Shakespeare: From Ecopolitics to Ecocriticism.* New York: Routledge, 2006.

Ferrara, Alessandro. *Modernity and Authenticity: A Study of the Social and Ethical Thought of Jean-Jacques Rousseau.* Albany: State University of New York Press, 1993.

Ferguson, Adam. *An Essay on the History of Civil Society.* 5th ed. London: T. Cadell, 1782.

Firchow, Peter Edgerly. *Envisioning Africa: Racism and Imperialism in Conrad's Heart of Darkness.* Lexington: University Press of Kentucky, 2000.

Flint, Kate. *The Transatlantic Indian, 1776–1930.* Princeton, NJ: Princeton University Press, 2009.

Flynn, Carol Houlihan. *The Body in Swift and Defoe.* Cambridge: Cambridge University Press, 1990.

Fulford, Tim. *Romantic Indians: Native Americans, British Literature, and Transatlantic Culture, 1756–1830.* Oxford: Oxford University Press, 2006.

Gallagher, Susan VanZantan. *A Story of South Africa: J. M. Coetzee's Fiction in Context.* Cambridge, MA: Harvard University Press, 1991.

———. "Torture and the Novel: J. M. Coetzee's *Waiting for the Barbarians.*" *Contemporary Literature* 29, no. 2 (Summer 1998): 277–85.

Gaston, Paul L. "The Gospel of Work according to Joseph Conrad." *Polish Review* 20, nos. 2–3 (1975): 203–10.

Gilbert, Sandra M., and Susan Gubar. *The Madwoman in the Attic: The Woman Writer and the Nineteenth-Century Literary Imagination.* New Haven, CT: Yale University Press, 1984.

Gillies, John. "The Figure of the New World in *The Tempest.*" In *The Tempest and Its Travels*, 180–200. Philadelphia: University of Pennsylvania Press, 2000.

———. "Shakespeare's Virginian Masque." *ELH* 53, no. 4 (Winter 1986): 673–707.

Girard, René. *Violence and the Sacred.* Translated by Patrick Gregory. Baltimore, MD: Johns Hopkins University Press, 1979.

Go, Kenji. "Montaigne's 'Cannibals' and *The Tempest* Revisited." *Studies in Philology* 109, no. 4 (Summer 2012): 455–73.

Goldberg, Jonathan. *Tempest in the Caribbean.* Minneapolis: University of Minnesota Press, 2004.

Goodridge, Frank J. "The Circumambient Universe." In *Twentieth Century Interpretations of Wuthering Heights*, edited by Thomas A. Volger, 69–77. Englewood Cliffs, NJ: Prentice Hall, 1968.

Gordimer, Nadine. "The Idea of Gardening." *New York Review of Books*, February 2, 1984.

Gowdy, John. "Introduction: Back to the Future and Forward to the Past." In *Limited Wants, Unlimited Means: A Reader on Hunter-Gatherer Economics and the Environment*, edited by John Gowdy, xv–xxxi. Washington, DC: Island, 1997.

Green, John. *The Anthropocene Reviewed: Essays on a Human-Centered Planet*. New York: Penguin Random House, 2021.

Gremillion, Kristen J. *Ancestral Appetites: Food in Prehistory*. Cambridge: Cambridge University Press, 2011.

Haggerty, George E. "Thank God It's Friday: The Construction of Masculinity in *Robinson Crusoe*." In *Approaches to Teaching Defoe's* Robinson Crusoe, edited by Maximillian E. Novak and Carl Fisher, 78–87. New York: Modern Language Association of America, 2005.

Halpern, Richard. "'The Picture of Nobody': White Cannibalism in *The Tempest*." In *The Production of English Renaissance Culture*, edited by David Lee Miller, Sharon O'Dair, and Harold Weber, 262–92. Ithaca, NY: Cornell University Press, 1994.

Head, Dominic. *J. M. Coetzee*. Cambridge: Cambridge University Press, 1997.

Hardt, Michael and Antonio Negri. *Empire*. Cambridge, MA: Harvard University Press, 2000.

Harris, Marvin. *Cannibals and Kings: The Origins of Cultures*. New York: Random House, 1977.

Heider, Sarah Dove. "The Timeless Ecstasy of Michael K." In *Black/White Writing: Essays on South African Literature*, 83–98. Cranberry, NJ: Associated University Presses, 1993.

Helm, June. "Does Hunting Bring Happiness?" In *Man the Hunter*, edited by Richard B Lee and Irven DeVore, 89–92. Chicago: Aldine, 1968.

Helvétius. *De l'espit: Or, Essays on the Mind, and Its Several Faculties*. London: Mr. Dodsley, 1759.

Herder, Johann Gottfried, *Reflections on the Philosophy of the History of Mankind*. Edited by Frank E. Manuel. Chicago: University of Chicago Press, 1968.

Hewish, John. *Emily Brontë: A Critical and Biographical Study*. New York: St. Martin's, 1969.

Homans, Margaret. *Bearing the Word: Language and Female Experience in Nineteenth-Century Women's Writing*. Chicago: University of Chicago Press, 1989.

Hulme, Peter. *Colonial Encounters: Europe and the Native Caribbean, 1492–1787*. New York: Methuen, 1986.

———. "Introduction: The Cannibal Scene." In *Cannibalism and the Colonial World*, edited by Frances Barker, Peter Hulme, and Margaret Iversen, 1–38. Cambridge: Cambridge University Press, 1998.

———. "Prospero and Caliban." In *Transatlantic Literary Studies: A Reader*, edited by Susan Manning and Andrew Taylor, 126–30. Edinburgh: Edinburgh University Press, 2007.

Hutcheson, Francis. *Collected Works*. 7 vols. Facsimile edition prepared by Bernhard Fabian. Hildesheim: Georg Olms, 1969–71.

Irvine, Robert P. "Enlightenment, Agency, and Romance: The Case of Scott's *Guy Mannering*." *Journal of Narrative Theory* 30, no. 1 (Winter 2000): 29–54.

Jordan, Peter. "The Ethnology and Anthropology of 'Modern' Hunter-Gatherers." In *The Oxford Handbook of the Archaeology and Anthropology of Hunter-Gatherers*, 903–17. Oxford: Oxford University Press, 2014.

Jordan, Peter, and Vicki Cummings. "Prehistoric Hunter-Gatherer Innovations." In *The Oxford Handbook of the Archaeology and Anthropology of Hunter-Gatherers*, 585–606. Oxford: Oxford University Press, 2014.

Joudrey, Thomas J. "'Well, we must be for ourselves in the long run': Selfishness and Sociality in *Wuthering Heights*." *Nineteenth-Century Literature* 70, no. 2 (September 2015): 165–93.

Kasdan, David Scott. "'The Duke of Milan/And His Brave Son': Dynastic Politics in *The Tempest*." In *Critical Essays on Shakespeare's* The Tempest, edited by Virginia Mason Vaughan and Alden T. Vaughan, 91–103. New York: G. K. Hall, 1998.

Kames, Henry Home, Lord. *Historical law-tracts*. 4th ed. London: Printed for T. Cadell, in the Strand, 1792.

———. *Sketches of the History of Man. A New Edition, in Three Volumes*. Edinburgh: William Creech, 1807.

Kettle, Arnold. "Emily Brontë: *Wuthering Heights*." *Twentieth Century Interpretations of* Wuthering Heights, edited by Thomas A. Volger, 28–43. Englewood Cliffs, NJ: Prentice Hall, 1968.

Kilgour, Maggie. "The Function of Cannibalism at the Present Time." In *Cannibalism and the Colonial World*, edited by Frances Barker, Peter Hulme, and Margaret Iversen, 238–59. Cambridge: Cambridge University Press, 1998.

Knight, Richard Payne. *The Progress of Civil Society. A Didactic Poem, in Six Books*. London: W. Bulmer for G. Nicol, 1796.

Kotze, Haidee. "Desire, Gender, Power, Language: A Psychoanalytic Reading of Mary Shelley's *Frankenstein*." *Literator* 21, no. 1 (2000): 53–67.

Lamming, George. "A Monster, A Child, A Slave." In *The Tempest: A Norton Critical Edition*, edited by Peter Hulme and William H. Sherman, 148–68. New York: W. W. Norton, 2004.

Lee, Richard B. "What Hunters Do for a Living, or How to Make Out on Scarce Resources." In *Limited Wants, Unlimited Means: A Reader on Hunter-Gatherer Economics and the Environment*, edited by John Gowdy, 43–64. Washington, DC: Island, 1998.

Lee, Richard B., and Irven DeVore, eds. "Preface." In *Man the Hunter*, vii–ix. Chicago: Aldine, 1968.

Leick, Gwendolyn. *Mesopotamia: The Invention of the City*. London: Penguin, 2002.

Le Mercier, Andrew, Rev. *The Church History of Geneva, in Five Books. Also a Political and Geographical Account of that Republic*. Boston: B. Green, 1732.
Lestringant, Frank. *Cannibals: The Discovery and Representation of the Cannibal from Columbus to Jules Verne*. Translated by Rosemary Morris. Berkeley: University of California Press, 1997.
Levin, Harry. *The Myth of the Golden Age in the Renaissance*. Bloomington: Indiana University Press, 1969.
Lévi-Strauss, Claude. *The Naked Man*. Translated by John and Doreen Weightman. New York: Harper & Row, 1981.
Levy, Anita. *Other Women: The Writing of Class, Race, and Gender, 1832–1898*. Princeton, NJ: Princeton University Press, 1991.
Locke, John. *Second Treatise of Government*. Edited by C. B. Macpherson. Cambridge, MA: Hackett, 1980.
Lodge, Sara J. "Literary Influences on the Brontës." In *The Brontës in Context*, edited by Marianne Thormählen, 143–50. Cambridge: Cambridge University Press, 2012.
Lubbock, John, Lord Avebury. *Prehistoric Times, as Illustrated by Ancient Remains, and the Manners and Customs of Modern Savages, Seventh Edition, Thoroughly Revised and Entirely Reset*. London: Williams & Norgate, 1913.
Lupton, Julia Reinhard. "Creature Caliban." *Shakespeare Quarterly* 51, no. 1 (Spring 2000): 1–23.
Malchow, H. L. *Gothic Images of Race in Nineteenth-Century Britain*. Stanford, CA: Stanford University Press, 1996.
Manning, Richard. *Against the Grain: How Agriculture Has Hijacked Civilization*. New York: North Point Press of Farrar, Straus & Giroux, 2004.
Marshall, Lorna. "Sharing, Talking, and Giving: Relief of Social Tensions among the !Kung." In *Limited Wants, Unlimited Means: A Reader on Hunter-Gatherer Economics and the Environment*, edited by John Gowdy, 65–86. Washington DC: Island, 1998.
Marshall, Tristan. "*The Tempest* and the British Imperium in 1611." *Historical Journal* 41, no. 2 (June 1998): 375–400.
Martin, Calvin Luther. *In the Spirit of the Earth: Rethinking History and Time*. Baltimore, MD: Johns Hopkins University Press, 1992.
Mayer, Ted. "The Weird Ecologies of Mary Shelley's *Frankenstein*." *Science Fiction Studies* 45, no. 2 (July 2018): 229–43.
Meek, Ronald L. *Social Science and the Ignoble Savage*. Cambridge: Cambridge University Press, 1976.
Melzer, Arthur M. *The Natural Goodness of Man: On the System of Rousseau's Thought*. Chicago: University of Chicago Press, 1990.
Meskell, Lynn, and Lindsay Weiss. "Coetzee on South Africa's Past: Remembering in the Time of Forgetting." *American Anthropologist* 108, no. 1 (2006): 88–99.

Millar, John. *The Origin of the Distinction of Ranks; or, an Inquiry into the Circumstances Which Give Rise to Influence and Authority, in the Different Members of Society*. London: J. Murray, 1779.
Miller, J. Hillis. *Fiction and Repetition: Seven English Novels*. Cambridge, MA: Harvard University Press, 1982.
Miller, Lucasta. *The Brontë Myth*. London: Jonathan Cape, 2001.
Mithen, Steven. *After the Ice: A Global Human History, 20,000–5,000 BC*. Cambridge, MA: Harvard University Press, 2003.
Montesquieu, Charles de Secondat, Baron de. *The Spirit of the Laws*. Translated by Thomas Nugent. New York: Colonial, 1900.
Morris, Ian. *Foragers, Farmers, and Fossil Fuels: How Human Values Evolve*. Princeton, NJ: Princeton University Press, 2015.
Morse, Jedidiah. *The History of America*. Fourth Improved Edition. Philadelphia: Thomas Dobson, 1808.
Morton, Timothy. *Dark Ecology: For a Logic of Future Coexistence*. New York: Columbia University Press, 2016.
———. *Humankind: Solidarity with Nonhuman People*. New York: Verso, 2019.
Moses, Michael Valdez. "The Mark of Empire: Writing, History, and Torture in Coetzee's *Waiting for the Barbarians*." *Kenyon Review* 15, no. 1 (Winter 1993): 115–27.
Mowat, Barbara. "'Knowing I love my books': Reading *The Tempest* Intertextually." In *The Tempest and Its Travels*, 27–36. Philadelphia: University of Pennsylvania Press, 2000.
Mumford, Lewis. *The City in History: Its Origins, Its Transformations, Its Prospects*. New York: Harcourt Brace Jovanovich, 1961.
Murphy, Robinson O. "Black Friday, Queer Atlantic." *Research in African Literatures* 49, no. 2 (Summer 2018): 182–98.
Nardizzi, Vin. "Wood." In *Fueling Culture: 101 Words for Energy and Environment*, edited by Imre Szeman, Jennifer Wenzel, and Patricia Yaeger, 376–78. New York: Fordham University Press, 2017.
———. *Wooden Os: Shakespeare's Theatres and England's Trees*. Toronto: University of Toronto Press, 2013.
Nilsson, Sven. *The Primitive Inhabitants of Scandinavia*. 3rd ed. London: Longmans, Green, 1868.
Novak, Maximillian E. *Defoe and the Nature of Man*. Oxford: Oxford University Press, 1963.
———. "Teaching *Robinson Crusoe* in a Survey of the Novel Course." In *Approaches to Teaching Defoe's Robinson Crusoe*, edited by Maximillian E. Novak and Carl Fisher, 191–97. New York: Modern Language Association of America, 2005.
Oles, Thomas. *Walls: Enclosure and Ethics in the Modern Landscape*. Chicago: University of Chicago Press, 2015.

Olsen, Lance. "The Presence of Absence: Coetzee's *Waiting for the Barbarians*." *Ariel* 16, no. 2 (1985): 47–60.
Orgel, Stephen. "Shakespeare and the Cannibals." In *Cannibals, Witches, and Divorce: Estranging the Renaissance*, edited by Marjorie Garber, 40–66. Baltimore, MD: Johns Hopkins University Press, 1987.
Pakenham, Thomas. *The Mountains of Rasselas: An Ethiopian Adventure*. New York: Reynal, 1959.
Palmeri, Frank. *State of Nature, Stages of Society: Enlightenment Conjectural History and Modern Social Discourse*. New York: Columbia University Press, 2016.
Pluciennik, Mark. "Historical Frames of Reference for 'Hunter-Gatherers.'" In *The Oxford Handbook of the Archaeology and Anthropology of Hunter-Gatherers*, 55–68. Oxford: Oxford University Press, 2014.
Post, John D. *The Last Great Subsistence Crisis in the Western World*. Baltimore, MD: Johns Hopkins University Press, 1977.
Prentice, Chris. "Foe." In *A Companion to the Works of J. M. Coetzee*, edited by Tim Mehigin, 91–112. Rochester, NY: Camden House, 2011.
Purchas, Samuel. *Purchas His Pilgrimage. Or Relations of the World and the Religions Observed in All Ages and Places Discovered, from the Creation unto This Present*. London: W. Stansby 1613.
Pye, Henry James. *The Progress of Refinement: A Poem. In Three Parts*. Oxford: Clarendon, 1783.
Raemaekers, D. C. M. "The Persistence of Hunting and Gathering amongst Farmers in Prehistory in Neolithic North-West Europe." In *The Oxford Handbook of the Archaeology and Anthropology of Hunter-Gatherers*, 805–23. Oxford: Oxford University Press, 2014.
Randel, Fred V. "The Political Geography of Horror in Mary Shelley's *Frankenstein*." *ELH* 70, no. 2 (Summer 2003): 465–91.
Redman, Charles L. *The Rise of Civilization: From Early Farmers to Urban Society in the Ancient Near East*. San Francisco: W. H. Freeman, 1978.
Redondo, María Valero. "*Wuthering Heights* and Kleist's *Novellen*: Rousseauian Nature, Spontaneous Love, Infancy, and the Performative Subversion of the Law." The Free Library, 1 July 2020. https://www.thefreelibrary.com/WUTHERING%20HEIGHTS%20AND%20KLEISTS%20NOVELLEN:%20ROUSSEAUIAN%20NATURE,...-a0645551830.
Reed, Donna K. "The Discontents of Civilization in *Wuthering Heights* and *Buddenbrooks*." *Comparative Literature* 41, no. 3 (Summer 1989): 209–29.
Reich, David. *Who We Are and How We Got Here: Ancient DNA and the New Science of the Human Past*. New York: Vintage, 2018.
Rhedin, Folke. "Interview with J. M. Coetzee." *Kunapipi* 6, no. 1 (1984): 6–11.
Rich, Paul. "Apartheid and the Decline of the Civilization Idea: An Essay on Nadine Gordimer's *July's People* and J. M. Coetzee's *Waiting for the Barbarians*." *Research in African Literatures* 15, no. 3 (Autumn 1984): 365–93.

Richetti, John J. *Defoe's Narratives, Situations, and Structures*. Oxford: Clarendon, 1975.
Rickel, Jennifer. "Speaking of Human Rights: Narrative Voice and the Paradox of the Unspeakable in J. M. Coetzee's Foe and Disgrace." *Journal of Narrative Theory* 43, no. 2 (Summer 2013): 160–85.
Rivkin, Julie, and Michael Ryan, *Literary Theory: An Anthology*. 3rd ed. Malden, MA: Wiley Blackwell, 2017.
Robertson, William. *The History of America, Fifth Edition, Vol. 2*. Edinburgh: Strahan, Cadell & Balfour, 1788.
Rousseau, Jean-Jacques. *A Discourse on The Origin and the Foundations of Inequality among Men*. In *Rousseau: The Discourses and Other Early Political Writings*, edited and translated by Victor Gourevitch, 111–246. Cambridge: Cambridge University Press, 1997.
———. *Essay on the Origin of Languages in Which Something Is Said about Melody and Musical Imitation*. In *Rousseau: The Discourses and Other Early Political Writings*, edited and translated by Victor Gourevitch, 247–99. Cambridge: Cambridge University Press, 1997.
Rowley-Conway, Peter. "Time, Change, and the Archaeology of Hunter-Gatherers: How Original Is the 'Original Affluent Society'?" In *Hunter-Gatherers: An Interdisciplinary Perspective*, edited by Catherine Panter-Brick, Robert H. Layton, and Peter Rowley-Conwy, 39–72. Cambridge: Cambridge University Press, 2001.
Sahlins, Marshall. *Stone Age Economics*. Chicago: Aldine-Atherton, 1972.
Sandars, Nancy K. *Prehistoric Art in Europe*. New York: Penguin, 1985.
Sayeau, Michael. "Work, Unemployment, and the Exhaustion of Fiction in *Heart of Darkness*." *Novel: A Forum on Fiction* 39, no. 3 (Summer, 2006): 337–60.
Scott, Heidi C. M. "Heavens and Horrors: The Island Landscape." *Interdisciplinary Studies in Literature and the Environment* 21, no. 3 (Summer 2014): 636–57.
Scott, James C. *Against the Grain: A Deep History of the Earliest States*. New Haven, CT: Yale University Press, 2017.
Seed, Patricia. "'This island's mine': Caliban and Native Sovereignty." In *The Tempest and Its Travels*, edited by Peter Hulme and William H. Sherman, 202–11.
Shakespeare, William. *The Tempest: A Norton Critical Edition*. Edited by Peter Hulme and William H. Sherman. New York: Norton Critical Editions, 2004.
Shelley, Mary. *Frankenstein: The 1818 Edition with Related Texts*. Edited by David Wootton. Indianapolis: Hackett, 2020.
———. "Rousseau." In *Lives of the Most Eminent Literary and Scientific Men of France, Vol. 2*, 111–74. London: Longman, Orme, Brown, Green & Longmans, 1839.

Shepherd, Paul. "A Post-Historic Primitivism." In *Limited Wants, Unlimited Means: A Reader on Hunter-Gatherer Economics and the Environment*, edited by John M. Gowdy, 281–326. Washington, DC: Island, 1998.

Shershow, Scott Cutler. "Agriculture as 'Writing': Some Thoughts on the Contemporary Relevance of Derrida's *Of Grammatology*." *New Cultural Review* 17, no. 1 (Spring 2017): 109–26.

Skura, Meredith Anne. "Discourse and the Individual: The Case of Colonialism in *The Tempest*." In *Critical Essays on Shakespeare's* The Tempest, edited by Virginia Mason Vaughan and Alden T. Vaughan, 60–90. New York: G. K. Hall, 1998.

Slotkin, J. S., ed. *Readings in Early Anthropology*. Chicago: Aldine, 1965.

Spencer, Herbert. *The Principles of Sociology, in Three Volumes*. Vol. 1. New York: D. Appleton, 1898.

Spivak, Gayatri Chakravorty. "Theory in the Margin: Coetzee's *Foe* Reading Defoe's *Crusoe/Roxana*." *English in Africa* 17, no. 2 (October 1990): 1–23.

Staten, Henry. *Spirit Becomes Matter: The Brontës, George Eliot, Nietzsche*. Edinburgh: Edinburgh University Press, 2014.

Sterling, Kathleen. "Man the Hunter, Woman the Gatherer? The Impact of Gender Studies on Hunter-Gatherer Research (A Retrospective)." In *The Oxford Handbook of the Archaeology and Anthropology of Hunter-Gatherers*, 151–73. Oxford: Oxford University Press, 2014.

Still, Judith. *Derrida and Other Animals: The Boundaries of the Human*. Edinburgh: Edinburgh University Press, 2015.

Stocking, George W., Jr. *Victorian Anthropology*. New York: Free Press, 1987.

Stoneman, Patsy. "Catherine Earnshaw's Journey to Her Home among the Dead: Fresh Thoughts on *Wuthering Heights* and 'Epipsychidion.'" *Review of English Studies* 47, no. 188 (November 1996): 521–33.

Sturgess, Keith. "'A Quaint Device': *The Tempest* at the Blackfriars." In *Critical Essays on Shakespeare's* The Tempest, edited by Virginia Mason Vaughan and Alden T. Vaughan, 107–29. New York: G. K. Hall, 1998.

Suzman, James. *Work: A Deep History from the Stone Age to the Age of Robots*. New York: Penguin, 2021.

Temple, William, Sir. *The Works of Sir William Temple, Bart., in Two Volumes, to Which Is Prefixed Some Account of the Life and Writings of the Author*. London: J. Round, J. Tonson, J. Clarke, B. Motte, T. Wotton, S. Birt & T. Osborne, 1731.

Thormählen, Marianne. "The Lunatic and the Devil's Disciple: the 'Lovers' in *Wuthering Heights*." *Review of English Studies* 48, no. 190 (May 1997): 183–97.

Tudge, Colin. *Neanderthals, Bandits, and Farmers: How Agriculture Really Began*. New Haven, CT: Yale University Press, 1999.

Van de Mieroop, Marc. *The Ancient Mesopotamian City*. Oxford: Clarendon, 1997.

Van Ghent, Dorothy. *The English Novel: Form and Function*. New York: Harper & Row, 1961.

Vattel, Emer de. *The Law of Nations, or, Principles of the Law of Nature, Applied to the Conduct and Affairs of Nations and Sovereigns*. Philadelphia: Abraham Small, 1817.

Vaughn, Alden T. "Shakespeare's Indian: The Americanization of Caliban." *Shakespeare Quarterly* 39, no. 2 (Summer 1998): 137–53.

Vaughan, Alden T., and Virginia Mason Vaughan. *Shakespeare's Caliban: A Cultural History*. Cambridge: Cambridge University Press, 1991.

Verey, Simon. *Space and the Eighteenth-Century English Novel*. Cambridge: Cambridge University Press, 1990.

Vine, Steven. "The Wuther of the Other in *Wuthering Heights*." *Nineteenth-Century Literature* 49, no. 3 (December 1994): 339–59.

Vital, Anthony. "Toward an African Ecocriticism: Postcolonialism, Ecology, and *Life & Times of Michael K*." *Research in African Literatures* 39, no. 1 (Spring 2008): 87–106.

Volney, Constantin-François. *The Ruins: Or Meditation on the Revolutions of Empires and the Law of Nature*. Project Gutenberg, [1791] 2006.

Von Sneidern, Maja-Lisa. "*Wuthering Heights* and the Liverpool Slave Trade." *ELH* 62, no. 1 (Spring 1995): 171–96.

Wade, Jean-Phillippe. "Review: Doubling Back on J. M. Coetzee." *English in Africa* 21, nos. 1–2 (July 1994): 191–219.

Warner, Marina. "'The Foul Witch' and Her 'Freckled Whelp': Circean Mutations in the New World." In *The Tempest and Its Travels*, edited by Peter Hulme and William H. Sherman, 91–113. Philadelphia: University of Pennsylvania Press, 2000.

Waswo, Richard. *The Founding Legend of Western Civilization: From Virgil to Vietnam*. Hanover, CT: Wesleyan University Press, 1997.

Watts, Cedric. "Conrad's *Heart of Darkness*: A Critical and Contextual Discussion." *Conrad Studies* 7 (2012): iii–153.

Westropp, Hodder Michael. *Pre-Historic Phases; or, Introductory Essays on Prehistoric Archaeology*. London: Bell & Daldy, 1872.

Wilkinson, Toby. *The Rise and Fall of Ancient Egypt*. New York: Random House, 2013.

Williams, Raymond. *The English Novel from Dickens to Lawrence*. London: Hogarth, 1987.

Winnifrith, Tom. *The Brontës and Their Background: Romance and Reality*. New York: Harper & Row, 1973.

Woodburn, James. "Egalitarian Societies." In *Limited Wants, Unlimited Means: A Reader on Hunter-Gatherer Economics and the Environment*, edited by John Gowdy, 87–110. Washington, DC: Island, 1998.

Woods, Derek. "Scale Critique for the Anthropocene." *Minnesota Review* 83 (2014): 133–42.

Wright, Derek. "Black Earth, White Myth: Coetzee's *Michael K*." *Modern Fiction Studies* 38, no. 2 (Summer 1992): 435–44.

Wright, Laura. *Writing "Out of All the Camps": J. M. Coetzee's Narratives of Displacement.* New York: Routledge, 2006.
Yoffee, Norman. *Myths of the Archaic State: Evolution of the Earliest Cities, States, and Civilizations.* Cambridge: Cambridge University Press, 2005.
Youngquist, Paul. "*Frankenstein:* The Mother, the Daughter, and the Monster." *Philological Quarterly* 70 (1991): 339–59.
Yu, Sheng-Yen. "'Ravaging the Earth, Wasting Our Patrimony': Excess Hunting, Landscape Depletion, and Environmental Apocalypticism in J. M. Coetzee's *Waiting for the Barbarians.*" In *Postcolonial Green: Politics and World Narratives,* edited by Bonnie Roos and Alex Hunt, 83–101. Charlottesville: University of Virginia Press, 2010.
Zeder, Melinda A. "After the Revolution: Post-Neolithic Subsistence in Northern Mesopotamia." *American Anthropologist* 96, no. 1 (March 1994): 97–126.
Zerzan, John. "Future Primitive." In *Limited Wants, Unlimited Means: A Reader on Hunter-Gatherer Economics and the Environment,* edited by John Gowdy, 255–80. Washington, DC: Island, 1998.
———. *A People's History of Civilization.* Port Townsend, WA: Feral House, 2018.

INDEX

affluence, 10, 44–45, 53, 112
After the Ice (Mithin), 45
agricultural development: overview, 1–5, 27–30, 38–42. *See also* farming; fixed-field agriculture
agriculturalist ideologies, 8, 12, 30, 31, 36, 58, 98, 110, 143–45, 179, 189
agricultural trap, 13, 15, 100, 106, 107, 109–13, 123, 190–91
agrognostic: as term, 8
Allistipus, 165
Amara, Mount: and Coleridge's "Kubla Khan," 182, 186–87; and Milton's *Paradise Lost*, 182–85; and Purchas's *Pilgrimage*, 182–84
ammonium nitrate explosion, 191
Amos (book of), 137
ancient Rome, 110, 165
Angel of History (Benjamin), 39–40
anthropophagy. *See* cannibalism
apartheid, 105–6, 155. *See also Life & Times of Michael K* (Coetzee)
Arens, Walter, 26, 128
Attridge, Derek, 120

barbarians, 86, 97–99, 102–3, 109, 114–15. *See also* cannibalism; savages
Bate, Jonathan, 132
Bearing the Word (Homans), 87–88
Beirut explosion (2020), 191
Benjamin, Walter, 39–40, 49
Berry, Laura, 77
Bertman, Stephen, 165
Blackstone, William, 20
Brantlinger, Patrick, 127
Brody, Hugh, 195–96
Brontë, Emily, 70–71. *See also Wuthering Heights* (Brontë)

Brown, Marshall, 170–71
bulwarks. *See* walls and wall-building
Burchell, William John, 107

Caesar, Julius, 23, 110
Calibanism: as term, 140
cannibalism, 25–26, 127–30; in *Foe*, 154–59; in *Frankenstein*, 67–68; in *Heart of Darkness*, 150–54; psychoanalytic views on, 126–27, 198n1 (chap. 5); in *Robinson Crusoe*, 146–50; in *The Tempest*, 140–41; in *Wuthering Heights*, 93. *See also* barbarians; savages
Cantillon, Richard, 19
capitalism: as precipitant of agriculture, 59–60, 125–26
Caribs, 23, 146
Carlyle, Thomas, 44, 176–77
Catlin, George, 93
cereals. *See* farming: of grains; grain domestication; grain hoarding
childhood: psychoanalysis of, 125–26
City in History, The (Mumford), 10, 27–29, 42
class distinctions, 48–50, 80–87. *See also* egalitarianism; inequality
Coetzee, J. M., 11, 97; *Foe*, 154–59, 176–86; *Life & Times of Michael K*, 6, 12, 97, 105–23, 155, 197n2 (chap. 4); *Waiting for the Barbarians*, 11–12, 54–55, 97–105, 107–8, 175; *White Writing*, 106, 188
Cole, Lucinda, 145
Coleridge, Samuel, 181, 182–83, 185–86
collecting. *See* foraging; hunter-gatherers
colo, 18
colonialism. *See* imperialism
Columbus, Christopher, 25, 140

215

communal bonds: within hunter-gatherer bands, 40, 50–52
Comte, August, 34
Conrad, Joseph: *Heart of Darkness*, 12, 150–54, 173–76; *Lord Jim*, 3
Coriolanus (Shakespeare), 142
crises: as spur to agriculture, 55–56
cultivating plants, 108–9

Dalrymple, John, 35
Davies, Stevie, 71
Defoe, Daniel, 12, 22, 23, 125. See also *Robinson Crusoe* (Defoe)
delayed-return activity, 36, 41, 52–53
Derrida, Jacques, 121, 165, 166
De Vattel, Emer, 23–24
Diamond, Jared, 26
diet and disease, 46–47, 48, 88–89, 122
Discourse on Inequality (Rousseau), 74, 92, 96, 168
disease, 46–47, 48, 79
domestication, 2; of animals, 3, 69, 111, 149, 163; Emily Brontë and, 95–96; human's self-, 31, 40–46, 73, 109; of plants, 47–49, 110, 160–61, 178; space and, 58
domus, 13, 40, 46, 66, 82, 83, 95–96, 110, 143, 149, 195–96
droit des genes, Le (De Vattel), 23–24
dual-use material, 191

Eagleton, Terry, 73, 80, 83, 86–87, 93
egalitarianism, 48, 91, 105, 112, 127, 159. See also class distinctions; inequality
Egan, Gabriel, 130
eliminationist attitude toward foragers, 18
Empire (Hardt and Negri), 105–6
enclosures. See walls and wall-building
Erasmus, 165
ethanol, 190–91
Ethiopia, 180–83

famine, 1, 21. See also nutrition
farmer: as term, 49
farming: class distinctions and, 48–50; of grains, 160–62; rise of, 42–43

farm labor, 80–81, 83–84, 115–16. See also stoop labor
Ferguson, Adam, 71, 93
fertilizer, 191
"First Affluent Society, The" (Sahlins), 43–44
fixed-field agriculture, 13, 27, 46, 53, 148, 167
Florio, John, 131–32
Flynn, Carol Houlihan, 150
Foe (Coetzee), 12, 154–59, 176–80
food and nutrition, 46–47, 48, 88–90, 122
foraging: abandonment of, 1–5; early literary depictions of, 17–26; *Frankenstein* and, 63–65, 66–70; in *Life & Times of Michael K*, 113–15; paleogeneticists on, 56–57; Sahlins on, 10–11, 42–45, 53. See also hunter-gatherers
fortifications. See walls and wall-building
four-stage theory, 10, 32–38, 70–71, 73–75, 85, 96. See also hunter-gatherers; stage-one imaginary
Frankenstein (Shelley), 11, 62–70, 167–73
Freud, Sigmund, 12, 26, 39, 124–27, 141, 154, 195, 196

Galbraith, John Kenneth, 44
Gallagher, Susan, 120
gaste, 22
gathering. See hunter-gatherers
Genesis (book of), 1, 69, 124, 161, 196
genetic mapping of human migration, 56–57
Geneva, 61, 67, 168–70
Gilbert, Sandra, 71, 88, 92
Girard, René, 141
global agriculture: as hyperobject, 7
Gnostic Gospels, 8–9
Gordimer, Nadine, 105
grain domestication, 160–61
grain hoarding, 142
Gubar, Susan, 71, 88, 92
gypsy, as term, 2, 3

Heart of Darkness (Conrad), 12, 150–54, 173–76

Heider, Sarah Dove, 120
Helvétius, 20, 32, 74
Herder, Johann Gottfried, 34, 40–41
Herodotus, 25–26
"hobo signs," 189–90
Homans, Margaret, 79, 87–88
Hottentots. *See* KhoiKhoi
Hulme, Peter, 146
Humankind (Morton), 198n1 (chap. 6)
hunger, transcendence of: in *Life & Times of Michael K*, 112; in *Wuthering Heights*, 89
hunter-gatherers: diet and disease among, 46–47; early literary depictions of, 18–26; Enlightenment prose on, 32–33; in *Foe*, 156–59, 185–88; *Frankenstein*'s Creature and, 63–65, 66–70, 171; in *Life & Times of Michael K*, 106–15, 119; paleogeneticists on, 56–57; Pye on, 32–33; in *Robinson Crusoe*, 125–26, 142–43; Rousseau on, 3, 24–25; Sahlins on, 10–11, 42–45; in *The Tempest*, 131–34; in *Wuthering Heights*, 81–95. *See also* foraging; four-stage theory; Neolithic period
Hutcheson, William, 35
hyperobject, 7, 168

imperialism, 5, 10, 12, 22–23, 54, 85, 97–98, 106–7, 124, 128–29, 131, 153, 154–55, 159, 198n2 (chap. 5)
incest, 11, 12, 18, 26, 68, 127, 140–41
inequality, 48–50, 80–81. *See also* class distinctions; egalitarianism; poverty
infantile: as term, 45, 124, 156, 198

Jericho, 49, 160–61, 162
Joudrey, Thomas, 87
Ju/'hoansi, 43, 44, 50, 51–52, 56

Kames, Henry Home, Lord, 20, 32, 35–36, 74
Kettle, Arnold, 90–91
KhoiKhoi, 106–7
Kilgour, Maggie, 128
King Lear (Shakespeare), 142
kingship, 167–68

Knight, Richard Payne, 20–21, 33, 74
"Kubla Khan" (Coleridge), 181, 182–83, 185–86

labor camps, 115
Lacan, Jacques, 12, 65–66, 87–88, 124–26
leisure, 20, 33, 51–52, 106–7, 127, 132
Lévi-Strauss, Claude, 26, 88, 127, 141
Life & Times of Michael K (Coetzee), 6, 12, 97, 105–23, 155, 197n2 (chap. 4)
Locke, John, 19, 25, 35, 36
loneliness: supposed of early humans, 73–74
Lord Jim (Conrad), 3
Lubbock, John, 22, 25, 129
Lyrical Ballads (Wordsworth), 94

malnutrition: as result of agriculture, 46–48
Malthus, John, 21, 32, 74
Manning, Richard, 57, 114
Man the Hunter conference, 10, 42–43, 53, 97
Marshall, Lorna, 50, 51–52
Marxism, 7, 9, 81, 85, 87, 92, 97
Meek, Ronald, 35, 36
Melzer, Arthur, 41, 65, 72
"Mending Wall" (Frost), 162
Mesopotamia, 48–51
migration: of farmers in search of land, 56–57, 195–96
Millar, John, 20
Miller, Christopher, 165
Miller, Lucasta, 71
Montesquieu, 19
Morse, Jedidiah, 19
Morton, Timothy, 7, 198n1 (chap. 6)
Mountains of Rasselas, The (Pakenham), 180, 181–83
Mumford, Lewis, 10, 27–29
Mundas Novus (publication), 141

Native Americans, 36–37, 84, 93–94, 129
Neolithic period, 22, 26, 29, 46–47, 49. *See also* hunter-gatherers

nomadism, 44–45
Novak, Maximillian, 64
nutrition, 46–47, 48, 88–89, 122. *See also* famine

obligate symbionts, 160, 164
Oles, Thomas, 161
Olsen, Lance, 99
"On Cannibals" (Montaigne), 131
On the Origin of Species (Darwin), 34
Ovid, 131, 137

Pakenham, Thomas, 180, 181–83
paleogenetics, 56–57
Paleolithic period, 22, 25, 50–51, 55
Paradise Lost (Milton), 182–83, 184
pastoralism, 10, 18, 19, 20, 32, 34, 35, 47, 71, 74, 86, 102, 106–8, 149, 167; in *Robinson Crusoe*, 143
Pauw, Cornelius de, 35
plough-boy, as term, 2
political quietism, 105
pottery, 49–51
poverty, 44–45. *See also* inequality
primitive communism, 92
primitivism, 93–96, 124, 195
primordial atomism, 38–40, 75, 92
prison camp, 115
private property, 35–36
Progress of Civil Society, The (Knight), 20–21, 33, 74
Progress of Refinement, The (Pye), 20, 33
Purchase His Pilgrimage (Purchase), 182–83
Pye, Henry James, 20, 32–33

racism, 93, 97–98, 105, 124
Recherches philosophiques sur les Américains (de Pauw), 35
Richetti, John, 148
Robertson, William, 23
Robinson Crusoe (Defoe): cannibalism in, 68, 142–50; on hunter-gatherers, 125–26; Shelley and, 64; wall-building in, 162–68

Rousseau, Jean-Jacques: on agriculture's rise, 38–42; Emily Brontë and, 72–73; *Discourse on Inequality*, 74; on domestication, 31, 69; four-stage theory of, 10, 11, 37–38, 96; on hunter-gatherers, 3, 24–25; on mankind's golden age, 107; on primordial atomism, 38–40, 75, 92; on savages, 197n2 (chap. 3); Shelley on, 63–65; on vulcanism, 39, 62
Ruins, The (Volney), 33, 64
"Ruth" (Wordsworth), 94

Sahlins, Marshall, 10, 43–44, 51, 53, 126, 128
savages, 37, 38, 93, 197n2 (chap. 3). *See also* barbarians; cannibalism
scale critique, 191–92
scarcity: as foundation of modern economics, 126
Scott, James, 52–53, 86, 109, 114
Scott, Walter, 71–72
sedentism, 38–39, 96, 111
self-domestication, 31
Serious Reflections of Robinson Crusoe (Defoe), 125. *See also Robinson Crusoe* (Defoe)
Shakespeare, William, 129–42, 195
Shelley, Mary, 10, 63–65; *Frankenstein*, 11, 62–70, 167–73
Shelley, Percy, 54–55
Shen-Yen Yu, 99–100
Shepherd, Paul, 194
Shershow, Scott Cutler, 121–22
Smith, Adam, 32, 93
Social Science and the Ignoble Savage (Meek), 32
solastalgia, 7–8, 127, 140, 152
South Africa, 105–16, 120, 128
speculative historians, 36
Spencer, Herbert, 25
stage-one imaginary: in *Frankenstein*, 11, 65, 67, 171; in *Wuthering Heights*, 75, 84, 88, 92–94, 197n2. *See also* four-stage theory
Still, Judith, 149

Stone Age Economics (publication), 43, 45
stoop labor, 14, 48, 51, 83–84, 108, 116, 117, 126, 133, 148, 161, 167. *See also* farm labor
Sumerian Ubaid culture, 51
supermarkets, 60

Tambora, Mount, eruption (1815), 62
Tempest, The (Shakespeare), 12, 129–42, 158, 177, 198nn2–3
Temple, William, 36

Unas, Pharaoh, 18

Van Ghent, Dorothy, 90–91
Verey, Simon, 167
Virginia Company, 129
Vital, Anthony, 105
Vitruvius, 165
Volney, Constantin-François, 33, 64
vulcanism, 39, 56, 62

Waiting for the Barbarians (Coetzee), 11–12, 54–55, 97–105, 107–8, 175
walls and wall-building, 12–13; in *Foe*, 176–80, 185–86; in *Frankenstein*, 168–73; in Frost's "Mending Wall," 162; for grain protection, 160–61; in *Heart of Darkness*, 173–76; in *Paradise Lost*, 182–84; purpose of, 59; in *Robinson Crusoe*, 162–68; in *The Tempest*, 132–33; in *Wuthering Heights*, 77–79
warfare, 21–22
wasteland: as term applied to any unplowed land, 22–23
Waswo, Richard, 18, 22–23
White Writing (Coetzee), 106, 188
Williams, Raymond, 91
Winnifrith, Tom, 90–91
Woods, Derek, 191–92
Wordsworth, William, 94
Wright, Derek, 105
Wuthering Heights (Brontë), 11; on agriculture's fallout, 41; bond between Catherine and Heathcliff in, 90–92; class distinctions in, 2–3, 70, 80–83, 84–87; Eagleton on, 73, 80, 83, 86–87, 93; food and nutrition in, 88–90; Homans on, 87–88; place and space in, 75–77; on primitivism, 93–96; Rousseau's theories and, 72–75; stage-one imaginary in, 75, 84, 88, 92–94, 197n2; on stoop labor, 83–84; walls and the Grange in, 77–80

Zeder, Melinda, 108
Zerzans, John, 193

www.ingramcontent.com/pod-product-compliance
Lightning Source LLC
Chambersburg PA
CBHW031812220426
43662CB00007B/612